THE PLEASURE POLICE

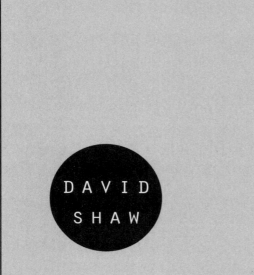

DAVID
SHAW

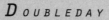

*D*OUBLEDAY

New York

London

Toronto

Sydney

Auckland

THE
PLEASURE
POLICE

How
Bluenose
Busybodies
and Lily–Livered
Alarmists Are
Taking All the Fun
Out of Life

PUBLISHED BY DOUBLEDAY
a division of Bantam Doubleday Dell Publishing Group, Inc.
1540 Broadway, New York, New York 10036

DOUBLEDAY and the portrayal of an anchor with a dolphin
are trademarks of Doubleday, a division of
Bantam Doubleday Dell Publishing Group, Inc.

Book design by Maria Carella

Library of Congress Cataloging-in-Publication Data
Shaw, David, 1943–
The pleasure police : how bluenose busybodies and lily-
livered alarmists are trying to take all the fun out of life /
David Shaw. — 1st ed.
p.   cm.
Includes bibliographical references.
1. Political correctness—Humor.   I. Title.
PN6162.S496   1996
814′.54—dc20   95-39581
CIP

ISBN: 0-385-47568-3

June 1996

1   3   5   7   9   10   8   6   4   2

First Edition

FOR LUCAS

CONTENTS

ACKNOWLEDGMENTS

In the course of writing any book—even one as personal and idiosyncratic as *The Pleasure Police*—an author inevitably requires the assistance of many other people. My primary debt of gratitude is to Bill Thomas, my editor at Doubleday, who responded to the idea embodied in my original proposal by making a counterproposal of his own, considerably broadening the focus of my examination. Equally important, Bill provided encouragement and support throughout the writing process, and he offered invaluable guidance, criticism and insight during the editing process. (It was also his suggestion that I avoid distracting the reader with endless footnotes; my sources are identified in the text itself and in the selected bibliography that follows.)

I would never have thought to write a book about those who seek to destroy or diminish the pleasure we should all find in everyday life had I not been fortunate enough to have a father who truly appreciated pleasure and who passed on to me his appetite for pleasure in every form. I shall also be forever grateful to all those friends and other intimates who have made my own life so pleasurable—and specifically to those who have introduced me to (and/or shared with me) all the pleasures that make life worthwhile.

In addition—and apart from those people specifically mentioned in the book itself—I benefited from the help and counsel of countless others. For their efforts in helping me to understand the Jewish perspective on human sexual relations, I thank Rabbi Steven Leder of the Wilshire Boulevard Temple, Rabbi Elliot Dorff of the University of Judaism, and David Lehrer, Pacific Southwest regional director of the Anti-Defamation League—all in Los Angeles. E. J. Dionne, Roberto Suro, Sam Fulwood III, Narda Zacchino and Betsy Amster graciously consented to vet other brief but sensitive sections of the book. Jacci Cenacveira was, as always, both enterprising and indefatigable in her research efforts on my behalf. My agent, Kathy Robbins, encouraged me to write this book and offered several sound suggestions on the manuscript.

My wife, Lucy, offered a few dozen excellent, constructive criticisms, and was, once again, my last and best reader-editor of the penultimate version of the manuscript.

I, of course, bear full responsibility for the views expressed in this book and for any errors of commission or omission and for any overstatements, understatements or misstatements.

One morning when I was about thirteen or fourteen, my father walked into my bedroom, pointed in the general direction of my crotch and—apropos of nothing that I could discern at the time or that I can recall now—smiled and said, "Until you're eighteen, you use that thing to take a leak with; after you're eighteen, come see me about it." Then he smiled again and walked out.

That was the beginning—and the end—of my sex education at home. Not that my father was either prudish or squeamish. He was demonstrably neither. He was sensual in every sense of that term. But he was fifty when I was fourteen, and I think he had long since forgotten how early (and how irresistibly) a young boy's testosterone levels begin their throbbing ascent. This was, after all, the mid-1950s. Hugh Hefner and Elvis Presley were brand-new to the national consciousness. *Deep Throat* was two decades away. Oprah was barely out of diapers. Madonna wasn't born yet. Nor were most of the other sexual revolutionaries who would ultimately make virtually everyone, of virtually every age, acutely and unceasingly aware of S-e-x. Besides, my dad knew how much I loved and respected him, and he was accustomed to my obeying him; I think he assumed that I would automatically do so in this instance as well and that I would come to him dutifully on my eighteenth birthday with a list of twenty questions (more or less) on birds, bees, breasts and balls.

He was half-right. I did follow the first part of his prescription-cum-proscription; I maintained my virginity until I turned eighteen. But I did so, in all honesty, less out of respect for my father's sage counsel than out of the same circumstance that has constrained adolescent males since evolution moved them from the limbs of trees to the backseats of cars: lack of opportunity. No girl of my acquaintance was remotely interested in having sex with me—assuming that I could have mustered the courage to ask, which I most certainly could not. But my concupiscence was more easily contained than was my curiosity. My best friend from the time I was seven until shortly before I turned eighteen was almost four years older than I was, and throughout my early teen years, I peppered him with questions on sex. (After all, when I was nine, Allan had carefully explained what "fuck" meant, so I figured he was a regular Dr. Kinsey.) I supplemented Allan's blend of instruction and speculation with readings in my father's extensive library. (*Sane Sex Life and Sane Sex Living* is the title I recall consulting most frequently.) Then, one bright, sunny morning just a few days after my eighteenth birthday, I was sitting in my freshman English composition class at the small, Christian college I had so foolishly chosen to attend. Suddenly, I heard a yelp of pain from the young woman seated directly in front of me.

"Ach, mein tochis," she screamed, leaping up and clutching her shapely (I couldn't help but notice) ass. Some lout who should have been in a reform school kindergarten class rather than college—Christian or otherwise—had put a thumbtack on her chair and she had sat firmly and unwittingly upon it. My head snapped up as quickly as she had jumped up—not initially, I must admit, out of sympathy for her pain or even admiration for her *derrière*. It was her Yiddish expostulation that suddenly riveted me. School had been in session less than three months, and with more than thirty students in this particular class, I hadn't really noticed her before. Now, hearing her speak and seeing her face—even in its reddened-with-rage condition—I had only one thought: "She's Jewish, too."

I jumped to my feet, held out my open arms and said, *"Landsman."* Beaming, she fell into my embrace and—to the utter bafflement of our classmates (and the utter consternation of our professor)—we bolted, hand in hand, from the classroom.

• •

Pepperdine College (now University) is a Church of Christ school, what would be known these days as a Fundamentalist Christian college. It was at Pepperdine that I first encountered the pleasure police of this world—the narrow minds, unbending wills, dictatorial ways, smug self-righteousness and determinedly dour approach to life that characterize the bluenose busybodies, the new Puritans and the congenital alarmists who, thirty-five years later, are increasingly trying to leech all joy from our daily lives. Granted, Pepperdine is in many ways a special case—a private institution, run by a church. No one forced me to go there. The church had (and has) every right to demand that everyone who attends its school obey the legitimate religious precepts and educational principles for which it stands. I should not have gone to Pepperdine in the first place. My mistake. But while I learned little academically at Pepperdine—and have been educationally disadvantaged ever since—I did learn a great deal about a particular mind-set.

Unsettling as it was at the time, my two-year experience at Pepperdine prepared me more than it did most of my peers for the rise of the New Right—first with the school's secular saint, Barry Goldwater, and the John Birch Society, later with Ronald Reagan and Jerry Falwell and now with Newt Gingrich, Rush Limbaugh and their illegitimate offspring. Pepperdine also prepared me—unintentionally, to be sure—for both the New Puritans and the burgeoning corps of scaremongers, some of them on the Left, who discovered sprouts and StairMasters in the past decade and who have decided that steak, cigars, alcohol, flirting and maybe even sex itself (the political spectrum does, indeed, come full circle) are verboten, most of them under penalty, quite literally, of death.

At Pepperdine in the early 1960s, smoking, drinking, dancing and swearing were prohibited both on and off campus, and kissing and holding hands—among many other things—were prohibited on campus as well. So how did I—a liberal, iconoclastic Jew—wind up at an ultraconservative, ultra-Christian college? I should have known better. Hell, I dated a Church of Christ girl while still in high school, and when I tried to give her a good-night kiss—on the cheek(!) after our eighth(!!) date—she screamed and bolted from my presence as if I'd dropped a live scorpion in her tampon box. But my high school English teacher had assured me that I would get the same-quality education no matter where I went, "if you just work hard." I can't believe I was naive enough—ignorant enough, dumb enough—to have believed her. But I wanted to go to a small school, one close enough to home that I could continue to live with and help care for my ailing father and keep my various part-time jobs. A high school journalism organization I belonged to offered me a full-tuition scholarship to Pepperdine, which was then located in South-Central Los Angeles, only twenty minutes from home. (It has since abandoned the inner city for the safer but sterile hills above Malibu.) I accepted the scholarship with only the slightest hesitation. I had known since I was ten that I wanted to be a newspaper reporter when I grew up, and I was convinced that the best way to become a good reporter and a good writer was to read and study good writing; I wanted to major in English literature, and I'd heard that Pepperdine had a good English department. That it did. But it lacked virtually everything else that an institution of higher learning should have. It also seemed to lack Jews—certainly not an academic essential but a circumstance that I, as a Jew, had noticed, which is why I reacted so enthusiastically when I heard my lovely classmate bemoan the state of her punctured *tochis* on that crisp January morning.

I was not then and am not now a religious Jew. I wasn't a bar mitzvah. I neither stay home from work nor go to temple on the Jewish High Holy Days. I don't go to temple at all, in fact, except for the weddings and bar mitzvahs of close friends and relatives. And I celebrate Christmas more actively than Chanukah. But I do think of myself as a Jew, culturally if not necessarily religiously, and when I found myself seemingly a lone Jew in the middle of three thousand Pepperdine Christians, I suddenly discovered a new empathy for General George Armstrong Custer. Thus, on that blessed day when I realized that there was at least one fellow Jew on campus—call her Bonnie—I instantly escorted her from our English class to the campus newspaper office. I was already an editor on the paper, and I took Bonnie into my office there, where we spent the rest of the afternoon comparing notes, two strangers in a strange Christian land. Bonnie was bright, frank and possessed of a delightfully bawdy sense of humor. We began to see a lot of each other after that, and on January 28, 1961—twenty-four days after my eighteenth birthday—we spent the day together at Disneyland, then had a pizza and went to a basketball game at my old high school. After the game, Bonnie and I spent an acrobatic two hours in the front seat of my 1953 Ford, at the conclusion of which time I was no longer a virgin.

Bonnie had long since abandoned that state of deprivation, and she subsequently told me that she had taken it upon herself to identify and service every other Jewish male on campus. (This was, remember, before AIDS.) Bonnie was a sort of sexual Red Cross—Clara Barton with condoms.

It turned out that there were thirteen male Jews at Pepperdine—eleven "Persians" (as they were then called), none of whom spoke English, plus a prematurely bald New Yorker and me. In the right-wing, rigidly Christian atmosphere of Pepperdine—where there was always more than a vague whiff of anti-Semitism in the fetid Christian air—the hairless New Yorker and I delighted in the delicious irony of having found a self-styled nymphomaniac committed to keeping thirteen Jews (and only the Jews!) sexually happy. We were truly, we decided, The Chosen People.

Bonnie soon realized that Pepperdine was not the ideal place for her, though, and she left after one year. Disappointed, I focused anew on my studies and on my work for the campus newspaper, the *Graphic*. The editor in chief and I had a great time, winning awards for journalistic excellence even as the administration and faculty fulminated about our lack of reverence for Pepperdine's hallowed halls; in the tradition of pleasure police everywhere, they tried their damnedest to suppress even the licit pleasures of good journalism and good writing. Henry Miller's *Tropic of Cancer* was the subject of an obscenity trial in Los Angeles at the time, and my editor friend asked Dr. Wade Ruby, the chairman of the school's English department, to review the book for the *Graphic*. Dr. Ruby, who taught me more about writing than any other teacher (or editor) I've ever had, was single-handedly responsible for the lofty regard in which the English department at Pepperdine was then held. Although he was, by Pepperdine standards, almost unspeakably liberal (he had once voted for Roosevelt, he confided to me in his office one afternoon), he was also a minister in the Church of Christ—and the official biographer of George Pepperdine, the founder of the college. His review of *Tropic of Cancer* was resoundingly negative. Despite that—and despite Dr. Ruby's high standing in the college and in the church community—the administration ordered his review withdrawn, on the eve of its publication, without explanation and without anyone from the administration having bothered to read it. We ran blank space and the word "CENSORED" in its stead, thus further endearing ourselves to the Billy Graham wanna-bes who ran Pepperdine. Suddenly indifferent to the school's straight-from-the-Bible motto ("Ye shall know the truth, and the truth shall make you free"), they threatened to revoke our scholarships. (Dr. Ruby stood up for us and they ultimately backed down.)

When I wasn't working on the *Graphic* or studying for class, I occasionally (and unsuccessfully) tried to find someone at Pepperdine to share and expand upon the carnal knowledge I had so happily acquired under Bonnie's expert tutelage in my freshman year. In a typical misadventure, early in my sophomore year, I took a very thin, very Christian classmate on a moonlit boat ride for two on a lake in a park in downtown Los Angeles. She was a minister's daughter, but as we cuddled in the boat, her affectionate murmurings encouraged me to casually slip my hand down the front of her blouse. Although a casual visual examination had already made it clear that I would not encounter anything mammoth lurking beneath my gaunt classmate's frilly bodice, I did expect to find something there. Nope. Nothing. I could see that she was flat-chested. But . . . Nothing? I leaned over further and further in the boat and plunged my hand further and further down and around her upper torso, trying frantically to find something. Anything. She seemed decidedly amenable to my quest—more than amenable, in fact, although I think she mistook my frenzied confusion for uncontrolled passion—until I leaned over so far that I capsized the boat and dumped us both in the lake. Once she realized that she was not going to drown, she began upbraiding me (and herself) for having behaved so immorally. God, she assured me, had overturned our boat and plunged us into the chill waters to punish us for succumbing to temptation. I debated pointing out that since I had never, as near as I could tell, managed to touch anything more intimate than her sternum, I didn't think we had done anything to offend even Pepperdine's extraordinarily rigid God. But I was afraid that would hurt her feelings, and since she was already convinced that she was hovering between pneumonia and purgatory, I settled for simply telling her that I thought God was much too smart and much too busy to waste a lovely spring evening hanging around an artificial lake in MacArthur Park. She was not assuaged.

On another occasion, I took a classmate—call her Janet—to a movie and then back to my apartment. I had first become aware of Janet one morning in our philosophy class, when her snug, amply filled lavender sweater began to distract me from Professor Thompson's eighth consecutive lecture on the fallacies of evolutionary theory. If God truly does work in wondrous ways, his miracles to perform, I thought Janet's structural engineering offered more compelling evidence of that than did anything Professor Thompson was saying.

When Janet and I walked into my darkened apartment, I was quite certain that there would be no repeat of the previous week's futile groping and searching. My first glance had told me that with Janet—to paraphrase Gertrude Stein—there definitely was a *there* there. Unfortunately, the instant I tried to touch what I had come to think of as her "Oaklands"—after what seemed like several hours of increasingly breathless and mutually pleasurable kissing—she displayed reflexes, both physical and theological, that immediately rendered moot the prominence of her manifest assets. She grabbed my right wrist, smiled and said, more in sorrow than in anger, "I think

God gave me these"—she thrust her chest out, as if I, poor, panting soul, didn't know exactly what she was so obliquely referring to— "for a very special reason."

"Yes, yes," I wanted to say. "I'm on God's side. I was—we were—about to do something very special." But it was clear that the evening's activities were at an end, however prematurely from my point of view, so I said nothing, yielded graciously and took her home.

I guess I can't really count either Janet or my lady of the lake as actual sexual encounters. But a year or two later, by which time I had come to my senses and fled Pepperdine for the more tolerant climes of UCLA, I received a most tantalizing telephone call from another girl I had dated, briefly and chastely, while we were both at Pepperdine. She—call her Christine—was still at Pepperdine, and she was representing the college at a journalism conference we were both attending at a hotel in Santa Monica. I was a delegate from UCLA, and I had just returned to my room after participating in an evening session of the conference. Christine wanted to know if I could come to her room. I politely declined. "I have to read *O Pioneers!* for my English class Monday," I said.

She persisted. A bit slow—and more than a bit gun-shy after my frequent failures in what I then thought of as my personal Pubic Wars—I patiently and sincerely explained the nighttime allure of Willa Cather in paperback. But Christine was not a minister's daughter (de Lawd be praised), and I soon caught her increasingly suggestive drift—at which point I threw the phone down and practically ran to her room.

I found her lying on her bed. With her roommate, Sally. When I walked in, Sally excused herself to go to the bathroom. When I sat down on the bed, Christine turned to me with a ferocity of purpose I had long hoped for but had never seen on our previous dates.

"But what about Sally?" I asked, suddenly shy now that Nirvana was finally within reach.

"Oh, she takes a very long time in the bathroom."

I didn't ask for details.

Soon our clothes lay in a tangled heap on the floor.

When we were through—still naked, still breathing hard but

through, for the moment anyway—Christine excused herself and went to the bathroom. Whereupon Sally returned, lay down next to me and began caressing me. You will have realized by now that my own substantial desires notwithstanding, I was not at that point in my life (and would never, alas, become) an *homme fatal*. I couldn't believe that one woman wanted me, never mind two.

"Christine will be back in a second," I whispered, gently removing Sally's hand from my left thigh.

"No she won't," Sally assured me. "We made a deal. If she could get you to come over, we'd share you."

Astonished, I jumped out of bed and leaped toward the bathroom—where I found Christine soaking in a tub, reading. She looked up and grinned at me.

I was convinced that I was the butt of an elaborate practical joke. But I couldn't figure out the punch line, so I went back to Sally, and she and I—and Christine and I and Sally and I and Christine and I—spent the rest of the night and early morning hours doing exactly the sort of things that must have made poor George Pepperdine positively fibrillate in his grave.

• •

California, in the mid to late 1960s, was the seedbed of the second American Revolution. The Free Speech Movement shattered the academic calm of Berkeley and sparked campus protests throughout the country (and around the world), although not, of course, at Pepperdine, which remained firmly imprisoned in the 1950s—or was it the 1850s? The Watts riot was the Fort Sumter of a new, urban civil war. Antiwar protesters and Black Panthers waged guerrilla movements against a smug establishment suddenly confused and frightened by the fierce determination of its young and disenfranchised. Longhaired hippies introduced the concept of free love, public love—a "bathless fuck" soon to be "zipless fuck"—to a nation founded by Puritans, steeped in Victorianism and convinced that cleanliness was next to godliness and that, by extension, washing a child's mouth out with soap and water was the most appropriate and effective parental response to the prepubescent utterance of one (or more) of the odious seven dirty words.

But on the eve of this social and political upheaval—a year before Watts, three years before the Haight-Ashbury "summer of love," a year or so after I had abandoned Willa Cather for Christine and Sally—an unknown Italian teenager, a waitress in a rock club in the North Beach section of San Francisco, made her own small but symbolic contribution to the forces that would soon transmogrify the nation. At the request of her employer, Carol Doda took off her blouse and her bra, donned the newest quirk in 1960s fashions— Rudi Gernreich's topless bathing suit—and danced onstage one night as a publicity stunt. She was an overnight sensation. Soon, she was dancing nine shows a night—bare-breasted—and the Condor Nightclub was packed with whistling, cheering, foot-stomping businessmen, tourists and assorted curiosity seekers for every single show. A few months later, Doda's employer suggested that she— and he—might be enriched still further if she took advantage of a silicone injection process he'd just heard about and had her heretofore more-than-adequate thirty-six-inch bust enlarged. Doda spent $2,500 of her own money for twenty weeks' worth of injections, and when she was done, she had rock-hard, eminently-visible-from-the-back-of-the-room, forty-four-inch breasts. Business boomed even more.

Soon, every club in North Beach had topless dancers, one of whom—a giant, neon marquee informed passersby—was a "TOPLESS MOTHER OF 8." While that marquee may have conjured surrealistic visions of a pitiable young woman, her immense, sagging breasts suckling eight infants simultaneously—Dali gone to the dogs—the topless craze quickly spread south and east, to city and suburb alike; within a year, bare-breasted women were dancing in bars, nightclubs, theaters and restaurants from coast to silicone-clogged coast. This was not the burlesque of my father's generation, which was a genuine art form (not to be confused, of course, with the paintings of Monet or the poetry of Milton), in which women in exotic costumes gradually stripped down to their pasties and G-strings, shedding one garment at a time—ever so languorously, ever so seductively, accompanied by appropriately bass- and brass-driven music

(David Rose's "The Stripper" comes to mind). That form was called striptease, and done properly, it required at least as much tease as strip. In "aboveground" burlesque houses—as opposed to private, "underground" stag parties—the women never did take everything off. Their nipples always remained covered, as did—it went without saying—their pubic areas. But that restraint only drove the patrons into greater frenzy—and imposed greater demands on the creativity, ingenuity and sensuality of the dancers. The best and most popular of the burlesque queens—Gypsy Rose Lee, Tempest Storm, Candy Barr—had whole routines, themes, a real act. They had wit and style; some had their own stand-up comics as warm-up acts. (My father used to insist, not terribly persuasively, that it was the comedians, not the semi-naked women, whom he went to the burlesque shows to see—much as the men of my generation would later say they subscribed to *Playboy* for the cartoons or the articles, not the nude photos.)

But no such pretense was possible with the topless dancers of the 1960s. They had only one thing—make that two—to offer their audiences: Breasts. Completely, totally bare breasts. Like Carol Doda, many topless dancers got silicone injections—compounding their assets, so to speak—but whether naturally or artificially endowed, they wasted little time in putting their breasts on display for the paying customers. No elaborate, choreographed routines—and certainly no pasties—for these ladies. No sirree. A few walked through a quick imitation of what a true burlesque artist used to do, but they knew no more about striptease than they did about high teas. Many didn't bother to try. When the curtain went up—if there was a curtain—they were seen just standing there, onstage, big breasts bouncing and pert nipples clearly visible. (Many topless dancers put makeup on their nipples to make sure that even the most nearsighted bozo in the last row wouldn't feel cheated; he'd know he'd seen The Real Thing[s].)

In time—and not very much time at that—the waitresses in topless bars went topless, too. Suddenly, the naked female breast—and soon thereafter the entire (and entirely naked) female body—were as ubiquitous as Old Grand-Dad in the barrooms of America.

It would, of course, be ridiculous to suggest that Carol Doda

was a revolutionary in the sense that Mario Savio or Stokely Carmi-
chael was a revolutionary—or that her comments about why she
became a topless dancer ("It was my only way to get into show
business, so I showed my business") belong in the history books
alongside Dr. Martin Luther King's "I have a dream." But Doda
was revolutionary, if only symbolically—revolutionary in what she
represented, if not necessarily in what she did. She was either the
beginning of the end or the end of the beginning. Or both. Contrary
to appearances (and accusations) at the time, it's now clear that she
foreshadowed the final, if drawn-out, stage of the voyeuristic, *Playboy* magazine culture of woman-as-mindless-sex-object; more important, she was a harbinger of the let-it-all-hang-out sexual liberation movement that brought forth not only "free love" but,
ultimately, a greater openness about all forms of human sexuality.
First came Carol Doda; then came *Hair, Oh! Calcutta!, I Am Curious (Yellow), Deep Throat, The Boys in the Band* and, later—tragically—*And the Band Played On* and *Angels in America*. Unwittingly, Doda also helped give birth to the mid-twentieth-century
pleasure police, the self-styled moral militia who would increasingly
seek to dictate just what their fellow Americans could—and could
not—do in virtually every walk of life. When they failed to stop the
topless troops of North Beach, they doubled and redoubled their
efforts in ensuing years and decades on every battlefield from intercourse to discourse. They started with sex, then moved on to dress,
hair length, diet, alcohol, exercise, smoking, joking, flirting, talking,
reading and thinking. Now, as I write this book, not a day goes by
that I don't see, hear, read about or encounter some manifestation
of their oppressive labors.

  Doda didn't see herself as a pioneer, of course. Betty Friedan's
landmark feminist manifesto *The Feminine Mystique* was published
a few months before Doda first bared her breasts for the edification
of the Condor clientele, and it had triggered a women's liberation
movement that would soon change the world. But all Doda could
think to say when feminists expressed outrage over her behavior
(and that of all other topless dancers) was, "They burned their bras;
I threw mine away. What's the difference?"

In a symbolic, superficial sense at least—mammary-as-meta-phor—Doda was to mid-twentieth-century America what Dada had been to early-twentieth-century Europe: a shocking, cynical, extreme reaction to the traditional values of the time, both artistic and humanistic. I don't mean to overstate this analogy any more than I wanted to overstate the comparison between Doda and the leaders of the civil rights, antiwar and Free Speech movements. She was, after all, merely clever, not Cleaver. The artists and writers of the Dadaist movement were intellectuals, committed to aesthetic if not political revolution. Doda had no artistic, intellectual or political pretensions; she was committed only to making money. To her, a revolution was what happened when tassels were pasted on a nipple and twirled rapidly. But in her own way, she was as absurdist—and as nihilistic—as Hans Arp, Tristan Tzara and the rest of the early Dadaists. Certainly, public reaction to Doda was every bit as enraged as it had been to the first Dadaists almost fifty years earlier, and maybe more so. Dada was largely an aesthetic challenge, the throwing down of an intellectual gauntlet; Doda's threat was far more personal—or so the horrified critics of the time contended. She was a threat to every value we cherished, everything from monogamy to motherhood. Bare breasts! In public! Onstage! And not even "real" breasts at that! It was as if her "twin 44s," as they came to be known in some circles, were not simply breasts (however engorged by the miracle of modern technology), but mammoth cannon, pointed at every church, every home, every school, every family in the country.

Not long after Carol Doda began hoisting her bogus boobs onstage, I began cultivating a news source who subsequently became a casual friend—a boyishly charming fellow who happened to be the district attorney in rapidly growing Orange County, the right-wing stronghold next door to Los Angeles. Mr. District Attorney—Cecil Hicks by name—always reminded me of Huck Finn gone slightly raffish. He had a perpetually playful smile and a mischievous glint in his eyes—eyes that were not displeased by the sight of an attractive woman. Cecil was at least as voyeuristic as the next man, which is to say that he loved looking at bare breasts as much as I did. But he was a political conservative, charged with upholding The Law, and when topless dancers wiggled their way south, into his very own county, he hit upon an ingenious tactic to combat this menace to democracy and family life. Most prosecutions of topless dancers, in California and elsewhere, had foundered on the inconvenient shoal of the First Amendment. Topless dancing, like dancing with one's breasts properly concealed, was held to be artistic expression, entitled to the full protection of the First Amendment to the United States Constitution, much to the red-faced, bluenosed chagrin of preachers and prosecutors across the fruited plain. But my friend Cecil found an obscure civil statute that had been used to close down bordellos on the Barbary Coast of Northern California in 1913, and with considerable success (and mounting vigor, as topless dancing became bottomless dancing became . . .), he applied this Red Light Abatement Act to the bars and other establishments that employed go-go dancers in various stages of undress.

As much as I liked Cecil and enjoyed his company, I was disappointed by his zealous determination to criminalize women for the simple act of flashing their private parts in front of willing adult males who were clearly part of Thoreau's "mass of men [who] lead lives of quiet desperation" (now at least temporarily relieved by a noisy and public perspiration). Cecil had seemed an exception to most conservatives—or at least to most moral conservatives. Some purely economic conservatives take a libertarian approach to issues of personal morality. But moral conservatives tend to be a grim and prudish lot. They seek to suppress fun wherever they find it. Conservatives want to "conserve," to preserve the status quo, to save things as they are, preferably for themselves. That's why so many rich businessmen are conservative—and racist and sexist as well. I am not saying that all or even most conservatives—or businessmen—are either racist or sexist or members of the pleasure police. Obviously, most conservatives, like most other Americans, are decent, caring human beings. Many conservatives are generous supporters of a wide range of charitable and cultural institutions. But conservatives do far outnumber liberals in the ranks of racism and sexism and in the suppression of sex in any form. *These* conservatives are not just conservative; they're exclusionary—and selfish. They don't want to share money or power or anything else of value. But pleasures, like most of the other good things in life, are best when shared (as Cecil himself certainly seemed to know).

I do not mean, in this very personal, very subjective book, to blame any one group or any one movement for the rise of the contemporary pleasure police. Their ranks are diverse. They come from both the Right and the Left. Some are devoutly religious; some are determinedly irreligious. Many mean well; some are simply mean. Some worry about secondhand smoke, others about steak, still others about sex. But in my everyday life over the past half century plus—and especially over the thirty-three years that span both my adulthood and my journalistic career—a growing number of people have become determined to make us all think that life is worse—less pleasurable, more dangerous—than it really is. In the process, they have made life a less joyous journey for us all.

I freely admit that I make these observations through my own particular prism, based on my own biases, perceptions and life experience. I also acknowledge that, given the dramatic shifts that have taken place in our economy and technology, in our family structure and in society as a whole, some measure of anxiety is understandable. One further caveat: I'm not black, brown, female, poor, physically or mentally handicapped (although some might dispute that latter claim). Were I any of those, I surely would find life much more painful than I do now. I would be worrying more about survival than about pleasure; fun might seem a foreign concept. But like most people, I *have* had my share of pains and problems. I grew up in a broken, lower-middle-class home with parents who fought constantly and divorced acrimoniously. I worked multiple jobs from prepuberty on to help support my father, whose heart condition forced him to quit work when he was forty-seven. I married foolishly the first time, got divorced, then remarried blissfully five years later and watched helplessly as my second wife died of cancer after we'd had only eight glorious years together. My father died relatively young—at sixty-two. One of my best friends—and mentors— died at fifty. But I have not become Chicken Little. The sky is not falling; indeed, the sky is not even as smoggy as it once was. I'm not Pollyanna but neither am I Cassandra. To me, the glass is almost always half-full, and I resent those who try to persuade everyone that the glass is not only half-empty but cracked—and leaking a fluid that is either a deadly poison or a dangerous aphrodisiac. Or both.

1

R I S K
A N D
R E A L I T Y

A couple of years ago, I happened across an observation by
the late political scientist Aaron Wildavsky that had me nodding my
head so vigorously in agreement that my teeth actually began click-
ing together, producing an odd sound not unlike the staccato burst
you might expect to hear from the castanets of a flamenco dancer
suddenly stricken by an epileptic seizure.

"How extraordinary!" Wildavsky wrote. "The richest, lon-
gest-lived, best protected, most resourceful civilization, with the
highest degree of insight into its own technology, is on its way to
becoming the most frightened."

A few weeks later, I read something similar by Lester Lave, an
economist at Carnegie-Mellon University in Pittsburgh. Thanks
largely to technology, Lave wrote, Americans are "safer than ever
before." Nevertheless, he said, we are "more concerned about
health and safety than ever before."

The following day, I found myself in Washington, D.C., speaking with Paul Portney, vice-president of Resources for the Future, a
think tank that specializes in environmental issues. Shaking his
head, muttering disconsolately about one exaggerated health hazard
after another, Portney finally threw up his hands in exasperation

and—clearly addressing forces beyond the four walls of his office—
said, "If everything is as harmful as we're told, how come we're
healthier and living longer . . . than ever before?"

Good question.

Two more good questions: Why aren't we happier? Why aren't
we having more fun?

Life expectancy in the United States is seventy-six years now,
up almost thirteen years since 1940 and more than double what it
was at the turn of the century. There are now more than fifty thousand people in this country over one hundred years old, more than
double the number just a decade ago. Deaths from automobile accidents and from accidents in the workplace are both down dramatically in the last quarter century. Since 1970, our infant mortality
rate has been cut in half, the death rate from heart disease (our
biggest killer) has dropped 27 percent and the death rate from
stroke (our third biggest killer) is down 44 percent. Death rates from
emphysema, tuberculosis, diphtheria, typhoid fever, pneumonia, diabetes, influenza and other once dreaded diseases have also declined
sharply. Polio and smallpox, long the scourge of childhood, have all
but disappeared. In 1994, the last year for which statistics are available, the overall death rate in the United States—the number of
deaths in relation to the total population—was the lowest ever recorded.

Deaths from cancer (our second biggest killer) have increased,
but that increase is largely attributable to smoking—which has led
to a doubling of the lung cancer death rate in the last thirty years—
and to two simple facts: (1) people are living longer, and (2) the
decline in fatalities linked to heart disease and stroke means that
other causes of death are rising proportionally. After all, the per
capita death rate for all causes combined is, ultimately, 100 percent.

Our much-brooded-over environment has also grown healthier in recent years. Lead emissions in the air are down 97 percent
since 1970. Untreated sewage is no longer dumped in the nation's
waterways. The amount of land set aside for wilderness or other
conservation purposes has multiplied more than fivefold. Most other
measures of health, wealth and well-being have improved almost as
significantly. Since 1970, the percentage of Americans finishing at

least four years of college has doubled, as has the number of two-car families and the average number of paid vacation days. The number of Americans finishing high school has increased about 50 percent. The size of the average new home has increased 35 percent. The average amount of time spent working, both in and out of the home, has *decreased* about 10 percent. The number of recreational golfers has more than doubled. Attendance at symphonies has more than tripled.

Despite these enormous gains, psychologists, sociologists and epidemiologists confirm what Wildavsky, Lave and Portney suggested: we may well be the most anxious, frightened society in history. Instead of enjoying the advantages of modern life, we spend all our time worrying about its (alleged) disadvantages. Almost every day, it seems, we read and see and hear about a new (purported) threat to our health, safety and happiness. We're warned about benzene in our Perrier, Alar on our apples and asbestos in our school buildings. We're told that popcorn, margarine and red meat—as well as Chinese food, Italian food, French food, Mexican food and junk food—all contribute to heart disease. Aluminum and zinc are reported to contribute to Alzheimer's disease. Alcohol is blamed for virtually every malady but the national debt. And everything, it's said, causes cancer: Birth control pills. Caffeine. Cellular phones. Dioxin. Hair dyes. High-power lines. The hole in the ozone layer. Hot dogs. Pesticides. Plastic water bottles. Saccharin. Secondhand smoke. Silicone breast implants. Vasectomies.

While we're fretting about the fat in our fettuccine Alfredo ("a heart attack on a plate," according to the Center for Science in the Public Interest), we are also being bombarded by terrifying tales of violent crime, crashing airplanes, a global warming trend and an AIDS "epidemic" among heterosexuals. From academe and the workplace, we hear one story after another about sexual harassment and date rape. From some radical feminists, we hear that pornography is not only degrading but dangerous—the equivalent of rape itself.

No reasonable person can deny that very real dangers lurk in all our lives—in our air, in our food and water supply and in other natural and artificial substances. Guns kill. Cigarettes kill. Toxic chemicals, excessively high fat diets and abuse of alcohol can kill. Nor can any reasonable person deny that sexism exists and that women are harassed, discriminated against and raped, in larger, more horrifying numbers than most men are willing to admit. But conditions have improved on almost every front. Not enough on many fronts but a great deal nonetheless. African Americans are still victimized by racism and poverty. They suffer in grotesquely disproportionate numbers from violence and AIDS. Now they're threatened anew by assaults on affirmative action and school desegregation—and by a Congress and Supreme Court determined to reverse many of the civil rights gains made in the past thirty years. Even most African Americans are largely better off, however, than they were a few decades ago, when Newt Gingrich and Clarence Thomas were more concerned with fighting acne than equity. Those who argue that Americans are worse off today than ever before are as wrong as Gingrich and his band of antigovernment reactionaries, who are busy trying to purge the various agencies and regulations that have helped to protect the American public after decades of neglect.

The laws engendered by the consumer and environmental movements are a major reason we are a healthier, safer society today. Smog has decreased substantially—down almost 50 percent in Los Angeles, for example, despite a huge increase in the number of automobiles—largely because the government forced stationary industries to reduce their polluting emissions and forced automobile manufacturers to produce cars that could run on lead-free fuel. Almost twice as many rivers and lakes are safe for swimming and fishing now precisely because of the passage, in 1972, of the Clean Water Act—a law that Republicans in Congress have recently done their best to eviscerate. Similarly, the release of toxic chemicals by U.S. industry declined more than 40 percent in the five years after Congress passed a law in 1988 requiring the disclosure of such pollutants, a law that Congress also tried to gut in 1995. But some regulations *have* gone way beyond what's reasonable. Many *have* failed to take into account any possibility of a cost/benefit ratio. Obviously, dollars are not nearly as important as lives. But dollars and (common) sense should not be ignored in the formulation of public policy.

Before Justice Stephen Breyer was appointed to the United States Supreme Court, he complained publicly that the government too often spent more money trying to clean up the last 10 percent of pollution in a given situation than it had on the first 90 percent. In his book *Breaking the Vicious Circle,* Breyer wrote about government efforts to allocate $9 million for the final cleanup of a toxic waste dump that was already "clean enough for children playing on the site to eat small amounts of dirt daily for seventy years without significant harm." Experts, Breyer wrote, "calculate that the EPA rules, regulating sources such as benzene storage vessels and coke byproduct recovery plants, save a total of three to four lives per year, at a cost of well over $200 million"—more than $50 million per life. Breyer and others have warned that the resources available to regulate and combat various health risks are not limitless. Money spent regulating minuscule risks is money that is then unavailable for research and treatment of more serious social, medical and environmental problems—prenatal care, childhood immunizations, day care, housing, education, highway safety, shelters for battered women, smoke detectors in low-income rental housing, hot lunches for poor children. One study has shown that vaccinating eighteen-month-olds against *Hemophilus influenzae* type B, the leading cause of bacterial meningitis, would save lives at a cost of only $68,000 each.

The risks that kill people and the risks that scare and anger people—and thus prompt government action—are frequently (and surprisingly) very different. William Reilly, chief administrator of the Environmental Protection Agency from 1987 to 1991, conceded in 1994 that only 30 percent of the EPA budget was actually spent on high-risk threats to the environment. As John Graham, the director of the Center for Risk Analysis at the Harvard School of Public Health, told Congress in 1995, "We regulate some nonexistent risks too much and ignore larger, documented risks. We suffer from a syndrome of being paranoid and neglectful at the same time."

Studies have repeatedly shown that the alleged hazards we

hear and worry about the most are often misstated, overstated, non-existent or of undetermined risk because there is just not enough scientific evidence today on which to base a sound evaluation. Breast cancer is one of the best examples of this syndrome. There is a widespread perception in this country that the effects of post–World War II environmental pollutants have created, in recent years, a new breast cancer epidemic among women. A *Mother Jones* magazine cover a couple of years ago pictured a woman, clearly distraught, naked to the waist—except for what appeared to be two gas masks hooked together to form a crude brassiere. "Breast cancer cover up," said the cover line. "Why scientists ignore vital evidence about toxins." Less graphic but no less alarming, many newspapers published stories in the fall of 1993 saying that scientists thought pesticides in the nation's food supply "may be contributing to an alarming surge in breast cancer," as the *Los Angeles Times* put it.

But in April 1994 the largest study on this issue to date found no evidence that breast cancer is caused by pesticide residues. (Early in 1996, a report based on seven separate studies in four countries found that another widely blamed "cause" of breast cancer—fat in a woman's daily diet—also had no relationship to the development of that disease.) That doesn't mean that a cause-and-effect relationship won't be found in the future. But science hasn't established that relationship yet, media hype and public paranoia notwithstanding.

Breast cancer *is* an epidemic. A horrible epidemic. More than 180,000 women a year are diagnosed with breast cancer—and 46,000 women a year die from it. My late wife, Ellen, died of breast cancer. My wife Lucy's mother had breast cancer. I am not speaking as some heartless, uninvolved male when I use words like "hype" and "paranoia" and when I point out that there is no persuasive evidence at this time that breast cancer is a *new* epidemic, occasioned by modern chemicals and fatty foods. The facts are clear: the age-adjusted death rate from breast cancer has remained almost constant for more than sixty years.

The *incidence* of breast cancer *has* been rising in recent years; studies suggest that there is now a one-in-eight lifetime risk of the disease. But most of the increase in the incidence of breast cancer is attributable not to the pernicious effects of technology, but to the beneficial effects of technology—specifically to new diagnostic tools like mammograms.

"There's been an enormous increase in screening, in early detection, an enormous increase in the number of mammographic machines around," says Malcolm Pike, chairman of the department of preventive medicine at the University of Southern California and a longtime specialist in the epidemiology of breast cancer. "Not all . . . [the increase in breast cancer] is due to that, but most of it" is, Pike says.

In other words, while there is some real increase in the incidence of breast cancer, most of the increase is a result of our now being able to diagnose and treat cases—many of them actually *pre-cancerous*—that we would not even have known about in previous generations.

Are more young women getting breast cancer these days? Yes. But again, while some of that increase is real, more of it is attributable to the improved diagnostic procedures cited above, and most of the increase is a function of demographics: there *are* more young women these days, baby boomers born between 1946 and 1964, so—inevitably, tragically—more young women are getting breast cancer. (As if to compound that tragedy, a 1995 study showed that breast cancer accounts for more medical malpractice claims than any other condition, largely because doctors often misdiagnose their patients, delay treatment and misread mammograms.)

But breast cancer still strikes older women far more often than younger women. The incidence of the disease among women in their seventies and eighties is more than four times higher than it is among those baby boomers who are now in their thirties and forties, according to SEER Program statistics for 1986 to 1990 compiled by the National Cancer Institute. The age-adjusted *death rate* from breast cancer is skewed even more dramatically toward the upper ages; it's more than eight times higher among women in their seventies and eighties than among women in their thirties and forties. The highest death rate of all from breast cancer is among women over eighty-five. In fact, the age-adjusted death rate from breast cancer actually *declined* 16 percent from 1970 to 1991 among women aged thirty-five to fifty-four, according to the National Cancer Institute and the government's National Center for Health Statistics. These statistics notwithstanding, women of all ages—and younger women in particular—are now so frightened of breast cancer that they vastly overestimate the likelihood of their getting it. A study in the *Journal of the National Cancer Institute* last year showed that most women thought they had a one-in-five chance of developing breast cancer within the next ten years; the real numbers: about one in forty-three. Women thought they had a one-in-ten chance of dying of breast cancer; the real numbers: about one in 250.

The real numbers are terrible—and terrifying—enough. A woman is twenty-four times more likely to die of breast cancer than she is to die in an automobile accident. But why make a ghastly threat seem even worse than it is? More than 95 percent of all women die of causes other than breast cancer. Although a woman is nine times more likely to die of a heart attack than of breast cancer, we hear far less about that threat.

Why are we so scared—and so often scared by the wrong things? And what motivates the fearmongers who work so diligently to exploit our every anxiety?

Violent crime is clearly one of the underlying causes of pervasive fear in contemporary society. Just look at how many people are buying guns, installing home security systems, putting up surveillance cameras, moving into walled and gated communities, voting in favor of three-strikes-and-you're-out ballot propositions. Two-thirds of all Americans say they have taken action to ensure their personal safety, even though violent crime has actually been decreasing in recent years. Murder—the best indicator of overall crime rates because virtually every murder is reported—has declined noticeably over the past five years. During the first six months of 1995, the number of homicides reported to police nationwide dropped 12 percent from the same period in 1994, the largest reduction in at least 35 years.

But there are valid reasons for people to be frightened. Murder—like all violent crime—remains far more prevalent today than it was thirty or forty years ago; per capita, violent crime has more than quadrupled since 1960, from 161 incidents per 100,000 people to 746. The United States Department of Justice has estimated that

83 percent of all Americans will be the victims of a violent crime at least once in their lives. Random violence in particular has increased markedly. Traditionally, law enforcement authorities have said that 80 percent of all murders are committed by a relative or acquaintance of the victim; now the figure may be closer to 50 percent. Robbers who were once happy with your wallet and your watch now want your life, too—for no apparent reason other than sheer thrills or drug-induced craziness. Increasingly violent young criminals contribute significantly to the random nature of our worst crimes. The number of people under 18 arrested for homicide and aggravated assault doubled from 1984 to 1994, according to the FBI; the number of people under *fifteen* arrested for homicide increased more than 50 percent in the same period.

These trends and statistics are a painful reminder of just how fragile and capricious life can be. But our legitimate fears are both exploited and exacerbated by politicians using scare tactics to win our votes and by police chiefs eager for bigger crime-fighting budgets. Local television news shows also play a major role in exaggerating the threat of crime, callously implementing the mantra "If it bleeds, it leads" with prominently featured stories on violent crime night after night. Even people living in communities with little violent crime see these reports and become convinced that rapists and murderers lurk around every corner. This pervasive fear of crime has contributed to a generalized climate of fear, which in turn breeds mistrust, both of other individuals and of our institutions, beginning with the police and extending to virtually all governmental and quasi-governmental entities. Television plays a further role in this process, as Robert Putnam, a political scientist at Harvard University, wrote in *The American Prospect* early in 1996. Several studies have shown that heavy television viewing, with or without violent images, induces passivity and cynicism, diminishing social trust and increasing viewers' pessimism about human nature.

At the same time, a radical restructuring of the economy and a widespread breakdown in the traditional family unit have combined to undermine the basic sense of security that most middle-class Americans long felt, indeed assumed, almost as a birthright. Divorce, single-family households, teenage pregnancy and out-of-wed-

lock births have all increased, while hourly wages for American production workers have decreased, labor unions have lost their
protective clout and large companies once regarded as invulnerable
have downsized, merged or collapsed, taking with them hundreds of
thousands of jobs and slashing benefits and stagnating salaries for
many of the jobs that remain. We feel exposed, defenseless, helpless.
We feel frustrated—and angry. That's why we're afraid. That's why
conspiracy theories flourish. That's why we have a climate in which
paramilitary paranoiacs run around the woods, practicing with au-
tomatic assault weapons. That's why we have Oklahoma City.

Americans have always had a weakness for conspiracy theories—dating back two centuries, to the publication of a book charging that a German organization known as the Illuminati Order was
secretly supporting Thomas Jefferson for the presidency. Senator
Joseph McCarthy conducted the country's most infamous witch-
hunt when he went after the "Communist conspiracy" in the State
Department in the 1950s, but at various times in our nation's history, Freemasons, Jews, Catholics and the CIA, among many others,
have been the target of conspiracy theorists. Conspiracy buffs have
been especially active since the assassination of John F. Kennedy,
and in recent years, conspiracy theories have been advanced for everything from the murder of O. J. Simpson's ex-wife and her friend
to the shoot-out in Waco between federal agents and members of the
Branch Davidian cult—not to mention every political campaign and
every corporate decision in between. Study after study has concluded, for example, that there is no evidence linking either high-
power lines or silicone breast implants to serious illnesses in humans, but many people remain convinced that both are extremely
dangerous and that we're being lied to, deceived by powerful interests—by the omnipotent and treacherous Them. The same is true
with breast cancer. Writing in the weekly *New York Observer* in
1995, Anne Roiphe said, "I tend to think that someone could have
stopped breast cancer if only they had tried harder. . . . I tend to
wax conspiratorial with the best of them about the reasons that
breast cancer has taken second place to AIDS in the great disease
sweepstakes run by our government and media."

More than people in other countries, Americans tend to measure the quality of our health in terms of life expectancy—and never mind that those final years may consist of being tethered to an oxygen tank, unable to feed ourselves, go to the bathroom unassisted or recognize our own children and grandchildren. Joseph Lelyveld, executive editor of the *New York Times,* says there is "something in the American soul that seems to think we should all live forever, and therefore, anything that can hurt you is part of a conspiracy to prevent that."

Conspiracy theories flourish when you have "a cleavage in the society," says Joyce Appleby, a history professor at UCLA, and a very deep cleavage is what we have today in the United States. No one trusts anyone anymore. No one feels safe—not even from the government, whose sole raison d'être is to protect us. After all, two of the most powerful and enduring figures in twentieth-century America—J. Edgar Hoover and Richard Nixon—kept "enemies lists" that included the names of honest, law-abiding, prominent Americans. The government lied about Vietnam, Watergate and the Iran-contra scandal, about arms sales to Iraq, "no new taxes" and more campaign pledges than Bill Clinton could count. No wonder more than 40 percent of the American public said in a 1995 survey that they think the federal government is out to get them.

At the same time that Americans seem trapped in this miasma of paranoia—much of it eminently understandable—technology has rapidly become so advanced that we can now detect minuscule risks whose existence we were previously (and blissfully) unaware of. Moreover, there is often a peculiarly American quality to the way in which this technology is interpreted. Americans insist on answers, reasons, solutions, no matter how random or inexplicable a given event may be. We're convinced there's a cause-and-effect syndrome in everything. We seem determined to fix blame, to find villains (and heroes). As a people, we are uncomfortable with uncertainty and ambiguity; we prefer black and white to gray. People are sick? It must be asbestos. Or dioxin. Or secondhand smoke. Never mind that scientists say the evidence isn't in yet. We want answers. Now. So we use whatever results technology makes available to us to provide those answers, even if the results and the answers are tentative, marginal, inconclusive or contradictory. This serves the further purpose of taking us, as individuals, off the hook for any problem we might have; we're not unhealthy or unhappy because we didn't take care of ourselves properly or pay enough attention in school or when choosing a mate or crossing the street. No, it's "their" fault—the people who make cigarettes or Hostess Twinkies or fast cars or booze or pesticides. No one in America seems to want to take responsibility for his own actions, to be held accountable for his choices—not the Menendez brothers, not Darryl Strawberry, not the chain-smoking, whiskey-swilling, drug-shooting Alibi Ikes who spend so much time pointing the finger of blame at parents, teachers, politicians and society at large that it's a wonder they have time left to indulge in their bad habits.

Besides, Americans—for some reason—regard any risk, no matter how small or how remote, as intolerable. They don't want to accept the fact that ultimately "Life is a sexually transmitted terminal disease," as Peter McWilliams put it in his 1993 book *Ain't Nobody's Business if You Do.* Americans seem to think that the Declaration of Independence included freedom from risk "among the self-evident rights to life, liberty and the pursuit of happiness," the late British journalist Henry Fairlie, wrote in 1989. "The idea that our individual lives . . . can and should be risk-free has grown to be an obsession, driven far and deep into American attitudes."

I should probably point out about now that I am not myself a big risk-taker—at least not in the physical sense. I don't ski. I don't ride horses. I don't sky-, skin- or scuba-dive. I don't argue with guys who look like they could (and would) pound me to a pulp. When I was a child, my father never had to worry that I would climb the tallest tree, tease the big dog down the street or play "chicken" with my first car. I have always, however, taken emotional and professional risks—putting myself on the line in human relationships, risking hurt and rejection even when I was most vulnerable and challenging and criticizing my peers, colleagues and, especially, my employers and other authority figures. I've never worried much about getting other people mad at me or having them think ill of me. Nor have I ever worried much about the kinds of daily "risks" that seem to obsess so many people I know. Whatever real problems I have in life, I'm too busy enjoying myself to worry about potential or imaginary problems.

Ironically, one explanation for the pervasive fear of risk in many quarters is that medical science and economic advancement have so reduced or eliminated many of our long-standing, legitimate fears—and so improved our standard of living—that we now have the luxury to worry about essentially peripheral and hypothetical problems. Most of us have a roof over our heads, food on the table, clothing on our backs, access to decent (if expensive) doctors and some measure of disposable income—which, by the way, has increased 50 percent, in constant dollars, over the past thirty years. As Donna Britt, an African American columnist for the *Washington Post,* wrote in 1995, "Even Americans of moderate means" have more "creature comforts . . . enjoy more leisure options and more technological marvels—TVs, cars, computers—than their parents dreamed. And they live in more fear of losing them—and their lives—than their parents dreamed, too."

A richer society can afford to worry more about *"de minimus* risks," says Bud Ward, executive director of the Environmental Health Center of the National Safety Council. "The wealthier we become, the better educated we become, probably the more risk-averse we're going to become."

Tragically, far too many people—in the United States and throughout the world—still lack the most fundamental necessities of life: Food. Proper housing. Clothing. Medical care. In this country, the gap between rich and poor has grown astronomically over the past twenty or twenty-five years. According to a cover story in *Washington Monthly* in the summer of 1995, chief executives of the largest companies in the United States, whose average income was 40 times more than the average worker's in 1972, now make more than 140 times what the average worker makes. According to *Current Population Report,* published by the Bureau of the Census, the income of Americans in the lowest 20 percent of the population dropped 3.6 percent from 1973 to 1989; the income for those in the top 20 percent increased 26 percent. (Although per capita income has increased more than 50 percent since 1970, in constant dollars, *median* household income has remained relatively stagnant over the same period, and it has actually declined slightly from its 1989 peak.) The Luxembourg Income Study, a nonprofit organization headquartered in Walferdange, Luxembourg, says that families in the top 10 percent in after-tax income in the United States now have almost six times more disposable funds than do families in the bottom 10 percent, the largest disparity by far among all industrialized nations.

Thanks to Reaganomics—and to the virtual collapse of organized labor, the effects of technology on unskilled workers and the dramatic growth in the 1980s of the stock and bond markets, where the rich invest and increase their wealth—the richest 1 percent of American households now control about 40 percent of the wealth in this country. That's more than double what the richest 1 percent controls in England, which has long been regarded as one of the most stratified of all Western societies. At the other extreme of the economic ladder, says Robert Greenstein, executive director of the Center on Budget and Policy Priorities, a research group in Washington, D.C., our child poverty rate is "four times the average of Western European countries." Figures from the Luxembourg Income Study last year showed that while the average income of affluent households with children is greater in the United States than in all other Western industrialized nations, the average income of poor households with children is lower in the United States than in any Western industrialized country except Israel and Ireland. The gap between income levels in affluent households with children and income levels in poor households with children was greater in the United States than in any other Western industrialized nation.

But poor people—the starving, the jobless and the homeless, whether here or abroad, with children or without—are not the ones demanding bans on smoking, silicone breast implants or oily popcorn in the local movie theater. The people of Rwanda don't worry about pesticides on food or the hole in the ozone layer or the "dangers" of pornography and sex education. No, the alarmists—the Cassandras who see death where'er they look—tend to be people with higher-than-average education and socioeconomic status, people who can afford a desire for what Aaron Wildavsky and his colleague, Mary Douglas, a social anthropologist, call "a sense of individual control over social forces"; they have enough of a stake in the world that they want to be absolutely sure they live long enough to enjoy it . . . except that they're so busy worrying that they don't have the time, energy or appetite to enjoy anything—and, in the process of trying to turn their personal anxiety into public policy, they are also depriving the rest of us of much of the pleasure we should be able to take from life.

In the preface to her book *Endangered Pleasures,* Barbara Holland says, "Subtly, in little ways, joy has been leaking out of our lives. Almost without a struggle, we have [allowed the] . . . spreading of a layer of forboding across the land." Perhaps we have some sense of guilt over our material success, and that makes us worry that our success is either undeserved or only temporary. Perhaps our Calvinistic roots have led us to believe that pain is more noble than pleasure, thus rendering us susceptible to arguments that everything we eat, drink, breathe, touch or see might hurt us. Whatever the reason, bad news always travels faster—and seems more credible—than good news.

The end of the cold war—and with it, at least temporarily, the suspension of fear about a nuclear holocaust—have further freed us to concentrate on anxieties of a far less catastrophic nature. Tim Weiner wrote in the *New York Times* in 1995 that the "cult of national security" has been supplanted by a "cult of personal insecurity." This has made it possible for the many alarmists and messengers of doom in our midst to get our attention just long enough to scare the shit out of us.

Since most of us are neither doctors nor scientists—nor avid readers of medical or scientific journals—we rely on the mainstream, general-interest news media for most of our information on health and safety. Whether out of ignorance, indifference or fear of offending their advertisers, these news organizations—daily newspapers, weekly and monthly magazines, local and network television stations—paid little, if any, attention to such matters until about thirty years ago. Then came Ralph Nader *(Unsafe at Any Speed)* and Rachel Carson *(Silent Spring)* and with them, the birth of the consumer and environmental movements. The news media, always more reac-

tive than proactive, gradually came to realize that these were good
stories; they hired consumer and environmental reporters. It was a
long-overdue move, and despite some early imbalance—consumer
and environmental activists were always righteously right in these
stories, big business and developers were always rapaciously
wrong—most of the coverage performed a valuable public service.
After all, most big corporations—be they food manufacturers, pesticide makers or oil, auto, timber, media or whatever companies—*are*
greedy; they *are* motivated by the bottom line. They care about
profits, not about public safety. Without news organizations as
watchdogs and the government as regulator, they would invariably
protect only their profits, not the public health and welfare. But even
as news media exposés and government laws and lawsuits have dramatically improved protection of both the consumer and the environment, the story remains largely unchanged, the same message
continuously repeated: Doom is nigh. The (polluted) sky is falling.
Life is dangerous. Don't do it—whatever "it" is—but especially if
"it" is fun; if it's fun, it must be particularly dangerous.

People on the East Coast are fond of poking fun at California
and its various health faddists for their seeming preoccupation with
being trim rather than enjoying themselves. Fair enough. But in this,
as in so much else, California has merely been the harbinger of a
national preoccupation. When I interviewed a reporter for the *Boston Globe* a couple of years ago, I thought it telling that she asked
me to meet her at a Thai restaurant in a suburban minimall "because it's right next to my exercise class." Several months later,
when I had lunch with a television producer in New York, I was
amused to hear him order "the turkey club sandwich—hold the bacon, hold the mayo and no fries." The last time I was in New York, I
saw a large sign on a bus stop that said, "Another Day, Another
Chance to Be Healthy." What kind of mantra is that for the Big
Apple—Fun City? The poster featured a full-color photograph of a
woman in a leotard, stretching—a Jane Fonda wanna-be if I ever
saw one.

For many years now, perhaps the strongest, most consistent
messages about the dangers of everyday life and the joys of abstinence, self-denial and eternal vigilance have come not from some

flaky, New Age, meditation-and-mushroom guru in Los Angeles, but from the pages of the *New York Times*—specifically from the "Personal Health" columns and other stories by Jane Brody. Although I've interviewed hundreds of reporters and editors over the past twenty-two years in my job as media critic for the *Los Angeles Times,* I've never met Brody. She is, by all accounts, a good person and a fine journalist. She has written many helpful, responsible stories, including those debunking the overstated threat of pesticides to the nation's food supply. But the crime of Ms. Jane Brody is that she is relentlessly depressing—terrifying—to read. One *New York Times* editor told me several years ago that while the paper kept entering her work in the annual Pulitzer Prize competition, he hoped she'd never win. "How the hell can you give a prize to someone who thinks it should be against the law to enjoy yourself?" he asked me one day.

To be fair, Brody is probably just doing her job as she and her editors define it—in effect, catering to the most neurotic among her readers. But if you obeyed all the strictures in Brody's weekly columns, you'd never leave the house. Hell, you'd probably never get out of bed. I was a Boy Scout, so—like Brody (who presumably wasn't)—I believe in being prepared. Calmly taking necessary precautions is one thing, though; being perpetually—paranoiacally—on the alert for imminent danger is quite another. There does not seem to be any substance, any season, any human activity, that does not call forth from Ms. Brody's mind and word processor some cautionary note.

Spring is a time for romance and rebirth, for baseball and the first bright rays of warm sunshine. But for Brody, spring is a time for "wheeze and sneeze . . . the runny nose and itchy eyes," as she warned allergy sufferers in her March 22, 1990, column.

"Summer," she wrote in the opening to her column three months later, "is fraught with hazards to the health of our most prized sensory organ: our eyes." (Of course, this was less off-putting, I guess, than her summer column two years earlier, in which her first paragraph noted that "The fine wrinkles on your face, the liverlike patches on your arms and legs, perhaps even some rough, scaly spots on your nose or hands are all signs of 'photoaging,' the damage done by repeated exposure to [the sun's] ultraviolet radiation.")

Some years, instead of warning her readers before summer, Brody will wait until autumn to tell them about the cruel damage that ultraviolet rays have perpetrated in the preceding months. Her October 1992 column suggested, "With summer over, now is a good time to assess the damage the sun has wrought upon your skin. . . . Skin repeatedly assaulted by the sun sooner or later begins to resemble elephant hide. It becomes progressively more wrinkled, leathery and loose. It may also become densely freckled, dry, yellowy brown and dotted with brown splotches called liver spots. Clusters of stretched and broken blood vessels that look like tiny spider veins may develop, especially on the nose and cheeks. Sun-induced blackheads commonly form around the eyes and nose."

But you were smart, right? You wore a hooded parka, sweatpants, thick socks and three pairs of Elton John's old sunglasses on the beach. Or you skipped the beach and traveled abroad. Oops. Brody has warned about the dangers of travel, too—about seasickness, diarrhea, blisters and back problems.

Christmastime is when Brody is at her festive, fun-loving best. "This is the season that puts millions of digestive tracts to the acid test," she wrote ten days before Christmas 1988. This was followed by more than a thousand words on the dangers of heartburn born of "overwork, the holiday rush with rich food and drink . . . and perhaps overindulgence in coffee to help keep you going."

Even if your only Yuletide overindulgence is gift-buying, Brody has concerns. "In the annual struggle to find appropriate and affordable holiday gifts, you may overlook an important consideration: allergic reactions to many of the most popular gifts, from fragrances and jewelry to food, furs, feathers and pets," she advised in 1988. Two Christmases later, she was back with another counseling session: "This holiday season, try giving family and friends just what the doctor ordered: gifts that can help them keep healthy."

What wonderful suggestions did she have for all the would-be Santas out there? How about a mammogram for your mother-in-law? (I'm serious!) Or "plastic food storage containers, perhaps with labeling pen and tape," to keep leftovers fresh? Or oven thermometers and acrylic cutting boards to prevent contamination from those dread microorganisms in our food supply? You say your friends love to eat? Well, Ms. Brody has just the thing for them—"assorted dried beans and peas" and "whole-grain crackers." (I was devastated when I read that column; how could my wife possibly appreciate the silver necklace and silk jacket I'd bought her when I could have given her Tupperware and a year's supply of kidney beans?)

"People of all ages," Brody assured her readers, "might appreciate a trial membership in an exercise class." Or maybe a tape player or concert tickets—not, I hasten to add, because Brody necessarily appreciates the pure joy of listening to music, but because music is "a time-honored stress-reducer." Besides, in yet another column, she warned of "virtual epidemics of occupationally induced ills" among musicians and other artists. You enjoy playing that fiddle? Well, be careful. "As many as three-fourths of professional musicians have been injured playing their instruments," Brody reported in 1989. Musicians who practice too hard may suffer from "crippled hands," she wrote, while "100 million Americans, including children and hobbyists, as well as professional artists, are exposed to dangerous art materials and rarely know it. Some of the materials are known or suspected to be carcinogens." The result: "outright poisoning. . . . Chronic headaches, extreme fatigue, muscular weakness and visual and emotional disturbances . . . reproductive problems, respiratory disorders, kidney and liver ailments and brain syndromes." Think of that the next time your kid brings home an art project from school! And don't try to help your little ones escape these hazards by sending them outdoors for some good old-fashioned American athletic activity. "Every day millions of young people participate in sports like baseball, football, basketball and soccer and in activities like skating, cycling, swimming and running," Brody wrote in the first paragraph of her May 24, 1995, column. "And every day, several thousand are treated in emergency rooms for sports-related injuries."

•   •

Jane Brody is not alone on the journalistic ramparts, of course. Because of the preeminence of the *New York Times*—it is the best and most influential newspaper in the country—she's just the most visible of the bad news bearers who are determined to help us protect ourselves from any danger, no matter how slight. Editors, reporters and news directors at most news organizations insist that it is their civic duty to serve as both educational forum and early-warning system for their readers and viewers. Well, yes. And no. News organizations, alas, have an even higher "duty"—at least in the eyes of their stockholders: making money. The only way to do that is to attract readers and viewers in such numbers that advertisers will come running, eager to peddle their automobiles and deodorants and beer and bras. But readers and viewers are increasingly going to other sources for their information and entertainment—to the Internet, to MTV, to videos, to interactive cable TV, to specialty magazines and newsletters. Since many people no longer turn as automatically as they once did to the traditional forums for news, the people who run those forums have begun acting like farmers with stubborn mules. You want the mule to go where you want? First you have to get his attention. So you whack him over the head with a two-by-four.

To attract the attention of readers and viewers, editors and news directors are whacking them over the head with megadoses of "news" that would once have been reserved for the *Police Gazette* and the *National Enquirer*. Tonya Harding and Nancy Kerrigan. Amy Fisher and Joey Buttafuoco. Eric and Lyle Menendez. John and Lorena Bobbitt. Heidi Fleiss. William Kennedy Smith. Michael Jackson. And—of course—O.J., O.J., O.J., morning, noon and *Nightline*. In an increasingly competitive and fragmented market, general news media standards are slipping. The very definition of "news" is shifting. The elite gatekeepers who once decided, autonomously and imperiously, what was worthy of the front page or the six o'clock news now yield that judgment—grudgingly but increasingly—to the decision makers at CNN, *Hard Copy* and supermarket tabloids that specialize in stories about Elvis Presley and Adolf Hitler teaming up with two-headed nymphomaniacs from Mars to find a cure for cancer. That's how stories like Bill Clinton's alleged twelve-year affair with Gennifer Flowers find their way into the mainstream media and the public consciousness: Flowers sells her story to a supermarket tabloid. CNN goes live to cover Clinton's denial. Bingo! Everyone decides they no longer have the right to withhold the news from their readers and viewers. A tawdry story that few reputable journalists want to be first on suddenly triggers a frenzied rush everywhere to be second.

The same impulse is largely responsible for the media's often overplaying, oversimplifying and sensationalizing "news" about risks of questionable scientific or medical legitimacy. News executives don't want to be perceived as having missed—or, worse, having "covered up"—a specific health scare story. They *do* want to be perceived as being of service to their readers, viewers and advertisers—of being "user-friendly," "civic-minded," "consumer-oriented," to use just a few of the buzz phrases that seem to have replaced "Gimme another double bourbon" as the most common expression heard these days wherever news executives gather. What these news executives want most of all, of course, is to attract and retain the attention of their readers and viewers. So they whack them over the head as often and as stoutly as possible with the two-by-four of the Big C—cancer—and with as many other alarms as they can muster on the dangers to which people are most vulnerable, either physically or psychologically or, preferably, both: what they breathe, what they eat, what they drink and, best of all, anything that can be depicted as being the slightest threat to the ability of their innocent young children to grow into strong, healthy, happy adults with glamorous, six-figure jobs and two innocent young children of their own.

Look at the panic the media helped create about apples and the pesticide Alar a few years ago:

"The most potent cancer-causing agent in our food supply is a substance sprayed on apples to keep them on the trees longer and make them look better."

So said Ed Bradley on *60 Minutes*—against a backdrop of a giant apple marked with a skull and crossbones—and so began a nationwide panic, fed by other media, which quickly followed *60 Minutes* with their own stories on the new killer chemical daminozide (better known under its trade name Alar). News media throughout the country, aided by public appeals and congressional testimony from that well-known molecular biologist Meryl Streep, almost made it seem that one bite of an Alar-treated apple or one swig of juice made from Alar-treated apples would mean instantaneous death.

Young children, the media reported, were most vulnerable because they tend to drink a lot of apple juice and because their digestive and immune systems are not fully developed. School boards in Los Angeles, New York, Chicago, Atlanta and many other cities banned apples and apple products from their cafeterias. Some parents raced after their children's school buses to yank apples from their lunch boxes. Supermarkets came under intense pressure to remove apples from their shelves. Uniroyal, the manufacturer of Alar, pulled the product off the market. Sales of apples plummeted, forcing many farmers to dump their crops or give them away, costing the industry more than $100 million, according to economists' estimates. Suddenly, "An apple a day keeps the doctor away" became "An apple? No way—or the doctor you'll pay."

But apples *are* good for you. Not only that, they taste good. And they're fun to eat. There's something almost atavistic about all that chewing and crunching. More to the point, at the time of the *60 Minutes* broadcast—which was viewed by an estimated 40 million Americans—industry was already moving away from Alar, and the nation's three major baby-food makers said they were using non-Alar apples.

The Environmental Protection Agency had been concerned about the safety of Alar for many years before *60 Minutes* broadcast its story, but the agency had decided that test results were either flawed, contradictory or insufficiently conclusive to warrant an immediate ban; formal action was delayed, pending public hearings. Although the EPA finally decided, well after *60 Minutes,* that "long-term exposure to Alar poses unacceptable risks to public health," many other public health experts disagreed. A panel of international experts concluded that Alar is safe to eat as a trace residue in food, and both the California Department of Food and Agriculture and Britain's Advisory Committee on Pesticides found that the risk of getting cancer from the small amount of Alar used on apples was minuscule.

Two years after the *60 Minutes* story, C. Everett Koop, the former United States surgeon general, said, "If Alar ever posed a health hazard, I would have said so then and would say so now. When used in the regulated, approved manner, as Alar was before it was withdrawn in 1989, Alar-treated apple products posed no hazards to the health of children or adults." Dr. Richard Adamson, director of the division of cancer etiology at the National Cancer Institute, said the risk of eating an apple that had been properly treated with Alar was "certainly less than the risk of eating a well-done hamburger. . . ."

So, is Alar completely harmless? No. There is some evidence that Alar, like so many other substances—natural and artificial—could cause cancer in humans, *at high doses,* doses unlikely to occur in normal, everyday consumption by adults *or* children. Even peanut butter, after all, contains a known carcinogen—aflatoxin.

But the story of the Alar apple scare is far more than just another cautionary tale about media excess and a resultant public panic. For all their power and all their flaws, the news media are ultimately mere messengers, middlemen—a conduit through which flow certain kinds of information. The forces most responsible for fear and anxiety in the contemporary body politic are the true alarmists, the people and organizations—the lobbyists, pressure groups, vested interests and concerned citizens—who use and manipulate not only that conduit but all the conduits through which society sends its myriad messages.

In the case of Alar, the prime mover was the Natural Resources Defense Council, an activist environmental group that took the Alar story to *60 Minutes,* in the form of a report titled "Intolerable Risk: Pesticides in Our Children's Food." Like many environmental and consumer groups, the NRDC generally has its heart (if not always its head) in the right place. As with most of its environmental/consumer colleagues, its avowed intent—to protect the public—is surely far more worthy than is the intent of most of the industries it criticizes, the vast majority of whom, as I've already said, seek only profits—the bigger the better—and public safety be damned. But it's one thing to call public and governmental attention to demonstrably unsafe conditions, as Ralph Nader did, for example, in his early critique of the automobile industry; it's quite another to sound the alarm over the most negligible and spurious "risks," as so many of Nader's progeny have done. Most of the undue alarmism these folks are responsible for arises from their well-meaning zeal, their admirable social conscience. Some no doubt stems from what Gregg Easterbrook, the author of *A Moment on the Earth,* calls their "institutional need . . . to promote doomsday as a concept"; they know full well that doomsday is "a much better fund-raiser than [the] guarded optimism" that Easterbrook thinks is often warranted.

But regardless of their individual motivation (mostly benign) or institutional need (sometimes less so), what is most interesting about the doomsayers who see danger and death everywhere, in everything from apples to alcohol and from steak to secondhand smoke, is that so many of them are on what passes for the Left in American society. In previous generations, most of the individuals and organizations that seemed determined to tell us what we should and (more often) should not do were on the Right. Many of the truncheon-wielding leaders of the pleasure police were (and still are) religious zealots and other conservatives preaching against the evils of sex. Now, however, we have the alarmists of the Left joining forces with the puritans of the Right for the suppression of fun in America. Their efforts, individually and collectively, have converted many in the apolitical middle to their joyless cause as well. The country, as Russell Baker has lamented in the *New York Times,* is "infested these days with a busybody puritanism determined to inflict wholesome goodness on the entire population."

I was in the small town of Three Oaks, Michigan, recently for a family reunion and was heartened to see, on the front door of a small butcher shop, a sign that said, "Enter at Your Own Risk— Ralph Nader Has Never Been Here." This kind of mocking notice used to be fairly common in an America that historically made light of risk and deterrence. Remember the tongue-in-cheek bumper sticker that said, "Everything I like is either illegal, immoral or fattening"? Remember "Eat, drink and be merry, for tomorrow we die"? The sign I saw in Michigan now seems both an anachronism and a reminder that the puritans and alarmists who surround us today are wont to say—with nary a trace of a smile—"Don't eat, drink, *or* be merry; in fact, don't do anything that's fun or tomorrow you *will* die."

A friend of mine, a sociologist named Barry Glassner, who's written on subjects ranging from fear to alcoholism to the physical-fitness fetish, just grimaces when he thinks about all this. One afternoon at my favorite Italian restaurant—over a modest lunch that included two bottles of wine, goose prosciutto, ravioli stuffed with fresh ricotta cheese, sauteed calves' brains, zucchini blossoms wrapped around *escargots,* a few bites of *parmigiano* and an assortment of *gelati*—Barry suddenly looked up and said, "Don't people realize . . . every scientific study shows that the single best thing you can do for your health is have fun?"

But the fun seems to have gone out of life for far too many people. Almost every day, it seems, I read or hear about someone saying life just isn't as much fun as it used to be. Even pregnancy, that most joyous of states (according to most mothers I know), has been turned into a job. Not that carrying a fetus for nine months was ever easy. But until relatively recently, the burdens of pregnancy were largely physical. Morning sickness. Backaches. Bladder pressure. Toting all that extra weight around. Now expectant mothers also have to worry about everything they put into their bodies or expose their bodies to.

"Years ago, women ate for two, smoked, drank black coffee, tea or alcohol and took aspirin during pregnancy (producing a generation of fast-track superachievers smart enough to blame every disaster to befall mankind on caffeine, diet foods and aspirin)," Barbara Klaus wrote in the *New York Times* not long ago. "Today, if you offer your daughter a cup of tea, the same person who only last year regarded orange juice as a kind of diet soda looks as if you are about to feed strychnine to your future grandchild."

"Years ago," Klaus continued, "prenatal exercises consisted of vomiting in the first trimester, trying on maternity clothes in the second and getting out of chairs in the third. Today there is prenatal aerobics, stretching, calisthenics and squats."

That's only the beginning. Some prenatal counselors urge expectant mothers to put tape recorders on their bulging bellies and play classical music and various educational tapes—ideally including a few in foreign languages—for the benefit of that Yale-bound fetus inside.

"Am I to believe that I have already short-changed a new life?" one pregnant mother asked plaintively in the *New York Times* after reading about such advice. "And what of the two sons I have already delivered without the benefit of intrauterine education? Will they not reach their full potential now?"

Parenthood itself—and, more important, childhood—is now seen, especially in many yuppie circles, as a top-speed marathon run. Mothers and fathers are urged to sign their infants and toddlers up for swim classes, art classes, gymnastics classes and dance classes. By kindergarten, many kids are also taking classes in science, computers, cooking, tennis and music—and playing in organized soccer, T-ball and basketball leagues. Having fun? Playing with toys? Don't be silly—unless, of course, they're educational toys. Gotta learn. Gotta study. Gotta be well rounded. Gotta hurry. Presumably, neither the Ivy League colleges nor the Wall Street law firms will bother with anyone who squandered his childhood on being a child.

Clearly, some of this cautionary behavior and some of these activities do benefit the child. My wife, Lucy—a smart, pretty, healthy Harvard graduate and a successful partner in a literary agency—once teased her mother that "I might have won the Nobel Prize if you'd put me in some of those classes and hadn't chain-smoked cigarettes and drunk all that vodka while you were pregnant with me." But in the process of making pregnancy, parenthood and childhood so goddamn safe and productive, haven't we sacrificed much of the sheer joy of all three? And aren't we compounding this sin by simultaneously overemphasizing the hazards of life to our children?

"The world's a dangerous place," says a friend of mine with a son about the same age as my son, Lucas. Well, it *can* be a dangerous place. And you aren't doing your job as a parent if you don't both prepare and protect your child accordingly. But I don't think you help your child by frightening him, by making him worry so much about everything that he comes to think of the world as a hostile environment. This friend doesn't do that. But I have several who do. How can a parent *or* a child take pleasure in a life that's made to seem as perpetually dangerous as downtown Sarajevo?

Work also seems to have lost much of its intrinsic pleasure. Almost everyone I know says he doesn't enjoy his work as much as he used to—or as much as his parents or his older colleagues say they did. To a certain extent, this is a function of the changing economy. People earn more than ever before, with more hardworking, two-income families than ever before, but—except, perhaps, for the very rich—hardly anyone seems to feel he has enough money to live as well as his salary should make possible. But workplace malaise involves more than just money, and it affects people in virtually every line of work, from manual laborer to white-collar executive. In my own life, I am particularly aware of the "this is not fun anymore" syndrome among newspaper reporters and editors who grumble that the professionalization of daily journalism—more education, higher standards, a greater ethical awareness—has been accompanied by a stultifying yuppification and political correctness that, combined with corporate bottom-line pressures, have taken much of the raffish, rough-and-tumble fun out of the business. I hear a similar complaint from editors at magazines and book-publishing houses who say they have been forced to give up the joy of working with writers and words and now worry only about marketing and profits. I hear the "no fun no more" lament most loudly from chef friends, whose creativity and sense of adventure are stifled by customers determined to eat nothing more caloric than cauliflower.

The fortunate few in any field who once found their jobs so much fun that they were astonished they actually got paid to do it may be the most hard hit by the demise of pleasure.

"It just wasn't fun anymore," Ryne Sandberg, the longtime, all-star second baseman for the Chicago Cubs, said when he (temporarily) retired from baseball in 1994, still healthy and still playing superbly. Many entertainers say the same thing. So do those doctors who are genuinely committed to helping their patients—there actually are some—but who grumble that between the avalanche of government-mandated paperwork and the anxiety over malpractice lawsuits, they no longer enjoy or have much time for the interpersonal contact that first attracted them to medicine. The kind of "fun" that both Barry Goldwater and John Kennedy envisioned having when they thought they would run against each other for president in 1964 died in Dallas; today, there is a meanness of spirit abroad in the land, and it has turned the political arena into a swampland of charge and countercharge, of cynicism and scandal—real and imagined. I was discussing this phenomenon with Mario Cuomo, the former governor of New York, in the waning days of 1995, and he said he saw a deep and troubling connection between the pervasive atmosphere of negativism and the frustrating stalemate we seem to have reached, as a government and as a society, in our efforts to solve our many problems. "You can't move forward," Cuomo said, "you can't innovate or develop new programs if everyone's saying 'No, don't, that's bad' all the time."

The news media have contributed significantly to this atmosphere. Politicians now have to worry that everything they do—or have ever done—will be subjected to intense scrutiny (and possible misinterpretation) by a mass media that is increasingly arrogant, scornful and knee-jerk adversarial. A record number of congressmen and senators have announced that they will not seek reelection this year; many of them blame the press for creating a climate that has severely undermined the pleasure and sense of accomplishment they once found in their work. "You make everything we do seem criminal," one congressman told *Newsweek*. Then, echoing Ryne Sandberg, he said, "The job just isn't fun anymore."

Of course, many people who complain about not having fun anymore can wipe the tears from their eyes with copies of multimillion-dollar contracts. It's difficult to feel sorry for a baseball player or movie star or rock singer who complains that what he does has been reduced to a mere business, while he simultaneously pockets more money for working one day than many people make in a year. When Ryne Sandberg retired—sixteen months before he announced that he was un-retiring—he criticized many of his fellow players for taking no pride in their work, for caring about nothing but themselves. "When I was coming up, we played baseball because we loved the game," he said in his 1995 autobiography. That's no longer true, Sandberg says, and after he announced his return to baseball, he revisited this theme, telling a columnist from the *Chicago Tribune* that players "should be enjoying what they're doing and having fun with it." But today's players don't chat after a game about whether the pitcher had good stuff or whether the umpires blew a call, Sandberg says; they talk about their stock portfolios and the designer clothes they saw in the local men's store. In recent years, several baseball players—new *and* old, Darryl Strawberry *and* Duke Snider (not to mention Pete Rose and Willie McCovey)—have cheated on their income tax by failing to report tens of thousands of dollars they secretly pocketed for selling autographs and other baseball memorabilia that players once gave away willingly to adoring young fans.

Like athletes, many of today's spoiled and arrogant entertainers have brought most of their problems on themselves. Callous, greedy doctors and corrupt, hypocritical politicians have done likewise.

Some people, however—in every line of work, in every avenue of life—are simply incapable of having fun, for any number of reasons, ranging from religious training to toilet training and from overbearing parents to an overweaning social conscience. Worse, they seem to resent anyone else having any fun, of any kind. By the same token, I think that some people who are not exceptionally talented—which, let's face it, means most of us—resent those who are exceptionally talented. To some of these bitter mediocrities, excellence is not a quality to be admired, but one to be scorned. When President Nixon nominated Harrold Carswell to the United States Supreme Court in 1970, some critics said Carswell was too mediocre for so august a position. But Senator Roman Hruska of Nebraska said, "There are a lot of mediocre judges and people and lawyers, and they are entitled to a little representation."

Envy—jealousy—provides the negative energy that drives many of the pleasure police. Remember when Michael Jordan announced that he was retiring from basketball to play professional baseball? Instead of being applauded for having the courage to leave a sport at which he was the best in the world, at the peak of his game, to take on a new challenge, he was ridiculed for being arrogant and presumptuous. Again, excellence scorned. Forget for the moment that Jordan wound up abandoning baseball after one, strike-shortened season and returned to basketball; didn't he deserve a chance to see what he could do, to see if the joy that he no longer found in basketball could be rekindled in baseball? Not according to many sportswriters and sports fans.

"There are those who believe that Jordan's mere presence may be just as much a sideshow as was the appearance of the 3-foot-7-inch [Eddie] Gaedel at the plate for the St. Louis Browns in a 1951 game," harrumphed Claire Smith, a sports columnist for the *New York Times,* in a blast typical of the sporting (and sports journalism) fraternity. "Bag It, Michael!" *Sports Illustrated* ordered, in bold yellow type on the cover of its March 14, 1994, issue. "Jordan and the White Sox Are Embarrassing Baseball," the secondary cover line said. Of course, all this was a month before Jordan had played a single game for the Birmingham Barons, the Chicago White Sox minor-league team to which he was ultimately assigned. And it was five months before baseball truly embarrassed itself with the appalling spectacle of an eight-month strike by spoiled, rich players against spoiled, richer owners who demanded the players help them do what they didn't trust themselves to do—stop overpaying undertalented ballplayers.

Some of the players ganged up on Jordan, too. It took George Brett, the class act from the Kansas City Royals, to put their sour grapes in perspective. "I know a lot of players don't want to see him make it because it will be a slap in the face to them," Brett said.

Kenneth Branagh, the talented British actor and film director, and his estranged wife, the gifted actress Emma Thompson, have encountered similar hostility and skepticism. Branagh and Thompson should be the toast of Britain. Instead, the British press actually criticizes them for being so successful. The British, Thompson said, "are terrible apologizers for success," and she theorized—only half in jest, I assume—that the perennially dreadful weather in England was to blame. "Everybody gets miserable," she said. "They say, 'Let's have a go at Emma because we're so miserable.' "

This analysis may seem as sophomoric as it is self-serving. But I've seen similar forces at work in the treatment of anything from the West Coast, especially Los Angeles, by the media and other opinion makers and culturemongers on the East Coast. Understandably, New York editors don't like being forever jostled on noisy, crowded streets and suffering through cold, snowy winters and hot, humid summers. But rather than admit that, they seem to take a perverse pride in battling and overcoming the elements, both natural and man-made. It's part of the hubris inherent in the self-congratulatory lyrics of the city's unofficial anthem, "New York, New York"—in particular, the line that says if people can make it in New York, they can make it anywhere. So New Yorkers make fun of the supposedly easy life in Los Angeles, of the sun and the palm trees and the swimming pools and the movie stars in "La-La Land." Never mind that most people in Los Angeles don't have swimming pools or work in Hollywood. Or that those who do work in Hollywood tend to work far longer hours than do those on Madison Avenue—as Lucy found out, to her shock and amazement, when she went from being an agent selling books in New York to being an agent selling movie scripts in Los Angeles. The basic attitude of most news executives in New York toward Los Angeles is, "You people are all sitting in hot tubs, wearing gold chains around your neck and eating alfalfa sprouts," says David Browning, who repeatedly encountered this mind-set when he was a senior producer for the *CBS Evening News* in Los Angeles, pitching stories to his bosses in Manhattan.

Of course, every February, when New York winter is at its freezing, sleety worst, it's amazing how many magazine editors suddenly find an excuse to visit Los Angeles, where they gleefully indulge in the very activities they then cite to prove how insubstantial life in Los Angeles really is. They beg their Los Angeles bureau chiefs to get them good tables at Spago and they "want to have dinners with Goldie Hawn and Raquel Welch . . . and they then go back to New York to talk about how shallow we are," Peter Greenberg, a freelance journalist, television producer, and former *Newsweek* correspondent in Los Angeles, told me several years ago.

The zealous-cum-jealous determination of many New Yorkers to ridicule Los Angelenos for their allegedly "laid-back" lifestyle—to try to make them feel guilty about finding pleasure in their back-

yard, rather than on the twenty-fifth floor of an office skyscraper—
manifests itself most clearly whenever there is a disaster in Los Angeles. Unfortunately, the riots, fires, floods, earthquake and recession of recent years have given New Yorkers ample opportunity to
suggest that the people of Los Angeles are somehow being punished
for having too much fun. The price of pleasure, they seem to suggest, is disaster. "Los Angeles has often been described as a city in
denial—of aging, of unhappy endings, of rain, of earthquakes," said
a front-page story in the *New York Times* three weeks after the city's
devastating January 17, 1994, earthquake. It was as if God had
unleashed forty justly deserved plagues on a modern-day Sodom and
Gomorrah. Indeed, the Sodom and Gomorrah analogy is apt, since
it was sex—licentiousness and perversity—that brought the wrath of
God down upon those two biblical towns, and it is sex—kinky sex,
hot-tub sex, gay sex, free-love sex—that helped ignite the New York
media's scorn of Los Angeles (and San Francisco) in the 1960s.

Perhaps because sex is the most fun—the greatest pleasure—
you can have on earth (and in heaven, too, I hope, or else I ain't
going), sex has historically been the human activity on which the
moral militia has come down the hardest. I'll have more—much
more—to say on matters sexual in chapter 5, but it may be worth
noting here that in their zeal to control everything from our eating
to our mating, in their determination to live even longer, "healthier"
lives, many people seem to forget that life, ultimately, is much like a
penis: how long it is matters far less than what you do with it.

2
—

YOU
ARE
WHAT
YOU
EAT

I have it on good and ancient authority—two good and ancient authorities, in fact, the original M&M's, Moses and Matthew—that man cannot live by bread alone. But the way things are going, lo these many centuries later, I expect the Center for Science in the Public Interest to announce any day now that not only is bread insufficient, it's unhealthful as well. After all, the center has already warned us off *chiles rellenos,* hamburgers, popcorn, pasta, *kung pao* chicken, submarine sandwiches and virtually everything else except brussels sprouts and tofu.

I know that too much fat can raise cholesterol and contribute to heart disease, prostate cancer and various other diseases. I realize that too many Americans are overweight and that too much weight can cause a wide variety of other serious illnesses, including diabetes. I'm aware of the sixteen-year study published in the *New England Journal of Medicine* in September 1995 that said one-half of all deaths from cardiovascular disease and one-third of all cancer deaths are attributable to overweight. That same study—of 115,000 female nurses—said that even a moderate weight gain significantly increases one's risk of dying earlier than one's thinner counterparts. Today, a third of all Americans weigh at least 20 percent more than

they should; that's about 30 percent more overweight people, proportionally, than we had a decade ago. That's cause for national
concern. But I don't think it's cause for what Julia Child has called a
"fear of food." I don't think people should look on food as the
Enemy.

Writing in *Time* magazine early in 1995, Barbara Ehrenreich
lamented that "Food, which once served primarily as a cure for
hypoglycemia, has become an entertainment medium." The only
thing wrong with that statement is that it's not true. Would that it
were. Wouldn't it be better to think of food as pleasure than as
medicine? Most of us—those of us fortunate enough to be able to
afford it—eat three times a day; why should we look on that activity
as therapy or treatment when it should be fun? To be sure, there was
a relatively brief period of time, from the late 1970s into the mid-
1980s, when *nouvelle cuisine* swept the land and people suddenly
began going to restaurants and cooking at home and talking about
food as if it were a combination of a remarkable new toy, a lifesav-
ing scientific discovery and the Holy Grail. Unfortunately, that silly
trend triggered an even sillier trend, and people are now being told
that eating is not only not fun—it's dangerous. "Beware—Eating Is
Hazardous to Your Health" could be the bumper sticker of the broccoli brigades.

Many people are actually afraid to eat. To them, every morsel
of food contains a potential, hidden carcinogen—or, at the very
least, a gram of fat that will somehow, simultaneously, attach itself
to their heretofore-svelte hips (or thighs or waist) and to the inner
wall of their main cardiac artery, where it will lie in wait, prepared
to clog that bloody thoroughfare and bring about instant death. I
know many other people who regard the act of eating as simply the
human equivalent of putting gas in the car; you have to do it at
regular intervals to keep the engine running, but that doesn't mean
you actually look forward to it or enjoy it. Other Americans of my
acquaintance are so indifferent to food that they resent having to
stop what they're doing to eat. The *Wall Street Journal* published a
story in 1995 on young singles demanding "grab-and-go" foods so
they can gulp down a quick bite while shaving, brushing their hair
or running out the door. "Many feel they are wasting time unless

they combine eating with another activity," the *Journal* said, quoting Saul Katz, a food anthropologist at the University of Pennsylvania.

Not me, babe.

For me, eating well—by which I mean eating that which I enjoy, from hot dogs to *haute cuisine*—is a hobby (okay—an obsession). Eating is sheer pleasure; it appeals to all my senses. I like the aesthetics of food—how it looks and smells on the plate as well as how it tastes and feels and even how it sounds in my mouth. To me, the texture of food is almost as important as its taste. I love things that are chewy or crunchy, not mushy. When I have a steak, I want a thick, blood-rare New York strip sirloin, not a filet mignon. Whenever someone describes a steak—or any piece of meat—as "so tender it melts in your mouth," my first thought is, "When I want something that melts in my mouth, I'll eat ice cream."

I claim no objectivity whatsoever where food is concerned. I love to eat. I love virtually every cuisine—fancy or plain—from virtually every country. I love *b'stilla* and *paella, pâté* and prosciutto, sushi and sausage, Peking duck and *pad Thai*. I love *kung pao* chicken, *tandoori* chicken, fried chicken, roast chicken and chicken *mole*. I love barbecued ribs and prime rib. I love fresh fruit and fresh vegetables, fresh fish and fresh bread. I love turkey with dressing, hamburgers with french fries, bagels with smoked salmon. I love steak, lamb chops, Caesar salads, lobster, submarine sandwiches, hot dogs, shrimp cocktails, chocolate chip cookies, lemon meringue pie, dill pickles, peanuts, pretzels, potato chips . . .

I love fine French food best of all, with *alta cucina* a close second. (Risotto with white truffles truly is, as my restaurateur friend Piero Selvaggio says, "the Lord's porridge.") Fine dining—the entire food and wine experience, in any cuisine—is my only extravagance. I'm not rich and I don't own a fancy watch or a boat or any original art. I kept my last car, a Honda, for eleven years, and I hope to keep my current car, a Toyota, at least that long. My home is modest and my wardrobe even more so. I do, however, spend a disproportionate share of my salary on food and wine, and I look forward to virtually every meal—elaborate or simple, at home or in a restaurant—with the enthusiasm of a kid going to the circus.

When I travel, I make restaurant reservations before I make airplane, hotel and rental car reservations, wherever I go, whether for business or pleasure. Nineteen times in the past eighteen years, I've gone to France, for periods ranging from four days to five weeks, on itineraries designed almost exclusively around restaurants. In my computer at home, I keep frequently updated lists of my favorite restaurants in France, as well as in Italy, Los Angeles, New York and Washington. For any airplane trip longer than two hours, I take my own food and wine on board.

It's a measure of how deeply engrained anxiety about food has become in our society that when I begin unwrapping my various airborne delicacies, the first reaction of most other passengers is that I must be a vegetarian or have allergies or some other health reason for bringing my own food. When asked, I say, "Yes, I am allergic—to the crappy food that all airlines serve." Then, having brought more food than any one person could or should eat, I always offer tastes to my seatmates. They almost always accept—eagerly and gratefully.

Like John Mortimer, the British novelist and playwright, "I refuse to spend my life worrying about what I eat. There is no pleasure worth forgoing just for an extra three years in the geriatric ward." Don't get me wrong. I'm self-indulgent, not self-destructive. I do not agree with the wag who once described Irish coffee as "the only beverage that provides in a single glass all four essential food groups—alcohol, caffeine, sugar and fat." I understand the need for a healthful diet. I realize that one reason for our increased longevity and our decreasing cardiac death rate is that many people are being more careful about what they eat. That's good. My father had his first heart attack when he was thirty-eight, and he fought high cholesterol for the next quarter century before dying at sixty-two, still grumbling about the sacrifice he'd made in shifting from pastrami sandwiches to brisket of beef. My own cholesterol has long been borderline high, and given my heredity and my decidedly type A personality, I recognize the ineluctable wisdom of occasionally displaying at least a modicum of good judgment at table. I don't eat most junk food, I seldom snack between meals and I eat a healthful breakfast virtually every day I'm home: fresh-squeezed orange juice, a slice of toasted French bread with olive oil, a bowl of fresh fruit, nonfat milk and oat bran O's—the latter, I confess, for their reputed cholesterol-fighting qualities, not for their (marginally tolerable) taste. (Not long ago, when the newest medical research suggested that soy was an even more effective weapon than oat bran in the cholesterol wars, I decided to try some soy pancakes for breakfast instead. I used soy milk and soy flour—no egg, of course, since egg has cholesterol and that would defeat the purpose of the exercise. Without the egg, though, the batter didn't bind, and what I wound up with was a gloppy mess. I tried to eat it anyway, while reading the morning paper. I should have eaten the paper instead. It wouldn't have lowered my cholesterol, but it sure as hell would have tasted better.)

For dinner at home, unless Lucy and I are entertaining guests, we generally have fish or fowl or pasta, followed by salad and fresh fruit. As much as I love a thick steak and a gooey hot fudge sundae, I probably don't have either of them more than once every couple of months or so. The same goes for a pastrami sandwich, liver, barbecued ribs and many of my other favorite, cholesterol-laden foods (except for hot dogs during baseball season). But I certainly wouldn't claim to be a health-conscious eater, not if you add up all those occasional treats *and* all the delicacies I consume that, while clearly less hazardous than hot dogs, could by no means be confused with kale. As two working parents with a five-year-old son, Lucy and I call our local Italian delivery service at least once every couple of weeks or so to order pizza (pepperoni for me!), and—more important—we usually go out to restaurants three or four nights a week.

There are, I know, people who boast of a unique strategy that they call "eating out defensively"—which generally means either (1) going to some health food emporium, ordering a soyburger with alfalfa sprouts and washing it down with a big glass of rutabaga juice, or (2) going to a normal restaurant and ordering "a green salad, no dressing, broiled fish, no sauce, no dessert, no wine and a cup of herb tea"—all of which raises the obvious question: "WHY DON'T YOU STAY HOME AND EAT YOUR GERANIUMS?!"

Dr. Stephen Gullo is a psychologist and best-selling author

who has turned "defensive" eating into a moneymaking specialty. On an eating expedition at New York's tony La Grenouille for a 1995 *New York Times* story, Dr. Gullo solemnly explained to his journalistic companion that he wouldn't eat bread or butter or order the smoked salmon, split-pea soup, pâté or even the grilled vegetables (they were—*quel choc!*—"prepared with oil"); nor would he order—among many other items on the menu—filet mignon, veal, oxtail, cheese soufflé or any dessert other than sorbet. Before going to a restaurant, Dr. Gullo advises clients to eat an apple or a no-fat yogurt or, once inside the restaurant, to "drink a tomato juice before ordering." Tomato juice, he says, is "a natural appetite suppressant." (I assume he also advises his clients to masturbate before making love.)

Naturally, all these defensive eaters miss—among many other treats—The Cheese Course. They also deprive *me* of the cheese course. There are few dining experiences more pleasurable than an assortment of cheese—Vacherin, Brillat-Savarin, St.-Marcellin, Brie, Epoisses—with bread and fruit and red wine. A formal cheese course has never been *de rigueur* in restaurants in this country as it is in France. It's just not part of our Velveeta culture. But when large numbers of Americans first became interested in fine dining in the late 1970s and early 1980s, some upscale restaurants in this country did offer cheese. Americans who order cheese in restaurants are rare these days, though, and few restaurants offer it anymore; the chefs know they'd just have to throw most of it away, at a considerable financial loss.

In an effort to be sensible—but not insensate—I, too, try to avoid an abundance of fatty foods in restaurants: no butter on my bread, few cream sauces on my pasta, more poultry than red meat. But I refuse to turn the exquisite pleasure of the dining experience into a ritual of deprivation and self-abnegation. I go to a restaurant—be it a hamburger stand, a trattoria or a gastronomic temple worthy of three stars from the *Guide Michelin*—to eat the best, tastiest food available at that particular establishment (although in the aftermath of the *E. coli* poisoning at several Jack in the Box outlets a few years ago, it's more difficult to get the best, tastiest hamburgers anywhere; the fearmongers and the lawyers have so terrified burger-cookers throughout the country that I practically have to sign a notarized waiver if I insist on the kind of fat, juicy, very rare burger I love).

Fortunately, by eating out a lot over the years, I've become friendly with virtually all the best chefs in Los Angeles, where I live, and with several of the best chefs in New York, Washington and France as well, and it's not uncommon for me to ignore the menu and just ask the chef to cook whatever he thinks I might like that night. Needless to say, such a liberating offer is not likely to bring forth from the kitchen a plate of steamed broccoli, a side order of wheat germ and a dessert of bok choy pie—certainly not at a time when many chefs are gnashing their teeth (and mashing their *toques)* over all the dreary orders they get from the aforementioned defensive (and increasingly offensive) diners. This is not to say that good chefs can't make healthful food. Many can—and do—rise to the challenge imposed by their demanding customers. Many chefs now substitute vegetable broths and purees for cream and butter. They use Asian herbs and spices to compensate for the loss of those flavors. They grill thick, meaty porcini and portobello mushrooms instead of steaks and chops. But chefs don't like artificial limits placed on their creativity. As Daniel Boulud, the superb chef at Restaurant Daniel in New York, put it in the course of a *New York Times* interview on the (allegedly) low-fat, low-calorie meals that many of his colleagues were serving: "Are the chefs telling you the truth? The chefs tell me they are dumping a lot of fat into the food."

Chefs—good, talented chefs—become chefs so they can cook, experiment, indulge their imagination, have fun—not to cater to a bunch of neurotic anorexics, most of whom are terrified of eating anything that isn't green, leafy and grown without the assistance of any technology created more recently than the Peloponnesian War. Instead of evolving normally, as primates, the forebears of these calorie-conscious cretins clearly—somehow—mutated into vegetable-chomping rabbits.

The most frenzied of these folks are not terribly pleasant to be around. Brillat-Savarin, the French gastronome of the late eighteenth and early nineteenth centuries, said, "Tell me what you eat, and I shall tell you what you are," which Bertolt Brecht, the German poet and playwright, modified a century later to "A man is just the food he eats." No wonder the nutrition Nazis all sound as if they have the IQ—and the disposition—of a turnip.

Moderation and common sense are as advisable and as admirable in eating as in any other human endeavor. But these mutants are not moderate; they're manic. No, they're beyond manic; they're paranoid. Worse, many are proselytizers. Worse still, they're enforcers, members of the food mafia. Except for a few animal rights zealots who regard the consumption of veal as the equivalent of a war atrocity and behave accordingly—one protester was crushed to death in 1995 when she threw herself beneath the wheels of a truck bringing live calves (i.e., veal) to a London airport—these culinary capos have not (yet) adopted the violent ways of their Sicilian brethren. But neither have they learned the value of *omerta*. They just won't shut up. Everywhere you turn, you're besieged by their dire warnings. They want to save your life—and your soul. Their smug sense of moral superiority as they nibble on their bran muffins is repugnant.

"These days, eating the wrong foods is almost tantamount to a character flaw," Karen Barr wrote in the *New York Times* in 1995. To avoid embarrassment, lying about what you eat has become "common," Barr said, and she quoted an expert on eating disorders as saying, "It's part of the culture we live in, which emphasizes health and fitness and eating right to the point that people who eat other things, these 'bad' foods, are viewed as sinful."

The new arbiters of our daily diet seem to think the road to heaven is paved with bean curd—and the road to hell is paved with fat. "Fat has become a four-letter word. There's a cultural notion that the lower the fat content, the better person you are," says Dr. Timothy Walsh, the director of the Eating Disorders Research Unit of the New York State Psychiatric Institute at Columbia Presbyterian Medical Center.

Hence, in a May 1992 *New York Times* article beneath the headline "The Dream of Low-Fat Baking," Marian Burros wrote, "For those of us who love sweets too much for our own good, the discovery of no-fat baking ranks right up there with the discovery of penicillin." To me, this dream seems more like a nightmare. The few low-fat pastries I've been induced to try all *tasted* like penicillin.

Burros concedes that desserts baked without fat "will never taste as good as desserts baked with fat. . . . The zucchini bread has a little rubbery spring in each bite. But it's amazing how quickly you can get used to such baking when you crave something sweet but don't want 20 grams of fat along with it." What's more amazing is that anyone would want to eat something that tastes like rubber. Of course too much fat is bad for you. We all know that. The Japanese are generally healthier than we are, in large measure because they eat only about 25 percent of the fat we do—until they move here and begin eating our fatty foods. But the solution seems simple: why not eat real sweets (or steak or pizza or whatever) but just do so less often? Why is it assumed that frequently consuming tasteless, ersatz food is "better"—smarter, more healthful, more virtuous—than occasionally consuming certain real foods? Why is it better to try to fool yourself and deprive yourself than to simply exercise a little restraint and common sense?

But fat—fat in any form or quantity—is the bête noire of the food mafia, as Burros's *Times* colleague, the redoubtable Jane Brody, reminded her readers on the day before Thanksgiving in 1992, when she disclosed this startling bit of news: "Numerous studies show that calorie-for-calorie, fat is by far the most fattening nutrient."

No shit! Or should I say, "No fat!"?

Eight years before that column, only 8 percent of American shoppers said they were more concerned about fat than about anything else in the food they ate; by 1992 that percentage had skyrocketed to 48 percent. That same year, as Michelle Stacey notes in *Consumed: Why Americans Love, Hate and Fear Food*, "1,257 new low-fat or nonfat products were introduced into supermarkets, making it the first year ever that more products boasted of being low-fat than of being low-calorie." By 1994, there were more than twice as many new "low-fat" and "nonfat" products as there were "low-calorie" products. Warnings from magazines like *Newsweek* helped fuel that trend: "The easiest way to make good choices when you walk into the supermarket or open the refrigerator is to remember just one fact," *Newsweek* said in 1991. "Fat, especially the saturated fat found in animal products, is the biggest troublemaker in the American diet." Thus, advertising about olive oil "no longer rhapsodizes about the antique terraced groves of Liguria in which the fragrant source of the golden liquid is hand-picked," laments Lionel Tiger in *The Pursuit of Pleasure.* "Instead, there is a grim medical report about saturated fats and the inner tubes of the buyer's arteries."

We have become a nation of fat-obsessed diet drones.

The newest magic bullet for the fat phobics is olestra, a synthetic oil that slides right through your system without being absorbed. This fat-free fat has a slight aftertaste, absorbs some of the nutrients and carotenoids that may help fight cancer and heart disease, causes flatulence and gives some people loose bowels. But now that the Food and Drug Administration has approved the use of olestra in snack foods, you can be sure that many Americans will rush out to buy the products that will be made with it. Trading fat for farts will be the odor—er, order—of the day.

Much of human history has been the story of the struggle for sustenance—for enough food to get through the day. In many parts of the world—including the ghettos, barrios and other poverty pockets of our own country—that struggle continues, every day. And yet, ironically, about 80 million Americans, more than a third of our population, struggle to eat *less* or, in extreme cases, to avoid eating altogether. Americans now spend almost $40 *billion* a year on diets of one sort or another. Most dieters fail—or they succeed temporarily, then fail; more than 90 percent of all dieters regain their lost weight within five years. In *Feeding on Dreams,* their denunciation of what they call "the diet con game," Diane Epstein and Kathleen Thompson say that only one in every 250 people who undertake a diet program loses weight in the long term. Dietmongers insist that's because most people don't really want to lose weight or lack the willpower to resist the fat- and sugar-laden concoctions that beckon so seductively from every menu, refrigerator, magazine and television commercial in the land. All of those factors are, no doubt, part of the problem. Many putative dieters do give up too easily, wailing, in effect, "It's not my fault; the devil's food made me do it." But some people *can't* lose weight. And I don't just mean the unfortunate few whose genes and glands have made them grotesquely, uncontrollably fat.

Genetics dictates a great deal about *most* people's weight. Some studies of twins have shown that at least 50 percent of the weight problems in this country are genetically determined. But "conventional dietary advice takes no account" of that, says Dr. Artemis P. Simopoulos, president of the Center for Genetics, Nutrition and Health in Washington, D.C. Researchers at the Howard Hughes Medical Institute at Rockefeller University in New York have found a gene in mice that they think tells the mouse when its body has consumed all the food it needs. The scientists theorized that this natural appetite suppressant may also exist in humans—and may be deficient or malfunctioning in humans who overeat. Subsequent research went a step further: scientists at three separate research centers discovered a hormone that speeds up a mouse's metabolism, suppresses its appetite and makes it lose weight. Since humans produce a similar hormone, which the scientists named *leptin*, from the Greek word for "thin," they theorized that obesity might ultimately be seen as a treatable metabolic disorder, rather than as the result of willful overeating. This would tend to corroborate a growing body of research that suggests that the human body—fat, skinny or in between—usually adjusts to its natural weight. People who are overweight often overeat in order to "maintain the weight that puts their energy metabolism precisely on target for their height and body composition," Dr. Jules Hirsch, physician in chief at Rockefeller University, told the *New York Times* in 1995.

This strongly suggests that many people may have far less control over their eating habits—and their weight—than the diet doctors would have them believe. It also suggests that millions of Americans are unnecessarily—and cruelly—being made to feel guilty, stupid, weak and self-destructive. This is all the more troubling given yet another, thoroughly insidious explanation for the inability of most people to lose weight: most diets are unscientific—as bogus as they are torturous. They prey on peoples' ignorance and vanity and on the guilt created by the diet promoters, health shamans and thin-thigh thickheads who increasingly dominate our social discourse. Eat only protein, says one diet. Eat only carbohydrates, says another. Drink booze, says a third. Drink powdered potions, says a fourth. Visualize your fat melting away, says a fifth. I'd like to visualize all diet books melting away. Fahrenheit 451 for the fat fetishists.

Almost every year, it seems, there's a new diet guru promising to lead the wandering chews out of the caloric wilderness into the promised gland. Adelle Davis and *Let's Eat Right to Keep Fit* begets Dr. Herman Tarnower and *The Complete Scarsdale Medical Diet,* which begets Judy Mazel and *The Beverly Hills Diet,* which begets Nathan Pritikin and *The Pritikin Program,* which begets Dr. Robert Atkins and the *New Diet Revolution,* which begets Dr. Martin Katahn and *The T-Factor Diet,* which begets Rosemary Conley and *The Complete Hip and Thigh Diet,* which begets Nancy and Dr. Ron Goor and *Choose to Lose,* which begets Michel Montignac and the *"foie gras* diet," which begets Dr. Dean Ornish and his low-fat vegetarian diet, which begets—well, I know I've missed a few of these maestros of the midriff. The latest is Dr. Stephen Gullo, the aforementioned New York psychologist who advises restaurant-goers to suppress their appetites—and who keeps a yellow, five-pound model of fat on his desk, presumably to remind his clients how attractive they are (a mirror for masochists, as it were). Dr. Gullo regards himself as more motivator than nutritionist, and as the *New York Times* noted in 1995, he is "big on sound bites," especially in the slogan-laden inspirational tapes he provides his clients, who pay $500 for an initial interview and $175 for each of the twenty-minute weekly sessions he provides thereafter. ($175 for twenty minutes? Why would anyone in his right mind pay $525 an hour to hear someone spout things like "Weight control begins with finger control." And "Change your head and weight loss will follow!" And "Think white and green! Fish and vegetables are the Concorde to thin!"?)

The ultimate irony of the unending quest to be thin is that studies now show that the elderly are better off being a little fat than a little skinny. According to a study reported in the *New York Times* in October 1995, researchers have discovered that "the risk is not there" even if you're twenty pounds overweight after passing your seventieth birthday. The risks only "begin to rise" for elderly people who are *fifty to seventy-five pounds overweight,* the story said. But the "risk of mortality [is] . . . high in elderly people who are underweight, rising sharply the leaner they are." Unfortunately, the pressure to be slender is so strong in our society that many elderly people think they are overweight when they are not—and many try to lose weight when they should not. It's difficult to reverse direction after being bombarded for decades by propaganda from the fat patrol, so people deprive themselves for years, experiment with one diet after another and finally—maybe—achieve Nirvana on the bathroom scales . . . just in time to start shaking their heads and muttering, "Say what?" when their doctor tells them, "You know, you should put on a few pounds; you'd be healthier."

The tug-of-war between self-indulgence and self-denial—between Rabelaisian gratification and Calvinistic abstemiousness—has been going on in the United States since before this country was officially a country. At various times in our history, various activities, conditions and substances—wealth, power, alcohol, drugs, leisure time, sexual promiscuity—have been seen as representative of the indulgence half of that equation; today, to many, fat is the ultimate (and ultimately evil) self-indulgence.

But "fat is what people really want, because it makes you feel good," says Dr. Adam Drewnowski, head of the human nutrition program at the University of Michigan. That's also one reason that many people crave chocolate. It makes them feel good. Some researchers say several of the more than four hundred natural and chemical compounds in chocolate induce feelings similar to that generated by love. Many women, suffering from diminished endorphin and serotonin levels just before the onset of each menstrual cycle, find that the fat, sugar and other compounds in chocolate increase those levels in the brain, relieving their lethargy and grumpiness and making them feel happy and energetic. And chocolate tastes good, too. Imagine that! So what happened when the American Medical Association released its winter 1995 gift catalog, which featured a one-pound, anatomically correct, solid milk chocolate heart? The fat fascists went crazy. How dare the AMA make such a wicked, death-dealing gift available, they howled. Chocolate is full of saturated fatty acids, the No. 1 villain on the FDA's Most Wanted list, the prime culprit in raising cholesterol levels, clogging coronary arteries and causing heart attacks. Does that mean a few bites of chocolate on Valentine's Day will put you six feet under by nightfall?

Gimme a fucking break.

Dr. Drewnowski is one of several academic nutritionists studying why people eat certain foods. As with chocolate, the answer is often a physiological craving—a biological need—rather than a conscious choice. Anyone whose pregnant wife has suddenly demanded a dill pickle at four o'clock in the morning will instantly understand this concept. But why must such understanding be limited to pregnant women? Aren't hormones active under other circumstances, in men and women alike? Might a man eat a steak not only because he likes the way it tastes but because his body needs the protein and the fat? The blindly self-indulgent, utterly lacking in restraint, could use this argument to rationalize any excess. That, obviously, would be foolish. But it's worth thinking about physiological cravings, as well as the pleasure they provide, before we rush to ostracize—and outlaw—all fat. After all, there has to be some reason that no nutrition researcher has ever found that his human subjects reported a deepseated craving for tofu or mung beans.

Sue Luke, a nutritionist in Charlotte, North Carolina, calls the alarming trend toward the avoidance of all fat a "fat phobia," and she warns dieters against worrying so much about fat that they surrender the pleasure of eating. "Food is meant to be enjoyed," she says, "and I think it's a sad scenario when we see people obsessing about what they are going to eat next, and worried about how fat it will make them."

Sensible folks like Luke are all too rare these days. The fat phobia is all around us, an excrescence upon the body politic. I was reminded of it yet again while driving through the predominantly Chinese suburb of Monterey Park, east of downtown Los Angeles. Looming just ahead of me, in one of those ubiquitous Southern California minimalls, was a large sign, in red letters, that could well have marked the headquarters of the food mafia:

SHUN FAT SUPERMARKET

I was particularly sensitive to the unintended message of that sign because my then-five-year-old son, Lucas, had suddenly begun reading to me—just two days earlier, in ominous tones—the fat content of various packaged foods that showed up on our breakfast and dinner table. I don't know where or how he became concerned about fat. Neither he nor his mother nor I is fat, and none of us had talked about fat—or about dieting of any kind. Quite the opposite. Because eating is an important part of our lives, we have shared with Lucas our view of eating as fun, and we have included him in the dining experience from, quite literally, the first day he came home from the hospital, when we put him on the kitchen floor at dinnertime, between our chairs, in a bassinet. We wanted him to appreciate—if only by osmosis at first—both the sensory and the social pleasures of dining. We wanted him to understand that mealtime is not just a pit stop but a time for pleasure and sharing, for conversation and togetherness, and that food is not merely fuel, not a threat or an obstacle or a challenge, but a joy. Lucas quickly graduated from bassinet to Sassy seat to high chair to regular chair. (For some reason, he skipped the booster-chair stage.) At first, Lucy nursed him, and we both fed him bottles. As soon as he seemed interested, we added commercial baby food and then—at six months— chopped, ground and mashed versions of whatever we were eating. He got used to eating off a plate and using a fork and spoon and drinking from a glass at an early age—and he got used to eating real food. In fact, he quickly came to prefer our food to his. He might start a meal with formula or a jar of baby food, but the instant we began to eat, he lost all interest in what he had and would eat only what we were eating—swordfish, chicken, leg of lamb, pasta, broccoli, salami, French bread, a fresh peach. We took Lucas to restaurants within weeks of his birth, letting him sleep in his Sassy seat or his car seat, on the floor or on a chair. As soon as he was able, we put him in a high chair and let him nibble on Sichuan eggplant and hamburger and tandoori chicken and *pappa al pomodoro* and anything else that seemed to interest him. He liked Italian food best of all, and once—when he was eight months old and Lucy ordered scrambled eggs for him during lunch at a local deli—he looked at his plate, smiled at her and said, "Polenta?"

A month later—on the same night that Lucas took his first, tentative steps—we took him out for his first fancy French dinner at Citrus, one of our favorite restaurants in Los Angeles. The chef, Michel Richard, is as warm and generous as he is creative; the father of five himself, he was delighted to see Lucas in his restaurant, and he made him miniature portions of everything we had. *Foie gras.* Diced, marinated Norwegian salmon served on a thin slice of raw potato and topped with caviar. Seafood sausage. Potato risotto. Sesame chicken. *Crème brûlée.* Lucas loved it all—especially the *crème brûlée.*

I wrote a short article about this experience for the *Los Angeles Times* and received several letters from outraged readers. They were horrified that we had encouraged our "poor little boy" to eat such fatty, cholesterol-laden foods as *foie gras* and *crème brûlée.* But when I asked our pediatrician about it, she first laughed, then shook her head. "They're perfect baby food," she said. "They're soft, easy to swallow, strong flavors, full of protein."

Lucas is six now and he has since had *foie gras* in Paris, steak in New York, hot dogs at Dodger Stadium and virtually everything in between, both gastronomically and geographically. He still likes Italian food best—at dinner one night recently, he referred to himself as "the linguini king"—but as much as he enjoys *calamari fritti* (his number one favorite) and such non-Italian specialties as escargots and steamed Maine lobster, he also likes most of the foods that other little boys like—peanut butter and jelly sandwiches, McDonald's hamburgers, pizza, cookies, ice cream. He and I have a deal: I'll take him to McDonald's occasionally, but I'll just watch while he eats; then he has to accompany me to a hamburger joint that I like, and *he* can watch while *I* eat. But when his mother has an evening business meeting, Lucas and I often head off for what he calls "boys night out" at one of our preferred French or Italian restaurants, and he enthusiastically consumes whatever exotic creations my favorite chefs put before us.

He has several foods of choice, and he's not shy about ordering them in any restaurant. Not long ago, having ordered a Caesar

salad, he turned to me after a few bites and said, "Dad, this isn't a
Caesar salad. Or else it isn't a very good one." He was right. It was
a simple mixed green salad. The waiter apologized. "The kitchen
made a mistake," he said. Since I had already told Lucas that the
chef was out that night, he turned to me and said earnestly, "See,
Daddy, that's why the top chef should always be in the kitchen."
Later, when he ordered a fruit tart for dessert, the waiter brought an
apple tart, with pastry crust top and bottom. Lucas looked puzzled.
"Doesn't a fruit tart usually have fruit on top?" he asked the waiter.
Then, innocently: "Or is this another mistake?"

The waiter laughed. I smiled. I was delighted that he'd ordered
the fruit tart, even if it was "just" an apple tart. Like most kids,
Lucas usually prefers sweeter concoctions, preferably those made
with chocolate. We don't let him drink Coke or most other soft
drinks, and we keep candy to a minimum, but he can have one
dessert a day, whatever he wants—if he has a full meal first, including vegetables and fruit. Because we eat a sensible, balanced diet, so
does he. Without our having to badger or threaten him. He *likes*
vegetables and fruits. He's disappointed when we don't have salad.
"Mommy, please make broccoli with my special sauce" is one of his
dinnertime chants. "Daddy, can we share a tangerine?" is another.

So whence cometh his sudden—and, I'm relieved to say, short-
lived—concern about fat? Why did he, for just a few days, begin
suggesting that he should have nonfat milk, rather than low-fat
milk, with his breakfast cereal? Got me. He was on the cusp of
reading at the time that he favored us with his first mealtime fat
bulletin, and he could recognize various words ("fat" among them);
he liked to find the sports section every morning to look at the
standings of whatever sport was in season, but I am fairly sure he
did not see and could not read the campaign launched about that
time by some outfit called the National Heart Savers Association.
The milk industry had been trying to promote the consumption of
milk by running a $35-million advertising campaign featuring pho-
tographs of Lauren Bacall, Glenn Close and other luminaries, all
wearing a "milk mustache"; so the National Heart Savers Association, in the person of one Phil Sokoloff, an Omaha businessman
whose campaign against fatty foods had previously targeted such

egregious offenders as McDonald's, began running its own full-page ads, parodying the milk industry ads. You may have seen Sokoloff's ads—a photograph of a chunky, young woman accompanied by the boldface challenge: "Would you let your child eat 9 strips of bacon a day." The ad charged that three glasses of low-fat (2 percent) milk have the same amount of saturated fat as nine strips of cooked bacon. "Drink skim milk!" the ads urged. "Don't drink 2% milk."

Child nutritionists quickly pointed out that young children need the extra calories in 2 percent milk and that it was absurd to equate a fatty food like bacon with milk, which is rich in vitamins, protein and other vital nutrients.

Regardless of whether Lucas saw or heard about the bacon/milk campaign, I have heard his comments on fat parroted by several other, equally young children in the past couple of years. Over dinner in a restaurant while on vacation two summers ago, a friend's slim, five-year-old daughter "treated" us to a disquisition on the dangers of fat. She rejected more than half the items we read to her off the restaurant menu, saying each time, "No, that'll make me fat. I don't want to get fat."

In mid-1994 the *New York Times* published a story about the increasing number of very young children who had become vegetarians, including one seven-year-old who had already been a vegetarian for four years. (Clearly, her parents had shielded her from the Bible; the Book of Deuteronomy says, "Thou mayest eat flesh, after all the desire of thy soul.") About the same time, the *Wall Street Journal* published the results of surveys in Chicago and San Francisco showing that 50 percent to 80 percent of *fourth-grade* girls in those cities were on diets. A year later, a *New York Times* story said that 80 percent of ten-year-old girls have dieted. I assume that these kids, like others I know, get their information on fat directly from their well-meaning teachers or from overhearing health-conscious parents (theirs or their friends') prattling on about diets, fat, health and exercise.

Anxiety about diet is in the very air we breathe these days—and especially so in many progressive, politically correct schools. I'm pleased that elementary schoolteachers are concerned with our children's health and well-being, but I could easily do without the lectures I've heard from Lucas and a few of his young friends and cousins on the dangers of coffee, red meat, wine and cigars. Sure—please—teach Lucas (and all young children) the importance of moderation and common sense and tell them that it's very important to eat a balanced diet and to avoid smoking cigarettes and taking drugs and drinking alcohol until they're old enough to handle it—and even then, not to drink too much of it. But don't leave them with the impression that their mothers are going to die if they have an espresso every morning or that their fathers are either stupid or suicidal—or both—if they drink wine with dinner every night . . . and if they occasionally have a steak and a cigar as well. I agree with Michelle Stacey, who wrote in the *New York Times Magazine* that she was "more afraid of my daughter's developing an eating disorder than I am of her being fat."

Parents who are picky eaters almost invariably have children who are equally picky—if not more so. Such parents will tell you with pride that their children just "don't like" desserts (or hamburgers or hot dogs or whatever); if they know that you're the sort who would look with skepticism on that allegedly spontaneous antipathy (hell, I'd regard it as a birth defect), they'll say, with their faces screwed up in seeming bewilderment, that they "just don't understand" why their child feels that way.

My mother may well be the pickiest eater on the planet. My sister, Barbara, is a serious contender for the title of second pickiest eater on the planet. Our parents were divorced when we were young, and I do not think it a coincidence that Barbara was raised by our mother, while I was raised by our father, a man who would eat anything that didn't eat him first.

I remember being in a French restaurant in San Francisco many years ago with Barbara. When the maître d' mentioned a special chicken dish, I ordered it immediately. Barbara asked, "How is it prepared?" The maître d' smiled and said, "It isn't Colonel Sanders. You, madam, would probably be happier sticking to the regular menu." At first, I was offended on Barbara's behalf; after all, she had asked a reasonable question, and he had responded with a rude remark. I love Barbara dearly and admire her greatly and I was tempted to tell the maître d' that he was out of line. But I was amazed by his sixth sense. He was as right as he was rude. He had never seen Barbara before in his life; how could he possibly have known that anything slightly out of the ordinary would not be welcome on her plate? I was reminded of this incident fifteen years later, when Barbara and I and our respective families were having dinner together in a casual restaurant in Los Angeles. Barbara's daughter, Lisa, then nine years old, ordered pasta. When it arrived, she said she didn't like the simple tomato sauce the restaurant had put on it. She didn't like any sauce on her pasta except soy sauce, she said. Barbara nodded understandingly, picked up the plate and took it into the ladies' room—where she washed all the tomato sauce off in the sink. When she returned, Lisa had a plate of pristine, if thoroughly dampened, pasta on which to sprinkle her soy sauce. (I don't recall just what Lisa's older brother, Tim, ate that night, but I do remember his lecturing me on the evils of wine, cigars and "smoked meat" after a barbecue dinner on an earlier visit, when he was about six.)

I don't know whether children acquire their parents' eating habits genetically, absorb them by osmosis or instruction or just overhear conversation about what's supposed to be good and bad to eat. (Not that there is always a cause-and-effect relationship between the words and actions of parents and children—in eating or anything else. One of my closest friends is even more passionate about food than I am and has taken a similar approach to food with her son that we have with Lucas, but her son, who is Lucas's best friend, has been a picky eater from the day he was born.) Some parents hound their children constantly about proper nutrition—a bizarre blend of the ("Eat! Eat!") Jewish mother and the ("Don't! Don't!") gastronomic gestapo. They sternly lecture their kids on the hazards of hamburger and the danger of dessert before they're in nursery school. I've seen too many parents use mealtime for dietary sermons, for what I've come to think of as building character through carrots—an enforced self-kelp program. Either they babble endlessly about the evils of fat and sweets or, worse, they force their children to eat fruits, vegetables and other healthful foods under such draconian pressure that it's no wonder many of these kids sneak sweets, abandon proper nutrition at the earliest possible moment and turn into prepubescent diet freaks—and, in the process, lose all sense of eating-as-pleasure and mealtime-as-social-event.

I realize that recent studies have shown there are more overweight children today than ever before—a mirror, if bloated, image of the adult population. But in my experience, it's not the genuine chubbettes—or even the potential chubbettes—whose parents nag them about their eating habits. It's more likely to be the neurotically thin parents, those whose primary goal in life is to Stay Slender and to see that their children do likewise, regardless of the psychic toll.

What a dreadful thing to do to young children—making them worry about getting fat before they've lost their baby fat, turning them into potential anorexics, force-feeding them the fear of food that has turned so many of their parents into dour denizens of the dining room. I can just imagine what will happen to many of these children, particularly the girls, when they reach adolescence, and peer pressure confirms what they have already heard from their parents and teachers about the dangers of fat.

It's interesting, although probably not surprising, that white girls seem to worry more about being fat than do black girls. In our society, African Americans are still forced to confront far greater problems than a few extra pounds; they don't have the leisure that many white girls do to worry about their thighs. That's one reason anorexia and bulimia are far less common among African American girls than among white girls. Sixty-four percent of the black girls surveyed for a study published in 1995 in the journal *Human Organization* said it was better to be "a little overweight" than underweight. The study also found that 90 percent of white junior high and high school girls said they were dissatisfied with their weight; only 30 percent of African American girls had the same complaint.

Maybe that's because, as *Newsweek* suggested in reporting on this study, black women's magazines don't tout "Ten Tips for Thin Thighs." But white women's magazines sure do, and the antifat message seems to intimidate their readers, no matter how intelligent or accomplished they are. Almost half the female medical students surveyed at Harvard University said they are preoccupied with their weight and engage in binge eating.

The overheated campaign against fat is waged everywhere in

the mass media and the popular culture. At the very moment that I spotted the "Shun Fat Supermarket" sign last year, I had—lying next to me, in the front seat of my car—the then-current issue of *Newsweek* magazine, with its cover story "The Skinny on Fat." Inside, as I had read that morning, were (1) an account by Patty LaNoue Stearns, the food writer for the *Detroit Free Press,* of having received a hundred phone calls from readers after writing about a fat-free pizza, (2) a comment by a Dallas woman about how she had spent a full hour in her local supermarket, "just looking at brownie labels," trying to decipher—and to decide among—the various "light," "fat-free" and "low-fat" options the store had thoughtfully made available to its customers and (3) a report on the amount of fat, in grams, contained in a blueberry muffin (34), a turkey sandwich (24.5), a cup of cappuccino (9), a serving of Caesar salad (38), a bagel with cream cheese (15), a serving of pasta salad (28), a piece of stuffed chicken (35), a slice of pizza (21) and a McDonald's Happy Meal (an oxymoron if ever I heard one) (26).

A few weeks earlier, I had read the *New Republic,* which departed from its traditional formula of cheering for Israel and jeering at various politicians to feature on its cover a photograph of a large stick of butter beneath the words "Fat City." Inside were two stories on America's increasing obsession with fat—with not eating fat and with not being fat.

There was a time when to be a bit heavy—it was called "stout" or "robust" then, not "fat"—was to be perceived as vigorous and prosperous, healthy and attractive. The voluptuous nudes painted by Rubens, for example, were thought to embody sensuality and desirability. This perception changed, temporarily, during the Victorian Age, when "Dainty food for neurasthenic bodies was accompanied by a widespread change in the view of the body itself," as Robert Clark wrote in his 1993 biography of heavyweight epicure James Beard. "Stoutness, once symbolic of plenty and success, was increasingly viewed as a sign of excess, ill health, sloth and a lack of self-control. Regulation of the body—through Houdini-like stunts, marathon fasts and bizarre dietary cults—was a running theme of late Victorian and early-twentieth-century life."

It is no coincidence that repression of the appetite for food occurred at a time when social forces also conspired in the repression of other appetites. In this, the Victorians emulated the original Puritans, who insisted that man's appetite—any appetite—was his enemy, an ungodly force to be restrained, controlled and denied; bodily pleasure, whether taken between the lips or between the legs, was to be avoided at all costs. Long before either the Puritans or the Victorians, of course, many organized religions—Islam, Judaism, Hinduism and Catholicism among them—saw a nexus between diet and morality, and they regarded the consumption of certain foods as sinful, just as they regard fasting for certain holidays as holy. For the Victorians, however, there was a clearly perceived (and vigorously condemned) linkage between the pleasures of the palate and the pleasures of the flesh. Meat was regarded as too "stimulating" for young Victorian women, and most adhered so closely to this prohibition that there was widespread suffering from chlorosis—iron-deficiency anemia, what the makers of Geritol would sixty years later call "tired blood." (In many Latin-based languages, the word for meat derives from the root *carn* ["flesh"], which English speakers associate more commonly with "carnal" or "carnality," a fleshly indulgence of a more intimate sort.) Meat aside, young Victorian women were expected to eat very lightly, daintily and without taking (or showing) any joy in the act. "Female discomfort with food, as well as with the act of eating, was a pervasive subtext of Victorian popular culture," writes social historian Joan Jacobs Brumberg in *Fasting Girls.* "Over and over again, in all of the popular literature of the Victorian period, good women distanced themselves from the act of eating. . . . To be hungry, in any sense, was a social *faux pas.* Denial became a form of moral certitude, and refusal of attractive foods a means for advancing in the moral hierarchy."

That figures. Both sex and eating are essential to the survival of the species, which is why the drive-cum-need for food and the drive-cum-desire for sex are the oldest, strongest and most primitive instincts in human nature. They are also among the most frequently linked—in word and deed, symbol and simile. In our natural state— i.e., before the guilt-ridden paranoia induced by our neighborhood nutrition nannies—most humans are in such a "high and chronic readiness for the pleasures of food," writes Lionel Tiger in *The Pur-*

suit of Pleasure, that "If the mouth were a male sex organ, it would be erect all the time."

When the James Beard Foundation presented its 1995 awards to the best restaurants and chefs in the country, one of the hosts of the program suggested that because AIDS had made the 1990s a boring, safe-sex decade, "food has replaced passion." These days, he said, no young man goes out on a date without first putting in his wallet a foil-wrapped . . . "condiment"—whereupon the host ostentatiously whipped out his own wallet and removed two small packets of catsup.

Four months later, the *New York Times* quoted Barbara Haber, the curator of books at the Schlesinger Library at Radcliffe College, making a similar point. "Food is the new sex—with the sin and the guilt," she said, "because people are more fearful of freer sexual activities."

But it's the French, in particular, who tend to equate sex and food. In *Serve It Forth,* M. F. K. Fisher writes of the "promiscuous" ladies in the court of Louis XVI—the courtesans-as-milkmaids— who "gave special drinking cups to their courtiers," so that the milk, "so pure, so chastely sweet," would taste sweeter; the cups were made of "the finest porcelain from impressions taken at the height of their owners' loveliness; each cup mirrored the curves of a woman's breast, wanton, fragile, evanescent" (much as the shape of the original, rounded champagne glass was said to be based on a mold of Marie Antoinette's breast).

As Peter Farb and George Armelagos point out in *Consuming Passions,* "More words from the lexicon of eating than from any other human activity have been used to describe sexual relations and organs." As enlightened citizens of the 1990s, we may find many of these terms ugly and offensive. But they have become part of the colloquial language: A woman is a "dish," a "piece of meat," a "hot tomato who looks good enough to eat"; her breasts are "melons"; her virginity her "cherry." A man's testicles are his "nuts"; his penis is a "hot dog" or a "banana." Buttocks are "buns." Having oral sex is "eating" someone. In several languages, the words for "hungry" and "horny" are identical, as are the phrases for having eaten or having had sex. Moreover, as Farb and Armelagos note, "There is

. . . a close parallel in the way the nervous system deals with both hunger and sexual excitement. . . . Some neurophysiologists see a correspondence between the sensory surfaces of the sex organs and the taste buds in the mouth. . . ."

After the Victorian interregnum, the natural link between food and sex (not to mention drinking and general revelry) resumed in the United States with the Roaring Twenties and endured for about half a century. Although Babe Paley, the wife of CBS founder William Paley, is reputed to have said, "You can never be too rich or too thin," most Americans seemed to accept only the first half of that aphorism until the contemporary rise of the palate patrol. As recently as the 1960s and into the mid-1970s, as my sociologist friend Barry Glassner writes in *Bodies: Overcoming the Tyranny of Perfection,* feminists "urged the acceptance of all women as beautiful, whatever their jeans size." Cyclical diet and fashion fads notwithstanding, it wasn't until the early 1980s that being thin and fit became a pervasive obsession virtually throughout society, feminists included. As Barry wrote in 1992, "In the issue of *Ms.* magazine that arrived as I was writing this chapter, a majority of the display advertisements were about staying beautiful, fit and sexy. Nearly every model in these ads was thin, gorgeous and young."

The implicit message—the calculated intent—in virtually every advertisement, regardless of the product or service being touted, is "You, too, can look/be/feel/smell as good/beautiful/happy as the person in this picture." In recent years, as the pleasure police have gained ascendancy, that message has been not-so-subtly transmogrified from "You can" to "You should"—or even "You must." More than ever, fat people are shunned and ridiculed, and anyone seen eating a large meal—or just, God forbid, a steak—is made to feel stupid, if not downright suicidal. If you don't exercise enthusiastically and more or less constantly—if you don't think fitness is next to godliness—you're made to feel like a moral imbecile.

Sure, extreme obesity is both unhealthy and unattractive. But in my experience, it's not the truly fat but the ever-so-slightly overweight (and the more-than-slightly overwrought) who are the most fanatic about what they (and you) eat.

Society has long conditioned women to think they must be

beautiful to attract a man, and now that our definition of beautiful begins with "thin," perhaps the female obsession with diet and exercise is inevitable. But more and more men share those obsessions. Medical specialists who treat bulimia and anorexia nervosa are finding that their patients—once virtually all women—now include a rapidly growing number of men as well. Women suffering from these disorders still greatly outnumber men—7 million to 1 million—but the gap is beginning to close. "Traditionally, women were twice as likely to seek weight-loss treatment," Dr. Randall Flanery, director of the eating disorders program at the St. Louis University School of Medicine, told the *Los Angeles Times* in 1995. "But now it looks like it's going to be more fifty-fifty. . . . I have men coming into my office telling me they're convinced they were passed over for promotion because the other guy was slimmer and they looked more like a beach ball."

It's bad—sad—enough that more men are becoming anorexic or bulimic, but at least anorexics and bulimics (generally) hurt only themselves. What's worse is that, like women, many men are now urging their pals and business associates to share their obsession with fitness and diet. "Let's skip lunch and go to the gym instead" is an all-too-common midday suggestion in corporate America nowadays. (Wouldn't it be healthier to take a break from hard work by relaxing over a simple meal rather than working even harder on Nautilus or the NordicTrack?) In ever-larger numbers, men run and lift weights and play handball and, come dinnertime, they forsake red meat for green vegetables, and if you offer them dessert, they regard their ability to say no as a test of their manhood. If *you* say yes, their disdain for your weakness is barely concealed.

The need-cum-zeal for exercise is a modern phenomenon. "The exercise required to catch our paleo-dinner made the cholesterol content of that dinner relatively unimportant because the exercise itself controlled levels of cholesterol," writes Lionel Tiger in *The Pursuit of Pleasure*. "Now this exercise must be carefully secured, often artificially and at cost of convenience, funds and, of course, time. Instead of running for our dinner, we jog before we have dinner."

I've always enjoyed sports, both participatory and spectator.

I'm more spectator than participant now—except when I play baseball or soccer with Lucas—but even if I had the time, I wouldn't go careening around a squash or racquetball court. That's because there are things I'd rather do with my limited leisure time, not because I've been slowed down by eating chocolate soufflés instead of chopped spinach. In fact, as a fan of food, fun *and* sports, I must admit that I have not been altogether displeased when a few of this modern generation's more health-conscious athletes ultimately stumbled over their own macrobiotic karma. I was a big fan of Bill Walton when he led my alma mater, UCLA, to two consecutive national basketball championships in 1972 and 1973. He was talented, unselfish and unspoiled. He seemed to genuinely enjoy playing basketball and helping his teammates be better than they really were. He was the living embodiment of what college sports are supposed to be but so seldom are: an exploration of the joy of competition and the gradual building of true character. Walton was also politically aware, and he got caught up in various campus protests. In my view, he was on the right side of all those controversies— against the Vietnam War and the suppression of free speech on campus, for example. But some of the people who espoused those worthy views also became the hippy-dippy promulgators of the back-to-nature, food-as-evil movement. Walton got caught up in that, too. He grew a beard, grew his hair long and began to resemble a lost (if uncommonly tall) lumberjack. That was fine. But he also became a vegetarian and began to take the whole organic food movement— and himself—so seriously that two things happened: (1) he no longer seemed to have fun playing basketball, and (2) he no longer dominated basketball.

Walton might have been the same kind of supreme presence in the professional National Basketball Association that he had been in college were it not for his bad feet and his bad diet. He began to worry so much about avoiding red meat, eating organic peanut butter and bringing his own pure drinking water to the bench that he sometimes seemed to forget that it takes a substantial amount of physical strength and psychological commitment to play hard in big-time professional sports every night. Several athletes who are friends, including that well-known carnal carnivore Wilt Chamberlain, just don't think an athlete can have the stamina necessary to survive the daily NBA grind if he doesn't eat more protein than Walton tried to get by on.

Todd Marinovich was an even better—worse?—example of this absurd and, I hope, aberrant phenomenon. Marinovich was raised by a martinet of a father who had him in training before he was born, insisting that his wife eat nothing but natural foods while she was pregnant. Daddy dearest—Marvin Marinovich—put his infant son through stretching and flexibility exercises while he was still in the cradle, fed him only fresh-cooked, strained vegetables (no Gerber's in the Marinovich household) and had him walking, running, throwing and kicking ("with both feet," Marvin boasted) before he was in preschool. To celebrate his fourth birthday, Todd ran four miles—at eight minutes per mile. He took ballet and gymnastics and played organized baseball and basketball before he was in the first grade. At birthday parties, he skipped cake and ate the carrots his mother sent along. And every day, he practiced, practiced, practiced. He settled on football as his sport of choice—Daddy had been a captain of USC's national championship team in 1962—and he became a high school all-star, bound for glory himself at USC. On the horizon: the Heisman Trophy, the Super Bowl, the Hall of Fame. But something went terribly wrong. He played well at times at USC—sometimes very well—but he was ultimately a disappointment, not an All-American. He, too, saw the fun go out of sports—assuming that his father ever let him have any fun. Shattered, he turned to drugs, recovered and lasted barely two seasons in the National Football League.

I'm neither a sadist nor a morbid practitioner of *Schadenfreude*. But I'd be lying if I didn't admit that I have to suppress a brief inclination to mutter aloud "I told you so" every time I hear about some marathoner or professional athlete with a body tuned like a Lamborghini and a diet based on nuts, roots and grains suddenly dropping dead of a heart attack. Whenever that happens, I'm reminded of astronaut Neil Armstrong's sage observation: "I believe every human has a finite number of heartbeats. I don't intend to waste any of mine running around doing exercises."

I've heard all about endorphins or betamorphins or Mighty

Morphin Power Rangers or whatever the fuck it is that strenuous exercise is supposed to release in your body to make you feel good. Hah! The only thing I feel after exercising is bored. And breathless. And tired. And sweaty. That doesn't mean I'm opposed to all physical activity, though. Far from it. I love sports and I played them regularly as a child and teenager. That's probably the only thing I miss from those years. Not that I was any good at sports. I was always too small, too skinny and too uncoordinated to be much of an athlete, no matter how much I enjoyed it. I was skinny for the first thirty years of my life, in fact, and I remained at least relatively slim for the next ten years or so. Then—like most men in their forties and fifties—I began to put on a little weight around my waist. I'm probably about five to eight pounds over my ideal weight now, but I'll be damned if I'll let that modest midriff bulge deter me from one of life's great pleasures. I've already said that I try to show some restraint *à table*. I also exercise. Always have. Moderately. Very moderately. I ride a stationary exercise bicycle for thirty to forty minutes while I read the newspaper most weekday mornings, pedaling just fast enough to break a sweat, not fast enough to dampen my Doonesbury. But I don't panic if I don't get a chance to ride, and if I'm traveling on business or vacationing in France (or anywhere else), without access to a stationary bicycle, I don't begin jogging frantically along the banks of the Seine, terrified that two or three weeks without regular exercise will turn me into a blimp bound for the local cardiac intensive-care unit. In fact, I have never gained weight on an eating trip to France—not even when I went for six weeks and had a grand, multicourse dinner every single night.

There is some medical evidence indicating that all our frantic exercise may be unnecessary—especially if, like me, you exercise primarily to avoid heart disease. A group of medical researchers from the University of Pittsburgh has pointed out that epidemiological studies "suggest that gardening three times a week is as effective as running for preventing heart attack." Of course, there was a massive study of 17,300 Harvard alumni that said you live longer only if you engage in vigorous exercise—fast cycling, swimming laps three hours a week, playing an hour of singles tennis three days a week, walking briskly uphill. But no one could explain why this study contradicted so many others that showed moderate exercise could prolong life. "Everyone is confused," Dr. Ralph Paffenbarger of Stanford University, a coauthor of the new study, told the *New York Times*. "Even the scientists are confused."

So what else is new?

. .

I have always taken some pleasure in the knowledge that our fattest president, William Howard Taft—he of the eight-course breakfasts—lived to be seventy-two, at a time when the average life expectancy was ten years less . . . and that Warren Harding, Taft's contemporary, died at fifty-seven, having frequented Dr. John Harvey Kellogg's well-known sanitarium in Battle Creek, Michigan, where the dietary fare was heavy on whole-grain cereals, and the normal routine included four to six enemas a day to purge the body of "toxins."

Dr. Kellogg, a sickly child, became a vegetarian at age fourteen, and a decade later, in 1876, he took over the Western Health Reform Institute and renamed it the Battle Creek Sanitarium. "Men and women," Kellogg wrote, "are subject to few diseases whose origins may not be traced to the kitchen." Because his fellow Americans ate too much meat, poultry and fish (which Dr. Kellogg somehow concluded were not "natural" foods), we were becoming, he said, "dwarfed and weazened, neurotic, daft, dyspeptic and degenerates." In addition to President Harding, such titans of commerce as John D. Rockefeller and J. C. Penney paid "restorative" visits to the Battle Creek Sanitarium. But they were in a tiny minority. This was before we, as a society, became obsessed with slimness—and before science both made us aware of the potential dangers lurking in our food supply and enabled us to measure those dangers, however infinitesimal.

As Michelle Stacey writes in *Consumed*, until the middle of the last century, "people had no means by which to analyze their food, no knowledge that the body could make different use of bread than of meat or vegetables. Nutritional values of various foods were thought to be basically equal, and nutritional advice centered on amounts rather than types of food. The science of nutrition as we know it now began in the 1840s, in Germany, with the scientist Justus von Liebig, who was the first to find a way to break down foods into proteins, fats, carbohydrates and minerals."

Almost fifty years later, a Wesleyan University chemist named Wilbur Olin Atwater, writing first in the *Century* magazine and then under the auspices of the United States Department of Agriculture, began talking about the havoc these various components could wreak on the human body. Atwater, like Kellogg, was an early advocate of the food-as-fuel, body-as-machine, pleasure-be-damned nutrition movement in this country. "In our actual practice of eating, we are apt to be influenced too much by taste, that is, by the dictates of the palate," he wrote in 1895. "We are prone to let natural instinct be overruled by acquired appetite." Today, a century after Atwater—a century and a half after von Liebig—we can not only analyze the natural components of food, we can detect the tiniest, one part per billion of some allegedly hazardous artificial substance in that food. The result: many Americans are striving desperately to ignore the "dictates of the palate," to eschew taste and to acquire not only an appetite for but an appreciation of "healthful" foodstuffs, many of which taste like a carefully concocted blend of sawdust, library paste and sorghum. (Have you ever eaten a turkey burger? A tofu hot dog? Pasta sauce made with cornstarch and nonfat yogurt? Were they yummy? Right.) The combination of advances in science and technology, a growing awareness of the relationship between nutrition and health and the collective efforts of the consumer, environmental and physical fitness movements has turned poor Dr. von Liebig's early work into the obsessive, pleasure-destroying apparatus we see around us today.

As agitated and obsessed as people have been in recent years over the fat/heart connection, there is, in many quarters, even more fearmongering about the (alleged) food/cancer connection. That is where modern science has been so "helpful," with its ability to measure carcinogenicity at the most minute levels.

Heart disease kills 40 percent more Americans than does cancer—700,000 a year to 500,000 for cancer. But cancer evokes special feelings of dread. A heart attack often strikes in the middle of the night. Boom! It's over. No warning but no suffering either. Cancer can be painful, debilitating, disfiguring; it can drain your strength and your spirit—and your life's savings. Around the turn of the century, cancer carried such a stigma that in some places, cancer cases were given other, less terrifying—albeit incorrect—diagnoses. The disease was not mentioned in polite company. Now there's a cancer fixation in this country; we can't stop talking about it. Almost every week, it seems, we hear about a new cause of cancer, many of them involving chemicals used in the nation's food supply. Consumer and environmental activists howl incessantly now about the hazards of pesticides and preservatives. Health food stores routinely boast of their "natural" packaged goods and "organically grown" fruits and vegetables—sales of which have increased 23 percent in each of the past five years. I was ordering dinner at a restaurant in Washington, D.C., a couple of years ago when the waiter interrupted to urge me to "skip the regular chicken sausages and have the organic chicken sausage. . . . There's a lot of persistent toxins out there in regular chickens."

There is a widespread perception that the United States is trapped in a cancer epidemic, created largely by exposure to synthetic chemicals. Wrong. Some pesticides and other chemicals *are* dangerous and should be regulated—or prohibited altogether. But some bring benefits, and not nearly as many are as dangerous to humans as the alarmists claim, based on their own fear of modern technology and their foolish extrapolation of laboratory tests on rats and mice that have been subjected to monstrously toxic megadoses of the sort that humans would never encounter. To begin with, according to the National Cancer Institute, the age-adjusted mortality rate for all cancers combined except lung cancer has been *declining* since 1950 among people under eighty-five. The death rate for stomach cancer, the cancer that should be the most closely linked to artificial chemicals in the food supply, has plunged 85 percent since 1930—which covers the period during which pesticides came into widespread use.

"Less than five percent of human cancer can be traced to causes that are within the jurisdiction of the U.S. Environmental Protection Agency," according to John Graham, the director of the

Center for Risk Analysis at Harvard University's School of Public Health. Moreover, Graham notes, the prices for pesticide-free, "organic" fruits, vegetables and other food products are generally 20 percent to 50 percent higher than for produce treated with pesticides. Since poverty is the single greatest health problem in this country—and since there is solid evidence that eating more produce makes you healthier—this is "not rocket science" but economics, nutrition and social policy "at the most basic level" in Graham's words. "If the prices of fruits and vegetables go up, people [poor people in particular] are likely to eat fewer fruits and vegetables." More frequent illness and greater social spending are the inevitable result.

But campaigns against pesticides continue to frighten Americans, intimidate politicians, distort national environmental priorities and waste scarce federal funds. It's yet another example of how some in our society are making everyday life seem more like a hazard-filled obstacle course than an opportunity for pleasure and relaxation. Stop and smell the roses? No way. You'll probably get cancer from the chemicals they've been treated with. Do I dare to eat a peach? If T. S. Eliot were alive to ask that question in 1996, the most likely rejoinder would probably be, "No—unless it's organic."

Bruce Ames, a biochemist and molecular biologist at U.C. Berkeley, says the three main causes of cancer are not the much-publicized pesticides or other chemicals developed over the past half century, but "smoking, dietary imbalances and chronic infections." Ames is the highly regarded director of the National Institute of Environmental Health Sciences Center. He also invented the standard laboratory test for cancer-causing agents. That made him the darling of the environmental movement. But now—to their shock and chagrin—he makes such provocative statements as:

"I don't think pesticide residues have anything to do with cancer."

Ames says, "Ninety-nine-point-ninety-nine percent of the pesticides we consume are naturally present in plants to ward off insects and other predators." The average American, he says, ingests ten thousand times more natural pesticides than artificial pesticide residues every day. But Ames thinks that fruits and vegetables,

which contain carotenoids and antioxidant nutrients such as vitamins C and E, suppress the cancer process. Other studies have
shown that the antioxidants in fruits and vegetables also decrease
the risk of stroke in middle-aged men.

Unfortunately, it often seems that for every encouraging study
like these, there are others that reinforce the alarmist trends so much
in vogue today. Science proceeds incrementally; almost every new
study is just a snapshot in time, not a definitive studio portrait.
That's one reason why, as Lawrence Altman pointed out in the *New
York Times* in 1995, "many landmark scientific discoveries win
prizes only years, even decades later," after peers have had an opportunity to verify the findings.

"Epidemiology is a crude and inexact science," Dr. Charles
Hennekens, a professor of epidemiology at Harvard's School of
Public Health, told the *New York Times* in another 1995 story.
"Eighty percent of cases are almost all hypotheses. We tend to over-
state findings, either because we want attention or more grant
money."

Journalists eager for a good story and activists eager for political and public support also tend to "overstate findings," to treat
each new study as if it *were* definitive (or, at the very least, clearly
cause for alarm and reevaluation). After hearing repeatedly about
the beneficial effects of such antioxidants as beta-carotene, for example, we were told last year that a massive study in Finland
showed that they may *not* help deter cancer or heart disease—and
might, in fact, contribute to both diseases in some people. Early in
1996, two large studies financed by the National Cancer Institute
reached a similar conclusion. We've also learned that margarine—
the (almost) all-purpose, low-fat substitute for butter, the weapon of
choice for many in the war on heart disease—is now known to
contain trans monounsaturated fatty acids that actually *increase* the
risk of heart disease. Meanwhile, a diet heavy in fish—so widely
believed to help fight heart disease that many Americans frantically
gobble down fish oil capsules as dietary supplements—was found to
have no impact whatever in preventing heart disease, according to a
Harvard study of 44,895 men that was released in 1995.

Whoops. A few months after the Harvard study, a study at the

University of Washington said that eating fish was beneficial to the heart after all. People who ate modest quantities of fish—as little as three ounces of salmon a week—were much less likely to suffer cardiac arrest than were people who ate no fish at all, the Washington study said. Dr. David Siscovick, the lead author of that study, said his findings did not really contradict those in the Harvard study since (1) his study compared the benefits of eating *some* fish with the benefits of eating *no* fish, while the Harvard study focused on eating a *lot* of fish rather than eating *less* fish, and (2) the Washington study looked at cardiac arrest, which is caused by a jumbling of the electrical impulses that regulate heart rhythm, whereas the Harvard study examined overall heart disease and heart attacks, which generally involve the blockage of an artery that prevents blood from reaching the heart.

Got that? Want some salmon? Smoked? With or without cream cheese?

In many ways, the biggest problem confronting the anxious eater/consumer/reader/viewer today is that the health warnings we receive one day are almost invariably rendered "inoperative" the next—to borrow a word from, appropriately enough, Richard Nixon's press secretary, Ronald Ziegler. Americans "increasingly find themselves beset by contradictory advice," Marcia Angell and Jerome Kassirer, editors of the prestigious *New England Journal of Medicine,* wrote in an editorial in 1994. "No sooner do they learn the results of one research study than they hear of one with the opposite message."

This syndrome is not limited to what we eat; in 1995, barely a month after a massive Harvard University study found an increased risk of breast cancer among women who underwent hormone replacement therapy, another study—at the University of Washington—concluded that no such causative link existed; in fact, the second study said, women who used hormones for at least eight years had a *lower* risk of breast cancer than those who had never taken hormones. Because the second study involved far fewer subjects than did the first, many epidemiologists were inclined to dismiss it. But a week later, yet another study found that hormone therapy could reduce a woman's risk of colon cancer.

Diet seems the most fertile field for contradictory scientific studies, though. There have been many stories in recent years about the health benefits of vitamin A. The *Washington Post* said it might be one of the "very few wonder drugs in the world . . . [a] dirt-cheap chemical" that can be used to treat measles and anemia, to prevent one of the leading causes of blindness, to "reduce the transmission of the AIDS virus from mother to fetus" and to "lower childhood mortality by about one-third in vast parts of the developing world." But on the day I sent this manuscript off to my editor, the *New York Times* published a front-page story that said a "large new study" had shown that women who "consume excessive amounts of vitamin A during the early months of pregnancy can cause serious birth defects in their unborn children."

My favorite revisionist view of what one should consume came earlier in 1995, also in the *New York Times*. For years, we had heard that carbohydrates were the answer to a dieter's dream. That made pasta the perfect food. No fat whatsoever. Everyone clamored for pasta. Everyone began cooking pasta. Even French chefs began including pasta dishes on their menus in the 1980s and early 1990s, even though most of them didn't change their opinion that all Italian food was, in the words of one *toque* of my acquaintance, "unimaginative baby food—a bunch of undercooked noodles and overcooked tomatoes." Then, on February 4, 1995, the front page of the *New York Times* carried this shocking headline:

So It May Be True After All: Eating Pasta Makes You Fat

There followed a story that continued through two full columns inside the paper explaining that many researchers were "beginning to wonder if a high-carbohydrate regime is appropriate for everyone, particularly overweight people and the 'insulin-resistant.' . . ."

How could anyone have written, edited or read that story without bursting into laughter at its unintended humor: researchers are beginning to wonder if pasta is fattening for fat people? But isn't it fat people who've been told for years that eating pasta would make them thin?

Much of the reaction to the *New York Times* story focused on the 25 percent of the United States population thought to be insulin-resistant and thus likely to overproduce insulin after eating sugar or starches. But I thought the most interesting note in the story was what it said about pasta, not what it said about people. Some nutritionists, the story said, were beginning to suspect that pasta is "not as innocent as it so recently seemed." Dr. Louis Aronne, the director of the Comprehensive Weight Control Center at New York Hospital–Cornell Medical Center, was quoted as saying, "People simply do not lose weight if they eat large quantities of pasta or rice."

So why have the diet doctors been beating the American public over the head with the pasta panacea all these years?

Almost before anyone could answer that question, nutritionists here and in Italy began attacking the science in the *Times* story. People who are insulin-resistant may find that pasta and other carbohydrates will raise the fat in their blood "but not necessarily in their bodies," Wahida Karmally of Columbia Presbyterian Hospital told *USA Today*. Karmally said that starches wouldn't make insulin-resistant people (or anyone else) fat "as long as they don't overconsume them."

The Italian newspaper *La Stampa* responded to the *New York Times* story with a front-page commentary under the headline "America, You Don't Understand Pasta." It's not pasta itself that's fattening, the Italians pointed out, it's the rich, copious sauces that many Americans heap on pasta. In Italy, pasta is lightly sauced; fettuccine Alfredo—pasta smothered with a rich sauce of butter, cheese and heavy cream—was popularized by Americans, not Italians, when tourists from the United States began ordering it in Rome (and then demanding it at Italian restaurants back home) after actors Douglas Fairbanks and Mary Pickford had eaten it regularly at a restaurant owned by Alfredo di Lellio during their honeymoon in Italy in 1920. It is the Americans, not the Italians—the greatest consumers of pasta in the world—who are facing an epidemic of obesity.

Pasta is but one of many comestibles that have been the subject of revisionist (and confusing) science. Remember the scares about saccharin? Fluoride? Red food dye? (M&M's abandoned red for ten years, from 1977 to 1987, after that scare.) All were ultimately given a clean bill of health. Sometimes it doesn't take long to put unwarranted fears to rest. That was the case with the great cranberry scare of 1959. Two weeks before Thanksgiving, minuscule amounts of a potentially cancer-causing weed killer were discovered in some cranberries grown in Washington State and Oregon. The *New York Times* put the story on page one five times in seven days. Other media followed suit. People panicked. Thanksgiving menus were revamped on the spot. Out with the cranberry sauce; in with— what? Pumpkin soufflé? But a nationwide inspection of cranberries disclosed no contamination other than at the original sites; not one case of illness from tainted cranberries was reported anywhere in the country.

More recently, parents, teachers and nutritionists have "known" that sugar makes many children hyperactive, aggressive, unable to sit still, concentrate, sleep or get along with their peers, parents and teachers. Well, several recent studies found no support whatever for the myth of the so-called sugar high. In these studies, delinquent boys who ate breakfasts heavy in sugar actually *improved* their performance on standardized behavioral tests.

Everyone knows that chocolate is bad for you, too, right? Now scientists aren't so sure. Although chocolate is full of saturated fats, it also contains stearic acid, and scientists think the human liver converts that specific kind of fat to monosaturated fat—like canola oil and olive oil—before it can begin the artery-clogging damage common to other saturated fats. Indeed, Dr. Penny M. Kris-Etherton, a nutritionist at Pennsylvania State University, came up with startling results a couple of years ago when she asked groups of healthy young men to sample different diets, rich—alternately—in cocoa butter, dairy butter, soybean oil or olive oil. After twenty-six days, each of the men underwent a cholesterol test. As expected, the men on the dairy butter diet had increased cholesterol levels. As expected, those on soybean oil had decreased cholesterol levels. As expected, those on olive oil maintained constant cholesterol levels.

But the men on the cocoa butter diet had the same result as those on olive oil—no change in cholesterol.

Olive oil is subject to confusion of its own, though: yes, it seems to help lower cholesterol, blood pressure and blood sugar levels. But it's fattening. Cholesterol itself is a maze of contradiction. We hear about the dangers of high cholesterol, but cholesterol can also be too low. Then there's the whole debate about good cholesterol vs. bad cholesterol. My friend Barry Glassner, the sociologist, further confuses matters by pointing out that the greatest "correlation" involving cholesterol is that between *low* cholesterol and highly violent behavior. So don't invite anyone with low cholesterol to dinner; he might stab you with a butter knife. (And maybe you should also think twice about taking drugs that lower your cholesterol; a study early in 1996 found that the two most widely used such drugs cause cancer in laboratory animals.)

Apart from that, what survival strategies should you follow to minimize risk and anxiety and maximize pleasure? What trade-offs are you willing to make? Do you use olive oil or not? Do you eat chicken instead of the beef or lamb you prefer—and thereby risk salmonella poisoning instead of a heart attack? Do you eat fish— and risk mercury poisoning . . . or worse?

And what about caffeine? In recent years, caffeine has been variously reported to cause cancer, to inhibit conception, to induce miscarriage, to cause birth defects, to increase cholesterol and blood pressure, to trigger irregular heartbeats and calcium loss, to aggravate ulcers and to increase urination. A front-page headline in my own newspaper two years ago said, "Study Finds Caffeine Has Qualities of Addictive Drug." But caffeine has also been reported to help people lose weight, to improve hand-eye coordination, to increase tolerance for exercise, to promote alertness and clearer thinking, to diminish drowsiness, to combat migraine headaches, to make children more attentive in school and to make adults less likely to suffer bronchial asthma or to commit suicide. You would think that with all the advances in modern medicine and technology, we could find a simple answer to the simple question "Is a cup of coffee bad for you?" But many people are afraid of technology, and many others have lost faith in it, and they've combined forces to confuse, confound and frighten virtually everyone who's ever dipped a spoon into a cup of java.

Under the headline "The Latest on Coffee? Don't Worry. Drink Up"—accompanied by a large photograph of six cups of coffee—Jane Brody, of all people, wrote a lengthy, prominently displayed story in the *New York Times* in 1995 that said, "A substantial amount of research . . . has turned up very little solid scientific evidence to indict a moderate intake of coffee or caffeine as a serious or even minor health threat." But Brody's story also repeated the warnings against caffeine consumption by pregnant women and cautioned dieters that caffeine induces hunger pangs by causing blood sugar to fall. In addition, the story ticked off the dangers of "heavier daily intakes" of caffeine, among them "heart attacks and bone loss in women." Typically—on the theory, it would seem, that even relatively good news must be accompanied by bad news—Brody devoted her regular "Personal Health" column that was published on the same day, in the same section, to bemoaning the agonies of caffeine withdrawal. ("I developed a headache so intense that if I had not known better I would have sworn I had a brain tumor or had suffered a stroke.") Brody ended her column by pointing out that the positive effects of caffeine are "associated with low doses" and that at higher doses "caffeine can produce negative effects like nervousness, anxiety, panic attacks and palpitations, especially in people who usually abstain from caffeine. It can also double the adverse effects of stress, aggravate stomach ulcers, interfere with sleep and increase the side effects of certain medications."

I rarely drink coffee myself, so the caffeine controversy doesn't affect me personally. But I'm so confused by now about conflicting reports on the safety of a whole range of food products that I'm not even sure that eating supposedly healthful food is always healthful. (If it is, why does virtually everyone who works in a health food store look as if he's suffering from terminal acne?)

A friend of a friend of mine used to complain all the time about how lousy he felt, even though he skipped meat and most other foods that are supposed to be hazardous to your health. Finally, his wife got tired of hearing him complain and suggested that he "start eating regularly." He agreed to give it a try.

Our mutual friend reported back a few weeks later: "He never felt better. He says his wife saved his life."

Remember Dan Quayle, Murphy Brown's favorite vice president? A couple of years ago, he was hospitalized in Indianapolis after a blood clot was discovered in his lungs. Quayle's doctor subsequently said he told his famous patient "not to eat as many green vegetables as he does, and eat a more regular, American diet." Green vegetables, it seems, contain vitamins that prompt clotting.

I sometimes wonder if we wouldn't all be better off if we just followed Mark Twain's advice: "Part of the secret of success in life is to eat what you like and let the food fight it out inside."

3

N A M E
Y O U R
P O I S O N

I was twenty-one years old when I had my first drink.
It was bourbon.
It was awful.

The occasion was a small going-away party for the editor of
my first daily newspaper. For some strange reason—maybe as a
practical joke—the staff of five editors and five reporters unani-
mously selected me, the youngest and newest member of our little
suburban paper, to be in charge of refreshments. I'd never done
anything like it before and didn't have a clue what to do. But I'd
read books and seen movies and heard stories about reporters and
their legendary love of hard liquor, so I went out and bought a lot of
Scotch and bourbon. But what do you eat with whiskey? I asked my
wife to bake some brownies. That got a few chuckles at the party.
But not as many chuckles as what I did with the Scotch and bourbon. Dimly recalling from some movie or other that most people
liked their whiskey "on the rocks," I decided that rather than waste
ice cubes and, ultimately, dilute my guests' drinks, it made much
more sense to just put the bottles of whiskey in the freezer the morning of the party. Then I forgot I had put them there until my guests
arrived.

"Omigod!" I said as the first few walked in. "I just realized—I froze the booze. Come in. Sit down. I'll get the bottles out of the freezer and put them in some boiling water. It shouldn't take long to defrost them—should it?"

The managing editor, a mild-mannered sort with a dry sense of humor, looked at me, his eyes wide with what I took to be uncharacteristic rage.

"Boil the bourbon?" he yelped. "It's fucking August. I don't want a fucking hot toddy in the fucking middle of fucking August."

Great. I was about to be the first man in history to play host to a newspaper party with no drinkable whiskey. My journalistic career was going up in smoke before I'd had my first anniversary on my first job. The ink was barely dry on my press pass and it was going to be yanked and burned—and me along with it. Then everyone burst into laughter. Distilled spirits, these veteran drinkers assured me, don't freeze—at least not at the temperatures reached in the freezer of a normal kitchen refrigerator; the alcohol content is too high. The whiskey would be too cold to be fully appreciated at first, they said, but it wouldn't be frozen; it would warm up and be drinkable before the evening was over.

My ice-cold booze notwithstanding, the farewell party ultimately went very well. One of the other reporters went to a nearby liquor store for ice cubes, peanuts, pretzels and room-temperature Scotch and bourbon to tide us over while mine warmed up, and before long, all my guests were exchanging increasingly hilarious journalistic war stories. Of course, when they finally induced me to try a glass of bourbon, I had to admit that it was my first-ever taste of hard liquor—and that I thought it tasted much like I thought Clorox would taste. That occasioned a few more hoots of derision—and a suggestion that I "try a brownie with it." But it was all good-natured fun, and to this day, more than thirty years later, I still remember fondly the names and faces of every single person at that party.

I'm somewhat more sophisticated about both liquor and entertaining now. But I still don't like the taste of whiskey. In fact, when Lucas recently asked me to describe the taste of the Scotch that Lucy occasionally drinks, I told him it tastes like a particular antibiotic he's taken—one that is so foul he can barely swallow it. He now refers to Chivas Regal as "Mommy's medicine."

I occasionally drink a margarita at a Mexican restaurant, and I'm not averse to a Bloody Mary at brunch every couple of years, but what I really like is wine. Over the past dozen years or so, I have become a wine lover—a wine drinker, a wine buyer, a wine collector. I have a twelve-hundred-bottle cellar in my home. I go to wine auctions. I take my own wine to most restaurants, as well as on airplanes. I ship cases of my wine ahead when I vacation in domestic resort areas.

Unlike many of my wine-drinking friends, I don't drink wine just to drink wine—to sip it, sample it and compare it to other wines sipped and sampled. I like making those judgments, but what I really like is drinking wine as a complement to food. I like the way food and wine taste together—the way a rich white Burgundy enhances the flavor of steamed lobster and the way a robust, almost chewy red from Bordeaux accentuates both the taste and the texture of a thick, blood-rare New York steak. I have friends who finish dinner, then open a new bottle and start drinking, tasting and talking all over again. I also have friends who rave about German Rieslings that are "great for sipping on a summer afternoon, while you're reading a book," and still others who wax positively poetic about the charms inherent in a big, hearty Cabernet Sauvignon from California. Not me, not me, not me. First of all, when I'm through with my meal, I'm through with my wine—even if I have a half-full glass left in front of me. Nor do I usually sip wine while reading books. (Well, maybe a glass of port with a cigar, but that's a different matter—and, in part, the subject of the next chapter.) As for California Cabernets, well, I find most of them too heavy and too alcoholic. They don't complement food; they overpower it. That's not why I drink wine.

Unlike some drinkers—beer and hard-liquor drinkers more than wine drinkers—I don't drink wine for the impact of the alcohol. I don't have a drink after work to unwind or before bedtime to help me sleep. Sure, I enjoy the slight buzz and the sense of well-being I get after my first few swallows of wine at the dinner table. But that's only momentary—and secondary. The real buzz I feel in those first few swallows is an appreciation of the flavor of the wine—and, more important, an anticipation of the gastronomic pleasure to come. I have absolutely no desire for escape, release, intoxication, feelings of omnipotence or whatever it is that makes some people want to get drunk. I have several friends who feel differently. One of them, Colman Andrews, is now the executive editor of *Saveur* magazine, which recently published an excerpt from Benjamin Franklin's list of 228 words and phrases "overheard in taverns to describe the condition of being drunk." (Franklin, you may recall, is the fellow who once pointed out, "There are more old drunkards than old doctors.") A couple of years ago, Colman wrote a story for the *Los Angeles Times Magazine* titled "In Defense of Getting Drunk." The title was more provocative than precise, since Colman said that when he spoke of getting drunk, he didn't mean "falling-down/throwing-up/screaming-and-flailing-or-sniffing-and-sobbing/out-of-control drunk." What he meant, he said, was drinking to "a state of pleasant inebriation."

"A lot of people who drink, and genuinely enjoy drinking, sometimes drink too much *(because* they genuinely enjoy drinking)," Colman acknowledged.

Why do they enjoy drinking? Why does *he* enjoy drinking?

Colman, who once wrote, "My body is not my temple; it's more like my bar and grill," said in his "Getting Drunk" story that he drinks because "I like the way alcohol smells and tastes. . . . I drink because I like the trappings of imbibing, the company it keeps—the restaurants and cafes and bars and (usually) the people who gather in them. And I drink, frankly, because I like the way alcohol makes me feel. I like the glow, the softening of hard edges, the faint anesthesia. I like the way my mind races, one zigzag step ahead of logic. I like the flash flood of unexpected utter joy that sometimes courses quickly through me between this glass and that one."

Colman said he only drinks excessively when the mood *and* the circumstances permit. He doesn't drive drunk, work drunk or get drunk every night. He hasn't abused, abandoned or neglected his wife and two young children. His drinking does not cause any problems for anyone else, and he is probably doing no more than minor damage, if that, to himself. So whose business is it if he drinks to excess on occasion? Isn't it perfectly appropriate for him to adopt the attitude implicit in the title of the classic Billie Holiday song "Tain't Nobody's Business If I Do"?

But even the moderate consumption of alcoholic beverages, wine included, is increasingly viewed as unacceptable in our society, regardless of the circumstances. People who drink are perceived in many quarters as weak, depraved and stupid, as wanton wastrels relying on an artificial and potentially deadly crutch. Beer or bourbon, Cabernet or Chardonnay—it's all the same, vile, corrupting Satanic brew to the neo-Prohibitionists. Bubbly water and iced (herbal) tea seem increasingly our national drinks of preference—as long as the tea and the ice cubes are made with filtered, purified, bottled water. How this came about is something of a mystery to me. Yes, I know that medical advances have enabled us to understand more about how the human body works now than we did in earlier generations, and this has led us to see how dangerous the abuse of alcohol can be. Nevertheless, there's a certain cognitive dissonance in the realization that in the 1950s, when the United States was a manufacturing and commercial behemoth—providing cars, steel, electronic marvels and other consumer goods for the entire world—the two-martini lunch was *de rigueur* for titans of industry, but now, when most of our business leaders drink iced tea, Perrier or Pellegrino at lunch, the strong currencies of the sake- and whiskey-drinking Japanese and the wine- and beer-drinking Germans dominate the global marketplace.

"If alcohol is indeed, as we are often told, 'America's number-one drug problem,' " Colman wrote, "it is also probably America's number-one scapegoat for societal ills—ills whose real causes don't come conveniently packaged in bottle form."

Not surprisingly, Colman's article engendered a considerable amount of angry mail. One letter-writer called his story "indefensible." Another said it was "the most well-written piece of denial, resistance, excuse-making and absurdity that I have ever read." I don't agree with any of those comments—except that the article was well written—and I would certainly not condemn Colman for his occasional "drunkenness." *Chacun à son* booze, as the French would no doubt say. But while I admire Colman greatly—as a friend, a sometimes colleague, a writer and a lover of food and wine—I don't share his appreciation of Scotch, beer or brandy, and I don't share his enthusiasm for inebriation.

Nor am I interested in recreational drugs of any kind. But I know many reasonable, responsible people who have smoked marijuana—or, on occasion, tried something a little stronger—without apparent harm to themselves or others; I wouldn't criticize them for doing so any more than I would criticize Colman or my other friends who like to get drunk. There are any number of (alleged) pleasures that hold no appeal for me. Skiing. Surfing. Gambling. Golf. Bowling. Gardening. Roller coasters. Horror movies. Opera. Ballet. Jazz. Science fiction. I don't have the right to—and don't want to—deprive others of those pleasures, though.

Marijuana is the only nonprescription drug I've ever tried. I did it three or four times, purely out of curiosity, in the late 1960s and early 1970s. It didn't do a thing for me. Many people obviously feel otherwise. Marijuana, the 1960s drug of choice, is making a comeback so vigorous in the 1990s that there is now an on-line head shop of sorts on the Internet. One study showed that marijuana use among eighth graders more than doubled from 1991 to 1995; another survey has shown that almost 40 percent of all high school seniors have tried it.

I'm not one of those who think that the use of marijuana automatically leads to the abuse of hard drugs. I think the opponents of marijuana have probably overstated its hazards about as much as the proponents of marijuana have overstated its benign-cum-beneficent effects. But I don't think young people should use recreational drugs of any kind. I was appalled when I read recently that the proportion of eighth-graders using illegal drugs had almost doubled from 1991 to 1995, according to a study conducted by the University of Michigan and funded by the National Institute on Drug Abuse. I can understand why a study conducted in 1995 by the Columbia University Center on Addiction and Substance Abuse found that adolescents considered drugs the greatest problem facing them today. As the father of a six-year-old boy, I am especially sensitive to the drug problem—all the more so because I live in Los

Angeles, where a 1995 study showed that children and teenagers are significantly more likely than children and teenagers elsewhere to experiment with drugs—and less likely than their age peers nationally to regard drug use as harmful.

For adults—in terms of marijuana alone—I'm inclined to believe that its legalization probably wouldn't result in the immediate collapse of the Republic. But this isn't something that I feel either confident about or strongly about—except to say that marijuana should certainly be legalized (and easily obtainable) for medicinal uses at the very least. Marijuana—*Cannabis sativa*—has been used to relieve pain and to treat various ailments for more than five thousand years, dating back to ancient China. In the United States, it had an honorable history as a painkiller on Civil War battlefields and as an ingredient in many patent medicines until around the turn of the century, when barbiturates and aspirin compounds were introduced. After the federal government slapped a huge tax on marijuana in 1937, it faded from use. But when carefully monitored, marijuana has proved beneficial in recent years in the treatment of symptoms related to many medical conditions, including epilepsy, glaucoma, migraine headaches, muscular dystrophy, multiple sclerosis, severe arthritis, spinal injuries, some types of cancer and the virus that causes AIDS. Marijuana can reduce nausea and vomiting caused by chemotherapy. It can ease crippling muscle spasms and chronic pain, prevent weight loss during debilitating diseases and, for glaucoma victims, reduce the eye pressure that gradually leads to blindness. But we are so paranoid about the "devil weed" in this country that federal regulations make it virtually impossible for most people who could benefit from marijuana to get it without risking arrest and imprisonment. In a bizarre, catch-22 sort of reasoning, federal authorities prohibit or severely restrict research on the therapeutic use of marijuana, then say marijuana cannot be used therapeutically because not enough research has been done to prove that it is safe and effective.

ABC News reported last year on the sad plight of Jim Montgomery, a forty-one-year-old paraplegic in Oklahoma, whose only brush with the law had been a speeding ticket and who smoked marijuana to relieve the pain from his broken back—until police found his "stash," in the pouch behind his wheelchair. They arrested him, and a jury sentenced him to life in prison. His sentence was ultimately reduced to ten years—still longer than the average time served in the United States for murder.

I've had no experience with LSD, peyote or any other "mind-expanding," psychedelic drug, just as I've had none with any hard drug. But my journalistic sidekick at Pepperdine was a big advocate of LSD when we were in school together. He used to rhapsodize about the LSD experience as "an orgasm of the soul," and while that sounded both poetic and tantalizing, I always told him I was quite happy—deliriously so—with orgasms emanating from the traditional organ. He argued that I only thought I was happy and that if I took LSD I'd find out that I wasn't really happy, after all, unless I took more LSD. Since happiness is, by definition, a state of mind, or at least a state of emotion, and since I clearly wasn't deluding myself and did have good reason to be happy most of the time, I saw no reason to join my friend in his experimentation with matter over mind. I decided that my exposure to possible bad trips would best be limited to driving the Los Angeles freeways at rush hour.

As I told my friend at the time, I've almost always managed to feel happy about my life and myself, despite my share of suffering—of death, divorce and disappointment. As I mentioned in the prologue, my parents fought bitterly and constantly throughout my childhood and then locked lawyers in an acrimonious three-year divorce that created enmities that last to this day, forty years later. My father suffered his first heart attack when I was three years old and he was sick most of my life and died before he could see me achieve the professional success that he, more than anyone else, had helped make possible. My second wife, Ellen, died after we'd had only eight indescribably happy years together. But I've never sought chemically induced relief from my emotional pain or problems, and I've never thought the potential risk of drugs was worth the temporary pleasure they are supposed to provide. I have absolutely no sympathy for big-name athletes whose salaries approximate the gross national product of a small Caribbean nation but who turn to drugs to escape the "pressures" of being adored by millions. Darryl Strawberry? Dwight Gooden? Steve Howe? Lawrence Taylor? Take away their fancy cars, big houses and investment portfolios and put them to work—incognito, at the minimum wage, cleaning toilets twelve hours a day in a slum housing project, with no support system of any kind, and all their children clamoring for the smallest scrap of bread. Then they'll see what "pressure" is.

I can understand why someone mired in poverty might turn desperately to drugs, seeking momentary escape from a dismal life. But most educated people surely realize that hard drugs can be tyrannically addictive, and I don't understand why anyone with the means to seek other, less dangerous diversions would try them. I don't understand why cocaine became a virtual party favor in Hollywood and various other yuppie circles in the 1980s. Cocaine, heroin and their derivatives have destroyed far too many lives to be tolerated in a humane society. I think they should remain illegal, and the people who sell them should be punished to the fullest extent the law allows. I do, however, favor a fail-safe system of doling them out under medical supervision to certain addicts who just can't quit. That's what doctors in Great Britain do and what several other European countries are experimenting with. Many European health officials think such programs reduce violence, crime and other antisocial activity, largely by taking both the profit and the taboo out of drugs.

I don't know if this approach would work in the United States, but I'd like to see it seriously studied. William Bennett, formerly the czar in the U.S. war on drugs, says Americans will never support legalization of drugs, under any circumstances. Given our puritanical roots, he may be right. Look at the vigorous resistance of so many Americans—and their elected leaders—to proposals as modest as trying to limit the spread of AIDS by allowing pharmacies to sell syringes without a prescription and permitting drug addicts to exchange dirty needles for clean ones. The proportion of new AIDS cases among gays has declined so significantly in recent years that the epidemic is now "clearly driven by infections occurring in the population of injection drug users and their sexual partners and their offspring," according to a study released in September 1995 by the National Academy of Sciences. The proportion of new AIDS cases attributed, directly or indirectly, to intravenous drug use more than doubled from 1981 to 1993; such cases now represent more than a third of all the AIDS cases in this country and two-thirds of those involving women. But even though studies clearly show that clean needles greatly reduce the spread of AIDS—without encouraging increased drug use—Congress has prohibited federal funding for needle exchange programs; Pete Wilson, the Republican governor of California, vetoed a bill in 1993 that would have legalized a needle exchange program in that state.

American parents will probably continue to abuse prescription drugs themselves, to swallow a veritable pharmacopoeia of tranquilizers, diet pills, sleeping pills and stay-awake pills, all the while lecturing their teenage children on the dangers of using drugs. That hypocrisy undermines both their argument and their children's respect for them in much the same way that Bennett's vaunted "war on drugs" undermined public respect for the government and its antidrug campaign. Bennett's approach reminded me of the one that folksinger Hoyt Axton used to recommend before singing "The Pusher": "I think they ought to take everyone who ever even thought about selling hard dope and bury them in the ground up to their necks and run over them with a power lawn mower." I have no sympathy for pushers—they are among the most despicable predators on earth—but Bennett's own rhetoric makes it clear that he would like to subject even casual drug users to the same grisly fate. Unfortunately, when Bennett had the power to actually *do* something about drug abuse—rather than just pontificate about it—he presided over a "war on drugs" that was more joke than *jihad*. As a California judge told ABC News in 1995, "The war on drugs has turned into a war on our people. We almost can't do it worse than we are today."

The "war on drugs" is not only a joke, it's a racist joke. Although Bennett himself has said, "The typical cocaine user is white, male, a high school graduate employed full-time and living in a small metropolitan area or suburb," it's big-city African American dropouts who are far more frequently arrested, prosecuted and imprisoned for cocaine use in Bennett's America. Powdered cocaine is the drug of choice among whites; crack cocaine is the drug of choice among blacks. Someone convicted of possessing five grams of crack cocaine gets a mandatory five-year prison sentence; but someone convicted of possessing powdered cocaine must have five *hundred* grams to receive the same sentence. Whites do use crack cocaine, too. In fact, federal statistics reported by the *Los Angeles Times* in 1995 revealed that there are more than twice as many whites as there are African Americans and Latinos combined who have ever used crack cocaine. But in more than half the federal court districts that handle crack cases, including seventeen states and such major cities as Los Angeles, Chicago, Boston, Miami, Dallas and Denver, not one white person was prosecuted for a crack offense, according to a 1992 survey by the United States Sentencing Commission. Nationwide, between 1991 and 1995, whites have accounted for fewer than 4 percent of those prosecuted in federal court for crack offenses; minorities make up 96 percent of those prosecuted in federal court. When whites *are* prosecuted, it is most often in state courts, where sentences are up to eight years shorter than in federal court, where many blacks wind up and where, since 1986, Congress has ordered stiff mandatory prison sentences for crack dealers. Moreover, the majority of those prosecuted in crack cocaine cases are low-level dealers, lookouts and couriers, not the big drug kingpins the police are always talking about.

Illegal drug use costs society $75 billion a year. But 92 percent of federal spending on entitlement programs for substance abuse and addiction goes for treatment of the consequences of abuse, including imprisonment, and only 8 percent is spent on prevention. Little real effort is made to cope with the drug crisis in the single most effective way possible: cutting drugs off at their source, interdicting them before they get into this country. Instead, the Reagan and Bush administrations—of which Bennett was a most visible and outspoken member—coddled Panamanian strongman Manuel Noriega for years (and paid him several hundred thousand dollars, through the CIA and the army), even as he turned a blind eye to the pervasive drug traffic between his country and ours. The Clinton administration, following the policies of the Bush administration, has been similarly reluctant to clamp down on the drug trade with Mexico. As the *New York Times* reported in 1995, American officials did not want to allow the drug issue to jeopardize the North

American Free Trade Agreement and "the new economic partner-
ship it symbolized." Rather than push for the prosecution of the
drug-related corruption in Mexico that helps make possible the flow
of illicit drugs into the United States, the Bush and Clinton adminis-
trations ignored or minimized the bribes, the rise to power of a new
generation of drug lords and the slow pace of the Mexican government in dealing with these problems.

It's probably a good thing that I have never been tempted by
drugs myself. I do have something of an addictive personality and,
worse, I am blessed with a liver that metabolizes all drugs (including
alcohol) very quickly. I couldn't possibly afford all the marijuana or
LSD or cocaine or whatever it would take to keep me high. Even
medicinal drugs don't have much effect on me. When I had my
appendix taken out about fifteen years ago, I warned the anesthesi-
ologist that he'd better "use plenty of that stuff on me or I'll wake
up in the middle of the operation." He thought I was kidding. But I
woke up just as the surgeon had finished putting the final stitches in
my lower abdomen. He and his colleagues were poised above me,
still wearing their masks and gloves and surgical gowns. I sat bolt
upright and began screaming—in pain and in a fury. Almost as
quickly as you could say, "I told you so, you goddamn-
stupidmotherfuckingcocksuckingmorons," someone jabbed me with
a needle the size of a baseball bat and I was unconscious again.

I've only gotten drunk—really drunk, falling-down drunk—
once in my life. And I've never had a hangover. Yes, I can recall a
couple or three times in the past thirty years when I've felt a little
too high to drive home with complete confidence after consuming a
great deal of wine at dinner. So I didn't drive. But I can drink substantial quantities of wine, when the occasion warrants, and remain
perfectly sober.

Two years ago, driving home late at night after a multicourse
dinner at which Lucy and another couple and I consumed five full
bottles of wine among us, I saw the driver in front of me make a
couple of erratic moves, then spin out of control and almost tip his
car over on the freeway off-ramp. I reacted quickly and managed to
avoid hitting him. Two police cars happened to be right behind us.
Red lights flashing, they screeched to a stop. Two cops jumped out

of the first squad car, jerked open the erratic driver's car door, pulled him out and handcuffed him in ten seconds flat. Another cop rapped politely on my window. When I rolled the window down, he gestured toward my steering wheel and said, "Pretty fancy driving."

"Thanks," I said, quite proud of myself.

The cop must have seen it differently. Or else he just figured it was two-for-one night.

"You always drive that way," he asked, "or have you had a little something to drink tonight?"

Uh-oh.

I felt absolutely sober and was convinced that I'd been driving safely, but I wasn't about to say, "Oh, sure, I just polished off the equivalent of a full bottle of wine and then some." So I told him I'd only had two glasses of wine (the standard lie), the last glass about two hours earlier (another standard lie). He insisted that I get out of the car and take a field sobriety test. I thought I did quite well, given that I'm not terribly well coordinated and couldn't have performed some of the maneuvers if it had been broad daylight and I'd just come from six weeks in an Olympic training camp. Then he asked me to blow into a Breathalyzer.

"This isn't admissible in court," he said, "but it helps us decide if we should take you downtown for the real test. You're considered drunk in California if your blood alcohol measures .08 or more." He grinned malevolently. "A little guy like you, even two glasses of wine might put you over the limit."

I snatched the Breathalyzer out of his hands and blew into it as hard as I could. The needle barely moved. It measured a mere .02.

Obviously disappointed, the cop let me go.

I was relieved. But the test only confirmed what I felt about my own state of solid sobriety. Dinner that night, like most of the relatively few events at which I consume more than a normal (for me) amount of wine, had lasted several hours and had concluded with the leisurely consumption of cigars and double espressos (about the only time I drink any kind of coffee); by the time I got in my car, whatever effects I might have felt from alcohol had long since dissipated.

The only time I was truly drunk was twenty-three years ago,

when my then-next-door neighbor asked me to demonstrate for her party guests the fine art of drinking an authentic margarita—licking salt off my fingers, gulping down a straight shot of tequila and biting into a fresh lime. Ever accommodating, I demonstrated this for each one of her guests. All eighteen of them. One at a time. I had eighteen two-ounce shots of tequila in two hours. But I didn't have to drive anywhere and I was very comfortable with my neighbor and her friends. I was totally relaxed, enjoying the limelight, with the normal censors and brakes completely off. I got drunk. No excuses. I got drunk. Not mean drunk. Clumsy, stupid drunk. I knocked over a large planter. I broke a glass. I spilled some tequila. And while gallantly escorting one of my neighbor friend's attractive female guests to her car at night's end, I groped said guest's breasts (both of them as I recall).

The guest called me the next day to suggest lunch "as soon as you can make it," so I guess she wasn't offended. But I was thoroughly embarrassed. As well I should have been. My behavior was boorish and stupid. I vowed never to let that happen to me again, and I've kept that promise.

Although most people who drink regularly probably get drunk more often than my once in a lifetime, most drinkers I know—especially wine drinkers, as opposed to some drinkers of hard liquor—are careful and responsible about their consumption of alcohol. In the not-so-old days, as my first newspaper colleagues would happily attest, this was not generally the case. Pint bottles of whiskey and cirrhosis of the liver were as common in most newsrooms as four-letter words and jangling telephones. Many newspapermen, like many men in other walks of life, measured their manhood by the number of drinks they could put away and remain standing (if only barely). My closest friend early in my journalistic career often boasted that he could down a quart of bourbon in the course of an evening's poker game without losing a moment's concentration—and that he had long held the record for drinking Manhattans at the Denver Press Club . . . twenty-three in a single night. But most newspapermen—again, like most other men (and women)—now realize that the excessive consumption of alcohol is, in a word, bad. It's bad for your health, bad for your work, bad for your relationships with other people, bad for just about everything. So except for an occasional binge—if that—most people I know drink moderately.

I realize that the people I know are a relatively small circle. I know the statistics on the larger circle: More than 100,000 deaths a year are attributed to alcohol, including more than 17,000 in traffic accidents. (That's 43 percent of all traffic deaths.) More than $110 billion a year is spent (or lost) on the treatment of alcoholism and its resultant problems. Thousands of children are born with birth defects from fetal alcohol syndrome—at a treatment cost of $1.6 billion a year. More than 8 million Americans are classified as alcoholic and almost 6 million more are regarded as having problems with alcohol. Some law enforcement officials say that alcohol is involved in more than half the homicides committed in this country—and in more than half of all arrests for any crime. Beyond the statistics, there is the human suffering. Lives ruined. Marriages and homes broken. Jobs lost. Self-respect shattered. As a lover of American fiction, I'm particularly aware of the dangers of alcohol; it helped destroy many of my favorite authors. William Faulkner. F. Scott Fitzgerald. Ernest Hemingway. John Steinbeck. John O'Hara. Tennessee Williams. Eugene O'Neill. As a society—and as caring people—we must do something about the dread scourge of alcohol abuse. But I think that what we must do is educate people about alcohol, beginning at an early age. And we must really (not halfheartedly) try to prevent alcohol sales to minors. And we must offer intelligent, compassionate treatment for those suffering from alcoholism. And, as I already said, we must impose severe penalties on drunk drivers (and anyone else who in any way harms others or commits crimes while under the influence of alcohol).

But even though the consumption of alcoholic beverages is lower than it has been in thirty years, 60 percent of all Americans still drink them, in one form or another, and I do not think that the proper or effective way to attack the devastating problems of alcohol abuse is to stigmatize every one of them as a potential alcoholic, drunk driver or baby killer; trying to frighten everyone into thinking that one sip of white zinfandel will be fatal, to fetus and graybeard alike, is both dishonest and, ultimately, counterproductive. But that's what many of the neo-Prohibitionists in our midst seem to want everyone to believe. They haven't read their history books *or* their medical books. They don't seem to realize what an abysmal failure Prohibition was the first time around. In the course of the fourteen-year ignoble experiment known as the Volstead Act—the Eighteenth Amendment to the United States Constitution and the only one ever to be repealed—per capita consumption of alcohol increased every year; it has never returned to pre-Prohibition levels.

Prohibition brought us rampant lawlessness and pervasive hypocrisy. It brought us bribery, corruption, smuggling, gang violence and murder. It brought us Al Capone, Pretty Boy Floyd, Legs Diamond, Dutch Schultz, Frank Nitti and Johnny Torrio. It brought us homemade moonshine and a wide range of deadly poisons—alcoholic beverages created by the endless ingenuity of the desperate American mind, drinks concocted from wood alcohol, perfume, hair tonic and antifreeze. (The antifreeze was drained from automobile radiators and contained a residue of rust that some drinkers said improved its flavor and gave their bodies "extra iron.") Prohibition also brought us blatant defiance of—and utter disrespect for—the law. In a speech to the alumni of the New York University Law School in 1923, Justice John H. Clarke of the United States Supreme Court, said, "respect not only for that law [the Volstead Act], but for all laws, has been put to an unprecedented and demoralizing strain in our country." Herbert Asbury, in *The Great Illusion: An Informal History of Prohibition,* went a step further. He argued that Prohibition engendered "contempt" for "all law."

• •

Although it was—appropriately enough—a Frenchman, Louis Pasteur, who discovered the nature of fermentation, in 1857, the natural process and its equally natural effects have been with us since long before Noah decided to try some fermented grape juice after having noticed several of his grape-nibbling goats staggering happily about. (As recounted in the Old Testament, Noah subsequently planted history's first vineyard.) Anthropologists Solomon Katz and Mary Voigt suggested in an article in *Expedition* magazine in 1987 that a fermented, beerlike beverage may have existed more than five thousand years before Noah—perhaps as early as 8000 B.C. The "most ancient documentary evidence for beer production" is much newer, dating from about 3000 B.C., Katz and Voigt say. But they note that "the world's oldest recipe is for beer . . . a highly detailed description of the brewing process in a Sumerian myth." They also mention a second ancient recipe for beer found in a hymn thanking Ninkasi, "the beer goddess . . . whose name is translated as 'the lady who fills the mouth.' " Katz and Voigt hypothesize that beer played a crucial role in early man's transition from a hunter-gatherer society to an agricultural society. According to them, early humans accidentally discovered that gruel made from cereal grains—barley and wheat—did not spoil when left to dry but instead fermented, creating a substance that "had distinct effects on the mind and emotions." This alcoholic brew both tasted good ("sweet") and represented "a substantial improvement in nutritional value over the unprocessed cereal grains."

"In biological terms," Katz and Voigt wrote, "beer drinkers would have had a 'selective advantage' in the form of improved health for themselves and ultimately for their offspring." In order to ensure a steady supply of this joyous, if serendipitous, brew, ancient man learned to plant, cultivate and harvest the necessary grains. Thus was agriculture born. And since agriculture required its practitioners to create an organized division of labor and to remain in one place rather than move on as each herd of animals was depleted, this theory would suggest that the discovery of and desire for alcoholic beverages helped lay the foundation for the farming cooperatives that became villages that became towns that became cities.

It may be more than a bit fanciful to suggest that beer gave birth to modern civilization. The so-called Eureka theory of the beginning of agriculture—whether it involved fermenting grains or the equally inadvertent discovery of seeds sprouting in a refuse heap—is not widely believed these days. Many archaeologists think that changing climatic conditions at the end of the Pleistocene era were a primary cause of the shift toward an agrarian society. Most anthropologists believe that "population growth was one of the main forces that brought the hunting-gathering way of life to an end," as John Pfeiffer writes in *The Emergence of Society*. Population growth brought many changes, including a greater need for food and for a sense of community than was required of the lone hunter. The Eureka theory underrates the ability of hunter-gatherers to adapt to their changing environment and to initiate, rather than simply stumble upon, the benefits of grains, fermented or not.

Regardless, alcohol *was* discovered early in the agrarian transition, and it did have both practical and ritual applications of considerable significance. "In general," Katz and Voigt say, "beer was an important food that was integrated into the mythology, religion and economy of the Sumerians."

Several thousand years later, alcohol also came to play an important role in early American history. Drinking was commonplace—and often excessive—in the American colonies. But alcohol itself was generally regarded as "a healthy 'gift' of God, with many curative and life-sustaining properties," according to Genevieve Ames of the Preventive Research Center in Berkeley, California, in "American Beliefs About Alcoholism," part of the definitive study *The American Experience with Alcohol,* which she edited with Linda Bennett of the George Washington University Medical Center in Washington, D.C.

Until the late seventeenth century, Ames says, most Americans made their own fermented beverages—"cider, ale and brandy"— from locally grown produce, and "an abundant stock of alcoholic beverages, laid in along with other consumable foodstuffs, was considered both a necessary staple of subsistence and a symbol of civility." Alcoholic beverages often replaced drinking water, which was regarded as "impure and too 'thin' for healthful human consumption," she says. Until well into the nineteenth century, alcoholic beverages were also cheaper than tea and coffee. (American colonialists did not, after all, revolt against King George III with a Boston Bourbon Party.) Like marijuana, alcohol had medicinal uses as well.

Puritan ministers were about the only critics of excessive drinking in the colonies. But they didn't object to habitual drunkenness as a falling-away from God; they saw it as an abuse of the "good creature of God" (i.e., God's healthful gift of alcohol), as Mark Keller wrote in "Problems with Alcohol: An Historical Perspective," published in 1976 as part of the study *Alcohol and Alco-*

hol Problems: New Thinking and New Directions. In other words, drunks—at least those who were neither criminals nor dependent on society for their care and feeding—were thought of as indulging in too much of a good thing, not as weak-willed addicts to a vile drug. It wasn't until the nineteenth century, when America began to transform itself from a colonial, agrarian society to a frontier society and then an urban, industrial society that drinking came to be—and to be viewed as—a serious social problem. One reason for this transformation was that people began drinking, and getting drunk, more often in public—in saloons rather than at home or at work—as the workplace "became more formal and the casual mixing of work and recreation, including drinking and socializing on the job, receded before the forces of organization and factory discipline," as John C. Burnham writes in *Bad Habits.*

The Quakers were among the first to regard alcohol as "demon rum" rather than as "God's good creature," Keller points out, but they were soon joined by other religious leaders, including those who allied themselves with the Women's Christian Temperance Union and the Anti-Saloon League. Religious leaders have remained in the forefront of the battle against booze to this day—a remarkable irony, given the long history of linkage between Holy Spirit and bottled spirits. (Jesus didn't turn water into grapefruit juice, did he?) Hugh Johnson, the eminent British wine authority, has suggested that the word "divine" may be derived from the French *de vin*—"of or from wine." Although etymologists are skeptical of this claim, Cistercian monks did plant the first grapevines for wine in Burgundy, and it was a Benedictine monk, Dom Pérignon, who discovered the method for making champagne. Monks have long produced the liqueurs Benedictine and Chartreuse as well as beer that many consider the best in the world. (I can't attest to this since I think all beer tastes like piss—a viewpoint I come to by means too repellent to describe here.) Fra Junípero Serra, a Franciscan missionary, planted the first grapevine in California, and the Christian Brothers still produce wine and brandy there. Wine is involved in many religious rituals, including the Holy Communion of the Catholic Church and the Passover Seder, the wedding vows and various other ceremonies and festivals celebrated by Jews worldwide. One ancient

Jewish teacher said that men should drink so much wine at Purim—
the festival commemorating the deliverance of the Jews from the
edict of death issued by Haman, adviser to the king of Persia—that
they would be incapable of knowing whether they were "cursing
Haman or blessing Mordecai" (who had been instrumental in saving
the Jews from Haman).

Although their gradual assimilation into the dominant Christian culture of the United States has begun to give Jews some of the
same problems with alcohol as the other members of that culture,
Jews historically have had low rates of alcoholism, notwithstanding
their relatively few taboos against alcohol and their relatively high
percentages of adult drinkers. In 1980 sociologists Barry Glassner
and Bruce Berg concluded that Jews have largely avoided serious
problems with alcoholism not *despite* the prevalence and tolerance
of alcohol in their homes and communities but—in part—*because* of
that prevalence and tolerance. "The Jewish family maintains . . . a
permissive drinking culture in which drinking is permitted, but excessive drinking is not," they said.

Charles Snyder, in *Alcohol and the Jews,* underscored that
point: "Where drinking is an integral part of the socialization process, where it is interrelated with the central moral symbolism and is
repeatedly practiced in the rites of a group, the phenomenon of
alcoholism is conspicuous by its absence." (It is worth noting, in this
context, that the standard Jewish toast is *"L'Chayim"*: "To life.")

For Jews, the perception of alcohol consumption as a routine,
ritual and life-affirming act begins in childhood, and Glassner told
me in an interview that this is extremely important. "Cultures that
introduce kids to alcohol at the earliest ages have the lowest rates of
alcoholism," he said. "Cultures that have the strongest prohibitions
[against alcohol] have the highest rates of alcoholism (with some
exceptions, like Mormonism)."

Why is this so? Easy. It's the lure of the forbidden fruit. Tell
someone—especially a willful child—that he can't have something,
and he wants it even more. Then, when he finally gets it, he may be
unable to handle it—may abuse it. I have tried very hard to avoid
this, with the stepchildren I had with my late wife, Ellen, and with
my own son. I allowed Jordy, my stepdaughter, to take a tiny sip of

wine the first time she asked, shortly after I entered her life. She was ten then. (Her brother, Christopher, was fifteen, and he'd already tasted his father's beer and decided that alcohol held no great allure for him.) If I'd come along sooner, I would have let both kids taste wine when they were even younger; I didn't stop my son, Lucas, from dipping his finger into a glass of wine and tasting it—no sips, no swallows, just licking his finger once—when he was two or three. His verdict: "Yuck!" He asked to dip his finger into my wine two or three more times as a toddler, and his reaction was always the same. "Yuck!" Jordy and Chris said approximately the same thing each of the few times they tried wine, and I can recall vividly—and proudly—the night Jordy called home during her first week of college, about a dozen years ago, and complained that she couldn't sleep or study because so many of the other students in the dorm were getting drunk and rowdy. "They never got a chance to try alcohol at home, so I guess they're rebelling and making up for lost time now," she said. I asked if she was drinking anything. "Of course not," she said. "You know I don't like the taste of alcohol."

Jordy and Chris are now thirty and thirty-five respectively. Except for a rare, small glass of wine with me, they still don't drink alcohol. Fine. They made that decision on their own. They weren't browbeaten by a paranoid parent. Lucas? He's only six, so it's much too early to say. After the novelty of the first few tastes of "Mommy's and Daddy's wine" wore off, he's had no interest in further tastes, and I have no more interest in proselytizing him than I do in prohibiting him. If he, too, decides not to drink as an adult, fine; if he winds up sharing my enthusiasm, well, I've got several cases of wine in my cellar from his birth year, and he'll have many opportunities to hone his palate as he grows older.

I'm not suggesting that parents encourage (or allow) their very young children to *drink* alcohol. That would be folly. Dangerous folly. An abdication—and violation—of parental obligation and good sense. Lucy and I have both told Lucas that drinking is for adults and that even adults must be responsible and moderate in their consumption of alcohol. We have told him, in very strong terms, about the consequences of alcohol abuse, just as we have told him how dangerous drugs and cigarette smoking are. He has become an obsessive baseball fan, and when Mickey Mantle needed a liver transplant in 1995, in large part because of his years of heavy drinking, we used that as an object lesson in our daily baseball discussions with Lucas, just as we used Darryl Strawberry's drug problems as an opportunity to discuss with him the destructive power of drugs. But I think it's foolish to paint alcohol as unremittingly evil—in any form, in any quantity, under any circumstances—and I think it's equally foolish to prohibit children from having any contact with alcohol until they're twenty-one, as every state in the Union began to do a few years ago; kids—they're not "kids" at eighteen, not in 1996—can drive, vote, get married, pay taxes, take out loans, pilot airplanes and fight (and die) in the armed forces. Why aren't they old enough to drink? Even before they turn eighteen, I think young people should be allowed to see that alcohol, in moderation, can be a normal part of everyday life—as when their parents drink wine with dinner. I think that an occasional, carefully supervised taste of wine—and once they're older, an occasional small swallow or two (or more, depending on their age and maturity)—would help demystify alcohol and rob it of the allure that taboo always provides. Most western European nations take this approach. Compared with the United States, kids in those countries start drinking younger—and per capita adult consumption is higher—but the rate of alcoholism and alcohol abuse is lower. As with the Jews, a connection seems both logical and likely.

We're determined these days to teach our children about safe sex. Good. Why not teach them about safe drinking, too? I'm convinced that if more parents were more relaxed about wine, we'd have fewer drunken rebels-with-a-cause, in adolescence and beyond. But religious leaders and medical "experts" have made it very difficult for conscientious parents to even consider this approach; frantic warnings that a single sip of any alcohol will turn a child into a drunken lout (or a corpse) have turned most parents into overprotective martinets.

Mothers Against Drunk Drivers (MADD) and Students Against Drunk Drivers (SADD) have been joined by what seems like Virtually Everybody Against Drunk Drivers. Everybody *should* be against drunk driving. Drinking and driving *don't* mix. Drunk drivers should be punished. Severely. I salute MADD, SADD and their colleagues for helping to reduce drunk-driving fatalities in this country by more than 30 percent over the past dozen years. I do not, however, think we should suspend the Bill of Rights and have police throw up roadblocks and sobriety checkpoints where drivers are randomly forced to roll down their windows and be sniffed for alcohol-tainted breath, without either probable cause or a judicial warrant. (I oppose random drug tests in the workplace and the schoolyard for the same reason.) Nor do I think that, except in extraordinary circumstances, bartenders should be held legally liable for damages caused by drivers they've served. This is yet another example of a troubling trend in our society: people increasingly seek to blame others for their own shortcomings. That's one reason we've become so litigious. You don't like something or someone? Don't bother to think about what you might have done (or not done) to contribute to the problem. Don't try to figure out how to solve the problem yourself. No. Just sue the bastards.

A Texas woman sued a tequila maker several years ago when her eighteen-year-old daughter died of alcohol poisoning after drinking more than twenty shots of tequila; she said the tequila maker was negligent in not warning customers that drinking too much too fast could be fatal. Under her reasoning, any parent whose eighteen-year-old was killed in a high-speed auto accident could sue the maker of the car for not having posted a notice on the steering wheel that driving at more than one hundred miles an hour could be fatal. Shouldn't people be required to exhibit at least a modicum of common sense and personal accountability? Must everything be someone else's fault? Apparently so. A jury awarded the Texas woman more than a million dollars. (An appeals court overturned the award in 1994.)

A few years ago, another firm that makes and markets alcoholic beverages, Anheuser-Busch, was sued for $10,000 by a man who charged that its beer ads on television were untrue, deceptive and misleading and that they had caused him physical and mental injury, emotional distress and financial loss. In essence, the man argued that TV commercials fraudulently led him to believe that if he drank Bud Light, he could enjoy the same kind of fantasy life that was depicted in the commercials featuring "tropical settings and beautiful women and men engaged in unrestricted merriment," as the courts phrased it in rejecting his suit.

Opponents of alcohol launched a more official attack on Budweiser in the state of Washington early in 1995 when the State Department of Health bought two minutes of advertising on the Super Bowl telecast to combat the "Bud Bowl" commercials that feature anthropomorphic bottles of beer in a mock gridiron showdown. The Department of Health commercials were intended to warn teenagers of the dangers of alcohol and to counter the "images of glamour, beauty and popularity" that the Bud Bowl commercials were said to confer upon beer drinkers, according to Dr. Mimi Fields, a health officer for the state of Washington.

Many neo-Prohibitionists want alcohol advertising banned from the airwaves altogether. The American Academy of Pediatrics and an outfit that calls itself Stop Marketing Alcohol on Radio and Television (SMART?) have both called for a total ban. The neo-Prohibitionists are pushing hard for a wide variety of measures to restrict the sale of and access to alcohol as well. They fight against the granting of new licenses to liquor stores, and they want to reduce the operating hours of existing liquor outlets.

In Colorado, state liquor authorities said in 1995 that wine could no longer be served at public art gallery exhibitions. In Georgia, several cities and counties now prohibit the sale of beer and wine in restaurants on Sundays. In Vermont, authorities began administering Breathalyzer tests to elementary school students without any specific cause for suspicion. Throughout the country, at every jurisdictional level, campaigns are under way for high "sin" and "luxury" taxes on alcoholic beverages. The federal government and all state governments tax alcoholic beverages, and many local jurisdictions do so, too. If you want to buy a bottle of wine in Chicago, you pay four separate taxes—federal, state, county and city.

Two hundred years ago, Thomas Jefferson argued that wine should be exempt from any such taxes. "I think it is a great error to consider a heavy tax on wines as a tax on luxury," Jefferson said. "On the contrary, it is a tax on the health of our citizens."

But Jefferson's arguments don't seem to carry much weight

these days, and indeed, it was during his lifetime that medical arguments against alcohol first surfaced in the United States. The opening salvo in this battle is generally thought to have been fired in 1784, with the publication of the pamphlet *An Inquiry into the Effects of Ardent Spirits on the Mind and Body,* written by Benjamin Rush, a signer of the Declaration of Independence and the surgeon general in George Washington's Continental Army. Rush is regarded in many quarters as the "intellectual and political founder of the temperance movement," as Genevieve Ames writes in "American Beliefs About Alcoholism." But his view of heavy drinking as disease, addiction and moral breakdown did not begin to have real impact until near the middle of the nineteenth century, when rapidly increasing immigration ignited a wave of xenophobia in the United States. Many middle-class, nativist Americans promoted temperance and abstinence as a lifestyle distinct from the drinking habits of the lower, working-class Irish and German immigrants, says J. R. Gusfield, in *Symbolic Crusade: Status Politics and the American Temperance Movement.* Many of these immigrants were Catholics, new to a country with a long, ugly history of anti-Catholicism—sometimes blatant, sometimes just beneath the surface—and that further fueled both the opposition to drinking and the characterization of drinkers as alien and deviant. By the end of the nineteenth century, Ames and Gusfield both say, the temperance movement had metamorphosed into what Ames calls "a self-serving political mechanism by which American Protestantism and the mainstream middle-class culture sought to deprive the growing immigrant population of power, with conflicting notions of values and ideology underlying the surface conflict over drinking behavior. The high point of this struggle was the passing of the Eighteenth Amendment to prohibit the sale of alcohol."

Within a decade after the repeal of Prohibition, the first generation of neo-Prohibitionists began agitating anew on the dangers of alcohol. They revived the medical model that Rush had introduced more than a half century earlier, and that is essentially the approach that the most effective critics of alcohol use to this day. To them, alcohol leads inevitably to alcoholism—a progressive disease of both will and body that leads just as inevitably to death. Regarding alcoholism as a disease is good in that it generally leads to a more compassionate attitude toward (and treatment of) those who suffer from it. Society tends to view victims more favorably than it does sinners and wastrels. But to see alcoholism solely as a disease over which the victim has no control also absolves the victim of any individual responsibility and may make it more difficult for him to recover. Some alcoholics—perhaps most—drink because of underlying physiological or psychological problems. But some may have those problems precisely *because* they drink. To let them rationalize their lack of will by saying, "I'm sick; it's not my fault; I can't do anything about it," does them, and society, a disservice.

I realize that some people who drink do become alcoholics— many through no fault of their own; they have an internal chemical imbalance, a genetic predisposition to alcoholism. I realize, too, that some people who are not clinical alcoholics drink too much for their own good—and for the good of their family, friends, coworkers and society at large—regardless of the reason. Alcohol can be abused. That's obvious. People who abuse it should be treated accordingly, whether as addicts, victims of a disease or criminals, depending on the circumstances and the consequences of their drinking. But most people who drink do not become alcoholics *or* drunk drivers. Drinking is just one of many things they do. It doesn't define their lives, and it doesn't poison their bodies. For many generations in this country, there was a culture of casual social drinking that encouraged the consumption of alcohol. Happy hours. Cocktail parties. A quick highball on the way home from work. A few beers with the guys on Friday night. Some people abused these opportunities, and we're all better off now that both the calculated glamorization and the careless consumption of alcohol have declined. But some people benefit from drinking moderately. Almost forty years ago, my father's cardiologist suggested that he have "a small schnapps" before bedtime every night to help him go to sleep. My wife, Lucy, like many other people, finds that a drink before dinner helps her relax. It's part of the "transition," she says, that starts the process of unwinding after a pressure-filled workday. For other people, a drink or two in a social setting may loosen inhibitions and self-consciousness and make it possible for conviviality to replace shyness. There have also been studies showing that moderate amounts of alcohol can increase resistance to the common cold and to adult-onset diabetes—and decrease the likelihood of depression.

Over the past three or four years, the most commonly discussed positive effect of alcohol consumption is what has come to be called the French paradox. In October 1992 the CBS program *60 Minutes* reported that the likelihood of a middle-aged, American male dying of a heart attack is "three times greater than [for] a Frenchman of the same age," even though the French "eat thirty percent more fat than we do . . . smoke more and exercise less."

Why?

It may well be because the average Frenchman drinks ten times more wine—mostly red wine—than does the average American; as Morley Safer, the *60 Minutes* correspondent, said, "For years . . . doctors in many countries [have believed] that alcohol—in particular, red wine—reduces the risk of heart disease."

The essence of the French paradox—originally reported eighteen months before the *60 Minutes* broadcast, in a lengthy article in the magazine *In Health*—is quite simple. People who drink alcohol regularly tend to have higher levels in their blood of high-density lipoproteins (HDLs), the so-called good cholesterol that carries dangerous fat out of the body. Red wine is believed to be the most beneficial alcoholic beverage because the chemical composition of wine also appears to inhibit the formation of blood clots. As Safer explained it, red wine flushes away the small blood cells (called platelets) that "cling to rough fatty deposits on the artery walls, clogging and finally blocking the artery and causing a heart attack."

Authoritative experts—French and American medical researchers interviewed by Safer, on camera—made strong, clear statements supporting Safer's report. (Dr. Serge Renaud of Lyons Centre: "There is no other drug that's been so efficient [in preventing heart disease] as a moderate intake of alcohol.")

I suspect that red wine alone is not responsible for the French resistance to heart disease. I wouldn't be surprised if subsequent studies show that the more *laissez-faire* attitude of the French, their genuine *joie de vivre*—there's a reason those two phrases are French—also help explain their lower death rate from heart disease.

Given what medical research has shown about the effect of anxiety, tension and stress on human health, I have always wondered how many people worry themselves to death, compared to how many drink themselves to death. But there seems little question that red wine does have a significant, beneficial effect on the human cardiovascular system. There have been a few studies showing that white wine may have a similar effect—and at least one large study showing beneficial health effects from drinking hard liquor: a Harvard study of 121,700 nurses showed a 50 percent drop in death rates from coronary heart disease in postmenopausal women who drank moderately.

But red wine has received most of the attention and has gained the most medical credibility in recent years, and the sales of red wine skyrocketed after the *60 Minutes* report. Unlike most Europeans, Americans have always drunk far more white wine than red. In most western European countries—France, Italy and Spain among them—90 percent of the wine sold is red; in this country, 75 percent of the wine sold is white. But in the first month after the *60 Minutes* broadcast, U.S. supermarket sales of red wine, which had been flat for several years, increased 46 percent over the same period the previous year, according to Infoscan data from Information Resources Inc. in San Francisco. Over the next seven months, red wine sales continued to increase—by 37 percent over the previous year— and in July 1993, when the *60 Minutes* program was rebroadcast, sales jumped still further: up 49 percent over the same month in 1991. However, when a few winemakers and wine merchants tried to capitalize on media coverage of the French paradox by referring to it in their merchandising, federal authorities stepped in. Beringer Vineyards in Napa Valley designed a tag to be hung on the necks of its bottles, quoting the *60 Minutes* program on both the benefits of red wine and the dangers of alcohol abuse. But after preliminary approval from the Bureau of Alcohol, Tobacco and Firearms, both the Food and Drug Administration and the Federal Trade Commission put a stop to it. When Draper & Esquin, a San Francisco wine merchant, began distributing to its wholesalers a small button that said, "Have you had your glass of red wine today?" the BATF (perhaps best known now for its brilliant handling of the Branch

Davidian standoff-cum-shoot-out in Waco in 1993) ordered the company to cease and desist. (Confronted by aggressive Draper & Esquin lawyers, the BATF ultimately backed down.)

Because of the pervasive bias against alcohol in any form in this country, many doctors and others in the neo-Prohibitionist movement make no distinction between wine and distilled spirits. To them, it's all booze—all evil—and never mind the paeans to wine by sources as diverse as Louis Pasteur, Beethoven, Michelangelo, George Washington and Plato (who said, "No thing more excellent nor more valuable than wine was ever granted mankind by God"). The all-booze-is-evil attitude inevitably influences the American public and helps explain why wine consumption is so low in this country. Per capita wine consumption in France is 17.6 gallons a year; in Portugal, it's 16.4; in Italy, 15. In the United States, it's 1.9. There are many explanations for this disparity, the most important probably being the cultural tradition of routinely drinking wine with dinner in many western European (and other) countries. In the United States, the pretentious prose of many newspaper and magazine wine writers has contributed to the sense that drinking wine is anything but routine, that it is only a special-occasion beverage, that the knowledge, purchase and consumption of wine is an esoteric rite, accessible only to the *cognoscenti*. But fear of the consequences of drinking alcohol in any form is the most powerful disincentive to would-be wine drinkers here, even though many scientific studies, dating back more than sixty years, have shown that wine is absorbed into the bloodstream in a different way than are beer and distilled spirits. The late Dr. Salvatore Lucia, chairman of the department of epidemiology at the University of California Medical Center in San Francisco, argued that the concentration of perhaps two hundred natural compounds in grapes and grape skins imbues wine with several health benefits. Leroy Creasy, a scientist at Cornell University, urges "drinking red wines [with] every dinner for the rest of your life." Indeed, Creasy's comment carries within it one of the most important distinctions between the consumption of wine and the consumption of other alcoholic beverages: the vast majority of the wine consumed in the United States is consumed at home, with food, not as a replacement for food or as a barroom escape to oblivion.

But how much wine should people drink? Even wine can be abused—*vide* the Thunderbird drunks on skid row in every major American city. At what point do the health benefits of moderate drinking give way to the health damage of excessive drinking? On this point, there is considerable, often heated debate. Most experts recommend no more than a glass or two a day. In 1995 a twelve-year Danish study of 13,285 men and women concluded, however, that the greatest benefit in terms of longevity came from drinking three to five glasses of wine a day. Among those who did so, there were, proportionally, 49 percent fewer deaths than among those who drank no wine at all. The number of participants who drank three to five glasses of wine a day was small—only sixty-two—so the authors of the study cautioned against making definitive judgments about the longevity benefits of that level of consumption. But much larger numbers of test subjects drank one or two glasses of wine a day or one glass of wine a week or a month, and at every level of consumption, the wine drinkers had lower mortality rates than did those in the study who didn't drink any alcoholic beverage or who consumed only beer or hard liquor.

"The risk of dying steadily decreased with an increasing intake of wine," said the authors of the study, led by Morten Gronbaek of the Institute of Preventive Medicine at Copenhagen Municipal Hospital. "Our finding, that only wine drinking clearly reduces both the risk of dying from cardiovascular and cerebrovascular disease and the risk of dying from other causes, suggests that other, more broadly acting forces in wine may be present. Antioxidants and flavonoids, which are presumed to prevent both coronary heart disease and some cancers, may be present in red wines. It has also been suggested that tannin and other phenolic compounds in red wine may have a protective effect."

In their study, published in the May 1995 issue of the *British Medical Journal*—and covered six months later by *60 Minutes*, as a follow-up to its 1992 "French paradox" story—the authors pointed out that while the overall consumption of alcohol in Denmark has been relatively stable for fifteen years, the percentage of wine as a share of total alcohol consumption has almost doubled; as wine consumption has increased 30 percent, deaths from heart disease have fallen 30 percent.

In early 1996, a joint committee of the U.S. Department of Health and Human Services and the Department of Agriculture said for the first time that the moderate consumption of alcohol may reduce the risk of heart attacks.

Spurred by all the talk about alcohol's potentially beneficial effects, Dr. Enoch Gordis, director of the National Institute of Alcohol Abuse and Alcoholism, has announced for the first time ever that the United States government is seeking research proposals to study the relationship between the consumption of alcohol and improved cardiovascular health.

It will no doubt be many years before we have definitive answers on this question and many related questions. In the meantime, the real paradox—the real dilemma—involving wine and health is that facing many women. Just as epidemiological studies show that drinking moderate amounts of red wine can help prevent heart disease, so epidemiological studies also show that consumption of alcohol in any form can contribute to breast cancer. Some scientists have suggested that as little as one drink a day may increase the risk of breast cancer.

Doctors urge women to make their decisions about drinking based on known risk factors. But what does someone like Lucy do? She has several high-risk factors for breast cancer: she started menstruating early, became a mother late and, worst of all, her mother had breast cancer. But Lucy also has several high-risk factors for heart disease: her father died of heart failure, and Lucy herself has a type A personality, a stressful job and a sedentary lifestyle. Should Lucy drink to protect her heart? Or abstain to save her breasts? Fortunately, she's sensible. She drinks moderately. She isn't sure she's doing the right thing—she worries about it more than a little—but the odds would seem to be on her side. As already noted, heart disease kills far more women than does breast cancer—by a margin of nine to one. Nevertheless, many in the medical community and, especially, the neo-Prohibitionist movement have been so alarmist about alcohol that Lucy and millions of other women have been made to feel that every time they have a glass of wine, they're taking a foolish step down the road to mastectomy, chemotherapy and death.

I'm neither a doctor nor a scientist. I can't guarantee you that it is 100 percent safe for women (or anyone else) to drink moderately—or to eat a steak every couple of weeks or to have coffee for breakfast every morning or to use a cellular telephone. Besides, as every scientist knows, it's literally impossible to prove a negative; you cannot demonstrate in a laboratory that any substance will never harm anybody under any circumstances. But I can tell you that too many people—well meaning or not—have made virtually everything we do seem so dangerous that one sometimes wonders if the only human activity that incurs no further risk is death itself. ("Warning: Death can be hazardous to your health.")

Perhaps no risk is so alarmingly portrayed as that of alcohol for the pregnant woman. Since November 18, 1989, all alcoholic beverages sold in the United States have been required by law to have, "in a conspicuous and prominent place," labels that say, "According to the Surgeon General, women should not drink alcoholic beverages during pregnancy because of the risk of birth defects." Alarmists and neo-Prohibitionists think that warning doesn't go far enough. One swallow of alcohol in any form, they seem to say, and a pregnant woman risks turning her fetus into an artichoke—physically handicapped, mentally retarded, incapable of leading a normal life. Just look at a few recent studies and statements from the most reputable and responsible sources:

- "Women should abstain from alcoholic beverages from the time they start trying to get pregnant until after their baby is delivered, the American Academy of Pediatrics advised on Monday."
- It's "not possible to advise women that any amount of alcohol is safe during pregnancy," says the American College of Obstetricians and Gynecologists.
- "To date, researchers have not established a clear threshold of daily drinking for alcohol-related impairments. For this rea-

son, women have been advised that abstaining from alcohol during pregnancy is the only known way to prevent alcohol-related injuries in offspring," says the National Institute on Alcohol Abuse and Alcoholism, in its eighth special report to Congress on alcohol and health.

- "Fetal alcohol syndrome—which afflicts infants damaged in utero by their mother's alcohol consumption—causes problems that last a lifetime, according to researchers at the University of Washington in Seattle."

- A study of women who drank alcohol during the last six months of pregnancy has found that their babies had a tenfold increased risk of developing leukemia during infancy.

Fetal alcohol syndrome (FAS) is the leading preventable cause of birth defects and mental retardation in the United States. Some advocates of abstinence estimate that 4,000 to 8,000 babies are born with FAS in the United States every year. Studies cited in the *Wine Spectator,* a consumer wine magazine which obviously has its own agenda, put the figure at "1,176 . . . out of a total of about 3.9 million live births"—in other words, about 3 in every 10,000 births. This big difference in numbers may be a matter of definition, with one school defining FAS very broadly and the other applying that label only to the most severe cases. But however one defines FAS itself, everyone agrees that many more infants—perhaps as many as 55,000—are born with the less severe cluster of symptoms known as fetal alcohol effects (FAE).

Whatever the numbers are—for FAS *and* FAE—they are too big. Fetal alcohol syndrome in particular is a national tragedy. Children suffering from FAS develop slowly, both physically and mentally. They are generally irritable, hyperactive, impulsive, antisocial, unable to concentrate. They have low IQs. The worst are retarded. Many are also short and underweight, with small heads and jaws, thin upper lips, short noses and low nasal bridges. The *Journal of the American Medical Association* has said that the lifetime cost of caring for one child suffering from fetal alcohol syndrome is $1.4 million.

I think that pregnant women who drink to excess are so stupid, selfish, thoughtless and cruel that they should probably be strangled with their own umbilical cords. But I also think we risk stretching the definition of fetal alcohol syndrome so far that it becomes meaningless. Some neo-Prohibitionists want to attribute every tantrum, every less-than-Harvard IQ point, every less-than-flawless act by every child, to the half a glass of wine his mother drank the evening after she probably got pregnant. In the process, they are frightening women who might benefit from the relaxing effects of an occasional glass of wine; they are also frightening women who do take that occasional glass of wine into thinking they are poisoning their children and destroying their future.

Not everyone agrees that pregnant women must abstain from drinking. French, Italian and Spanish women, among many others, have routinely consumed wine throughout pregnancy without a noticeably higher incidence of fetal alcohol syndrome. When Lucy and I were traveling in France while she was six months pregnant with Lucas in 1989, waiters looked utterly befuddled each time she declined wine and explained that she was *enceinte*. She didn't decline every night, though; her pediatrician had said it was perfectly okay for her to drink a couple of glasses of wine a week when she was pregnant, and Lucy gratefully did just that. Lucas certainly shows no ill effects from her modest imbibing. He's healthy, sunny, well behaved, amazingly adaptable and endlessly energetic. At three, he could identify every dinosaur by name and eating habit. At four, he could recognize, in the morning newspaper, the names of every major-league baseball team and of every player on the Los Angeles Dodgers. Now six, his knowledge of baseball statistics and strategy repeatedly astonishes the fans who sit near us at Dodger Stadium, and he has used his interest in baseball to essentially teach himself to read and to do relatively simple arithmetic in his head. (This week—spontaneously, completely unprompted—he launched a new breakfast-table exercise: adding up, in his head, all the runs scored in the previous day's major-league games. This morning, sports page in hand but without either pencil or paper, he ticked off the individual and cumulative scores, concluding with the matter-of-fact an-

nouncement that since there had been eighty-eight runs scored yes-
terday in the American League and fifty-eight scored in the National
League, "That means all the teams got a total of 146 runs.")

Lucas's single-minded passion for baseball notwithstanding,
he also managed, about five months after his fifth birthday, to mem-
orize the names of all forty-two presidents of the United States, in
order, and to learn three or four facts about each of them. I suppose
that some critics of alcohol consumption might argue that his obsessive behavior—and his inability, so far, to demonstrate physical
baseball skills equal to his baseball knowledge—are somehow a developmental shortcoming clearly linked to his mother's drinking
during pregnancy. I, on the other hand, would blame something
else. Me. I'm obsessive, too. And my hand-eye coordination and
general athletic skills have always been about on a par with Helen
Keller's. Since my mother didn't drink, though, my shortcomings are
clearly genetic, not alcoholic, in origin. So, I suspect, are Lucas's.

Personal anecdotes do not, of course, make good science. Even
the most fanatic promoters of temperance will admit that some ge-
niuses have been born of alcoholic mothers. That proves nothing.
But many medical researchers have supported the notion that moderate drinking is not harmful to the fetus. A seven-country study of
8,500 mothers and babies, sponsored by the European Commission,
concluded in 1992 that one drink a day "does not appear to have a
detrimental effect on fetal growth." In the summary to its report, the
scientists said, "There was no evidence that the development of children of mothers who drink [that amount] was impaired either mentally or physically at age 18 months." Ruth Little examined a number of epidemiological studies for the *Journal of Substance Abuse* in
1991 and concluded that fetal alcohol syndrome occurs "only with
heavy or alcoholic drinking."

Dr. David Whitten, coauthor of *To Your Health: Two Physicians Explore the Health Benefits of Wine,* said in 1994 that there
was no reason why a woman who regularly drank a glass of wine a
day should "abandon that healthy, delightful habit during pregnancy." Whitten's coauthor, Dr. Martin Lipp, concedes that their
book is not a "scientific treatise" and he says, "We don't argue that
there are not risks involved in alcohol consumption, even at these

sensible levels. But it's important to ask: Risky compared to what? There are risks involved in every activity, even those we consider good for us, like exercise." Whitten and Lipp argue that "the risks and benefits associated with light, regular wine consumption compare quite favorably with most other activities of daily life."

The bottom line, it seems to me, is that women should be free to decide for themselves if this is a risk they want to assume. Obviously, doctors and scientists have varying opinions; the effects of alcohol may also vary from woman to woman, just as some studies suggest they differ depending on when in the course of pregnancy a woman does drink. But no woman is really "free" to weigh the various personal factors and pieces of scientific evidence and decide for herself whether to drink if she's constantly being bombarded with alarmist, guilt-inducing harangues wherever she looks. Before long, I expect to see the modern-day equivalent of the WCTU adopting the tactics of the Operation Rescue antiabortionists; they'll start harassing pregnant women in liquor stores and blocking the grocery store aisles whose shelves hold wine. Something like that has already happened in at least one instance that I know about.

Tukwila, Washington, is a small suburb south of Seattle. Seattle is home to the University of Washington, where researchers were the first to report on the condition now known as fetal alcohol syndrome. The good people of Seattle and environs are an especially health-conscious, politically correct lot, and two of them demonstrated this moral superiority in an especially odious fashion five years ago when a pregnant woman sat down in a restaurant with a friend and ordered a strawberry daiquiri with dinner. The woman's baby was a week overdue and this was the first drink she had ordered since becoming pregnant. But the waiter who took her order didn't think she should drink any alcohol. He twice asked her if she'd like a "virgin daiquiri" instead. When she insisted on her original order, he shared his concern with a female coworker. The coworker then asked the customer if she was sure she wanted that drink. She was. The waitress showed her a pregnant-women-shouldn't-drink warning label from a beer bottle. When the woman still didn't rescind her daiquiri order, the waitress left the label on her table.

The pregnant customer was, understandably, shaken and irate. "They tried to make me feel like a child abuser," she told the *New York Times*. "I had been very careful throughout the whole pregnancy, and I thought it would be safe to have just this one drink, which I ordered with dinner. I've always made it a point to read everything I could find about alcohol and pregnancy. I felt guilty enough as it was for ordering the drink."

When the woman complained to the restaurant's management, the waiter and the waitress were both fired. They then helped launch a campaign to persuade the Washington liquor control board to adopt clear rules telling restaurant staffers whether they have the right to refuse to serve alcohol to pregnant women. Leaders of the women's rights movement instantly opposed the proposal. Such a rule, they said, would violate a woman's right to privacy and her right to make her own choices. "Any form of government has to stay out of women's reproductive rights and individual lives and bodies," said Lindy Cater, a lawyer at the Northwest Women's Law Center in Seattle.

The woman customer gave birth to a healthy, seven-pound twelve-ounce baby boy. But the next thing you know, one of the busybody extremists in the abstinence movement will adopt yet another tactic of the antiabortionists: he'll gun down a wine merchant or a bartender for selling alcohol to a pregnant woman.

Or maybe the antidrinking forces will borrow a stratagem from the antismoking forces and sponsor letter-writing contests in junior high schools. A seventh grader in Southern California won one such contest for writing a letter urging that pregnant women be prohibited by law from smoking. The student, Monica Martinez, won an all-expense-paid trip to Washington, D.C. . . . where she presumably shared her medical and political expertise with Congress, the White House and the Supreme Court.

4

O F
PANATELAS
AND PARIAHS,
SECONDHAND
SMOKE AND
SECOND-CLASS
CITIZENS

*T*here I was, sitting in my season's seats, high above and behind home plate at Dodger Stadium, two hot dogs and a Sprite already under my belt, game time still almost forty minutes away and several empty seats around me on all sides. It seemed the ideal time to smoke a cigar. I leaned back, a smile on my lips and an unlit stogie in my hand, contemplating the pleasure that awaited me.

Within nanoseconds, I heard a loud, ugly snarl from what seemed like twenty or twenty-five feet away, to my left and many rows farther back:

"Put that smelly thing out."

I turned in the direction of the voice. It belonged to a woman who looked to be in her midthirties, although her face was reddened and twisted in a paroxysm of such rage that it was difficult at first to be absolutely certain of anything—her age, her gender, even her species.

"I said put that goddamn thing out," the leather-lunged charmer repeated when she saw me looking in her direction. "It stinks to high heaven."

I held the cigar aloft so she could see it clearly.

"I haven't lit it yet," I said, as reasonably as I could. "You can't possibly smell it. There's nothing to smell. Besides, it's a good cigar, and good cigars don't stink, not even when they're lit."

"I can smell it, all right," she shouted back, "and I can smell you, too. You both stink."

I was convinced that she couldn't smell anything, except perhaps her own bile (it *was* a warm evening), but as much as I usually enjoy the dialectic, I make it a policy never to argue with fanatics on three subjects—religion, politics and cigars. I put my cigar back in its wooden case.

This happened about five years ago. Things have gotten worse since. The Dodgers—and twenty-one of the other twenty-seven major-league baseball teams—now ban all smoking from the seating areas of their stadiums. This is, alas, part of the larger movement in society to ban smoking anything, anywhere, to turn smokers—cigar smokers, cigarette smokers, pipe smokers, even barbecue smokers, for Christ's sake—into social pariahs. Every state in the Union and seventeen hundred U.S. cities, counties and other localities now have ordinances of one kind or another restricting smoking. One city, Sharon, Massachusetts, passed an ordinance in 1995 forbidding smoking in *outdoor* municipal recreation areas, including all beaches and parks.

The first recorded warning about smoking came from King James I, whose 1604 treatise described smoking as "a custome lothsome to the eye, hateful to the Nose, harmefull to the braine, dangerous to the Lungs." These are essentially the same arguments that animate the campaign against secondhand smoke today. Simply put, people are afraid that smoke—someone else's smoke—will give them cancer. Nor do they like the way smoke smells (not even in the great outdoors of Dodger Stadium, where it quickly dissipates). I'll deal with both those issues in some detail later in this chapter. But it's worth remembering that the modern antismoking campaign in this country, which really began with the 1964 report by United States Surgeon General Luther Terry, was originally based on the threat of cigarette smoking to the cigarette smoker. So let me begin there, too.

For the record, I have never smoked a cigarette, would never smoke a cigarette, can't understand why anyone would smoke a cigarette. The only time I was tempted to do so was when I was in my early teens, and my best friend, Allan—the guy who had earlier told me what "fuck" means—was sneaking a smoke in his backyard one afternoon.

"Let me have a puff," I said.

"No."

"Why not?"

"Because it's bad for you."

"You're doing it. Besides, I'm curious. I just want one taste."

"No. You're supposed to be the smart one on this block. Don't do something stupid just because I do."

Allan and I had an unusual relationship. Although he was four years older than me, he was not nearly as good a student as I was. I helped him with his homework, and he—being eight inches taller and forty pounds heavier than me—protected me from Dennis, the neighborhood bully. But when I told Allan that if he wouldn't give me a puff of his cigarette, I'd get one from someone else, he said, "You do that and you can deal with Dennis yourself from now on."

Allan may not have been a good student, but he was no dummy. He knew that I would find his argument just as persuasive as the one that my father was making about the same time. "If you ever smoke anything," Dad said, "I'll break both your arms off and beat you to death with them."

Except for my momentary weakness in Allan's backyard, I never considered violating my father's order until one evening in 1980, eleven years after he died. My late wife, Ellen, and I had just finished our dinner in Davos, a small Swiss mountain resort about forty miles from St. Moritz. She was sipping espresso. V-e-r-y s-l-o-w-l-y. I was drumming my fingers on the table. Very impatiently.

"I really like my espresso," Ellen said. "It's the perfect way to end a wonderful dinner. Can't you find something else to do with your hands so I won't feel guilty, like I'm keeping you from doing something important?"

"What did you have in mind?" I asked. "You know I don't like either coffee or after-dinner drinks."

"How about smoking a cigar?"

I told her of my father's admonition.

She knew how much I loved and respected my father, so she didn't say anything for a few minutes. Then she said, tentatively, "How much harm could one cigar a day do?"

I got up from the table, walked to a pay phone and called my doctor in Los Angeles to ask him the same question. He said he didn't think one cigar a day would pose any threat to my continued good health. I returned to the table, summoned the waiter and was soon puffing on a Davidoff from Havana, "the Rolls-Royce of cigars," the waiter assured me. It was wonderful. Mild but full-flavored. To my great surprise, I found it enormously relaxing. I was still smoking—and still smiling—when Ellen finished her second espresso.

After returning to Los Angeles, I began looking through the medical literature. Ellen and Dr. Cornfield were both right about the safety of a one-cigar-a-day habit, and in a 1983 report that repeated and expanded upon the 1964 surgeon general's condemnation of cigarette smoking, Surgeon General C. Everett Koop made it official, and even broader: he said research had shown that cigar smokers and pipe smokers "do not appear to experience substantially greater risks than non-smokers."

What's the difference between cigars and cigarettes? For one thing, cigarettes are addictive; cigars are not. That means that one can be a moderate cigar smoker; I've only known one or two moderate cigarette smokers. The vast majority of cigarette smokers smoke a lot of cigarettes—a pack, two packs, three packs a day, often using their last cigarette to light their next, with nary a clean breath in between. I've never known a "chain" cigar smoker. Equally important, most cigar smokers don't inhale, so while some nicotine is inevitably absorbed through the mucous membranes in the mouth, the amount is infinitesimal compared with the amount that cigarette smokers inhale into their lungs with every puff. Last year, an editor at *Cigar Aficionado* magazine took a blood test for a new life insurance policy after a week in which he had sampled fifty or sixty cigars, smoking the equivalent of fifteen or twenty full cigars, so he could help rate their quality for a forthcoming issue. The blood test was designed in part to detect nicotine, to see if applicants lied about smoking cigarettes.

The nicotine level in the editor's blood was zero.

In the interest of full disclosure, I should point out that I have written four stories for *Cigar Aficionado* since its inception almost four years ago. Indeed, a few relatively brief passages in this chapter are adapted from two of those stories. But I've never been part of a *Cigar Aficionado* tasting panel, and I've never smoked fifteen cigars in a week. After my epiphany in Switzerland, I smoked one a day, most days, for about nine years, almost always after dinner. Since Lucas was born in 1989, I've found myself more eager to play with him after dinner than to smoke a cigar. Not wanting to blow cigar smoke in his face for an hour a night, I've cut my cigar consumption dramatically. (Clearly, I'm not as obsessive about my cigars as was Marshal Ney, Napoleon's chief of staff, who lit up before giving the order to the firing squad for his own execution.) But when I do smoke a cigar—once or twice a week, often less, seldom more, unless I'm on vacation—I find it truly, utterly relaxing, more so than anything else I do. As H. L. Mencken put it, on the poster hanging in my bathroom, "I smoke cigars when I'm relaxed and happy." Even if there is some mild health risk, I am reasonably certain that for someone like me, with a family history of heart disease and a tendency to rush around trying to do three things at once, that minimal risk is more than offset by the completely stress-free, anxiety-free hour that it takes to smoke a cigar while doing absolutely nothing else. It's a lot better than psychotherapy—and about $100 an hour cheaper. Maybe that's why Freud himself smoked cigars and why, all through history, writers have been especially fond of cigars: it helps them relax when they face that most terrifying and stress-inducing of obstacles—the Blank White Page. Mencken. Kipling. Tennyson. Byron. Twain. Sir Walter Scott. Robert Louis Stevenson. All smoked cigars. A lot of cigars.

Most cigar smokers these days—writers or not—tend to smoke more moderately than did these literary titans. According to a survey by *Cigar Aficionado,* the average is about ten cigars a week. Among cigar smokers of my acquaintance, the number is smaller, perhaps two or three a week, and while there is no doubt that heavy cigar smoking increases the risk of cancer of the lip, mouth, larynx and esophagus, I have yet to see a study that says light cigar smoking poses a significant health hazard.

The science on cigarette smoking is clear. It has been clear for more than thirty years. SMOKING CIGARETTES CAUSES LUNG CANCER. Period. No toady from the $50-billion-a-year tobacco industry is going to convince me otherwise. From the 1960s to the 1980s alone, the death rate for lung cancer among men who smoked almost doubled; among women, it increased 600 percent. Several studies have shown that smoking cigarettes also contributes to breast cancer, colorectal cancer, heart disease, stroke, emphysema, fetal death and impotence. So why do more than 40 million Americans continue to smoke cigarettes? In part because the doughboys of World War I, the romantic heroes of Hollywood and the GIs of World War II smoked them, popularized them and glamorized them. Until 1880, cigarettes were "an almost inconsequential aspect of the tobacco trade, then dominated by chewing tobacco, cigars and pipe tobacco," as Gordon Dillow wrote in *American Heritage* magazine in 1981. Vile rumors inhibited the spread of cigarettes. "Cigarette papers were said to be saturated with opium, arsenic and other poisons," Dillow wrote. "Cigarette tobacco reportedly was gleaned from cigar butts retrieved from urban gutters by derelicts and street urchins. More revolting was the widely circulated report that cigarette-factory workers urinated on the tobacco to give it 'bite.' "

No wonder twenty-six states had banned cigarettes by the 1890s.

Although cigarette smoking did increase in the final years of the nineteenth century and the early years of the twentieth century, it was World War I that suddenly made puffing seem patriotic. Cigarette smoking was so widespread among American soldiers during the Great War that General John J. "Black Jack" Pershing cabled Washington in 1917, "Tobacco is as indispensable as the daily ration. We must have thousands of tons of it without delay." Within a year, the War Department made tobacco an official part of the daily rations for U.S. soldiers. One army surgeon, treating injured American soldiers in France, said, "As soon as the lads take their first 'whiff,' they seem eased and relieved of their agony."

During and immediately after the war, many states—among them, Oklahoma, Wisconsin, South Dakota, Tennessee, Iowa, Arkansas, Nebraska and Idaho—repealed their cigarette prohibition laws. By the time World War II broke out, the movie industry had further legitimized cigarettes. Soldiers—real and make-believe—aided by cinematic cops, cowboys, private eyes and others had made the cigarette "an indelible part of the . . . tough-guy image," as John C. Burnham writes in *Bad Habits*. (John Wayne may ultimately have undermined this image a bit, not only by dying of lung cancer in real life, but also by his pivotal scene in the World War II pop classic *Sands of Iwo Jima*. Having led his troops to victory in a savage battle, Wayne says, "I never felt so good in my life. How about a cigarette?"—whereupon a Japanese sniper shoots him dead.)

I think the glamorization of cigarette smoking is shameful. I think tobacco industry spokesmen are lying through their nicotine-stained teeth when they say they have no advertising campaigns designed to lure children into smoking, to replace the adults who are giving up smoking—or dying. In 1988 the R. J. Reynolds Tobacco Company introduced a cartoon character named Joe Camel in its advertising for Camel cigarettes; I suppose it's a coincidence that while the percentage of adult smokers who chose Camels remained the same over the next five years, the percentage of smokers aged twelve to eighteen who chose Camels increased more than 60 percent, according to a 1995 story in the *Los Angeles Times*. I suppose it's also a coincidence that cigarette brands marketed primarily to women use words like "slim" and "thin" in their advertising and promotion—and that most teenage girls who smoke do so because they've been induced to believe that cigarettes are an effective means of weight control.

After more than a decade of relatively stable smoking rates among young people, a study conducted by the University of Michigan in 1995 showed that since 1991, smoking had increased by one third among eighth-graders and by one fifth among high school seniors. Like the generations of adolescents before them, these teen-agers have taken up smoking in part as a means of exercising their newfound freedom and in part in defiance of parental disapproval. But unlike earlier generations of young smokers, they should know, unequivocally, that smoking is unhealthful. Instead, according to Dr. Lloyd Johnston, director of the Michigan study, an increasing number of young people think smoking is *not* harmful. As the *New York Times* reported, Dr. Johnston identified several possible causes for this attitude, among them the glamorization of cigarette smoking by movies and television programs and the $5 billion the tobacco industry spends annually on advertising, "much of which affects children." A study by the California Department of Health Services, also in 1995, found more tobacco advertisements in stores near schools than in stores farther away. The study also found more tobacco ads near candy counters in stores near schools. Those ads were often displayed at levels lower than three feet—the better to be seen by young eyes.

I think that any cigarette advertising campaign designed to appeal to children should be prohibited. Let's face it: the death and health toll that smoking takes on smokers is heinous and horrifying. We should be educating people about that danger, not tempting America's youth to follow the perilously ignorant path of their elders.

I'm delighted that the number of Americans who smoke cigarettes has dropped from 42 percent in 1955 to about 25 percent today. I wish it would drop to zero. Discouraging children from smoking is the best way to advance toward that goal. Ending government subsidies of tobacco growers would help, too. But I know that many adults truly enjoy smoking cigarettes. They like the way they taste. They like the way they feel in their fingers and between their lips. Reputable scientific studies have also shown that nicotine increases alertness, sharpens short-term memory, enhances the ability to concentrate and stimulates the limbic system of the brain, the system that stimulates neurotransmitter flow and "encourages the individual to reproduce, to eat and to perform all the basic drives," according to Dr. Lorna Role, a neurobiologist at the Columbia University College of Physicians and Surgeons, whose study was published in the journal *Science* in the fall of 1995. "These pathways in the brain encode information that essentially says, 'That was good! Do it again!' "

In other words, nicotine induces the brain to command a repeat of actions—like smoking—that will maintain the nicotine levels necessary to make the brain feel good. That may help explain both the physiological and the psychological nature of nicotine addiction.

Richard Klein, in his 1993 book *Cigarettes Are Sublime,* concedes that cigarettes are "harmful to health" and he says, "The world can only be grateful for the precision and insistence with which doctors remind it of the dangers of smoking poison." But Klein argues that cigarettes have "beauty and benefits" nonetheless. He speaks of the sheer joy, of the serenity and sensuality that can come with smoking a cigarette and of the "mastery [that] cigarettes provide in moments of stress or fear." Like soldiers in wartime, urban police officers often find themselves in need of just that sort of mastery, of that relief from tension and stress. In purely practical terms, they say the smell of cigarette smoke helps screen out the stench of death (which didn't stop the Los Angeles Police Department in 1995 from ordering its officers not to smoke at crime scenes or inside their squad cars. Of course, that's not nearly as bad as what happened to a couple of police cadets just down the coast from Los Angeles, in Huntington Beach, around the same time: three instructors at the Criminal Justice Training Center at Golden West College smelled smoke on the clothing of one cadet; the cadet and a classmate who also admitted smoking were ordered to bring their cigarettes to class, put them between slices of bread and take two bites each. After their cigarette sandwiches, they were ordered to do 250 push-ups and 50 pull-ups. Both cadets vomited. One collapsed and was taken unconscious to the hospital. Both recovered. Their instructors are no longer employed at Golden West College.)

Klein links the right to smoke with other civil liberties—and the suppression of smoking with the reign of tyrants. "It is probably no accident," he says, "that in April 1945 women received the right to vote in France two weeks after they had received cigarette rations for the first time since the war." I think Klein—who teaches French at Cornell University—is stretching a point there, almost as much as he is when he declares cigarettes "a great and beautiful civilizing tool and one of America's proudest contributions to the world." In fact, that's more than stretching a point; exporting billions of our coffin nails to the rest of the world is something we should be ashamed of, not proud of.

But I think Klein is absolutely right to attribute much of the antismoking hysteria in the United States today to a culture "descended from Puritans . . . legislating moral judgments under the guise of public health." Don't get me wrong. I do not for a moment doubt that most people opposed to smoking and secondhand smoke are truly concerned with safeguarding their health and that of their families, friends, neighbors, colleagues and society at large. Nor do I question the sincerity of most of those who say they can't stand the smell of tobacco smoke. I am convinced, however, that there is also something else operating here, especially among a small but growing number of fanatics who take (and propose) the most extreme antismoking measures, including an outright ban on making, selling or advertising cigarettes. As with so many of our other pleasures, it seems to me that they represent the puritanical streak in America that seeks to deprive smokers of their pleasure.

The first antismoking ordinance in this country came in the 1630s, among the Puritans who settled the Massachusetts colony. Antismoking crusades have erupted periodically in the United States ever since, often both prompted and accompanied by extensive moralizing. Orson Fowler, the nineteenth-century eugenicist, charged that tobacco was an aphrodisiac and warned, "Ye who would be pure in your love-instinct, cast this sensualizing fire from you." A pop song warned against "cigareetes and whusky and wild, wild women," and indeed, early-twentieth-century opponents of smoking included members and supporters of the Women's Christian Temperance Union (WCTU), who sought to draw a cause-and-effect relationship between smoking and drunkenness. As a Johns Hopkins doctor wrote in 1913, puritans object to tobacco "because it gives its users contentment, peace and a healthful, animal sort of enjoyment, a sublime callousness to the ethical and theological puzzles which fret and frazzle its enemies, a beautiful and irritating indifference to all but pleasant things of life."

We know now that smoking cigarettes is not "healthful"—to put it mildly—but I think that apart from that egregious misperception, the good doctor had a good point. More recently, John Burnham, whose 1993 book *Bad Habits* is subtitled "Drinking, Smoking, Taking Drugs, Gambling, Sexual Misbehavior, and Swearing in American History," labored diligently, if unsuccessfully, to link all these "bad habits" in a "minor vice-industrial complex" that he sees leading to a degeneration of America's moral fiber.

Early American critics of smoking also blamed tobacco for various health problems, including hemorrhoids and insanity. There may be some logic in those diagnoses: you do have to be crazy—or have your head up your ass—to smoke cigarettes. Smoking cigarettes *is* deadly. But the question, it seems to me, is whether society has the right to stop you from fatally polluting your own lungs. If so, does society also have the right to stop you from fatally clogging your own arteries? Are we going to outlaw butter? Require warning labels on ice cream? Impose high taxes on steak? Sure, smoking and smoking-related illnesses cost society billions of dollars a year. But for the most part, smoking doesn't kill people in the prime, productive years of their lives; it kills them, as Peter Huber pointed out in *Forbes* magazine in 1993, "before they live long enough to burden the social welfare system." Dennis Zimmerman, an economist for the nonpartisan Congressional Research Service, says that smokers cost society the equivalent of seventy-two cents per pack; that's what we pay for smokers' (1) medical bills, beyond what they pay themselves through insurance or other means, (2) excess sick leave, (3) excess fire and life insurance premiums and (4) tax revenues lost because they die prematurely. But because cigarette smokers die early, society saves the equivalent of thirty-nine cents per pack in Social Security and pension fund payments not made and nursing home and Medicare expenses not incurred. That leaves a net monetary cost to society of thirty-three cents per pack—less than the current, average per-pack cigarette tax of fifty-six cents. So, in purely economic terms—ghoulish though it sounds—society comes out ahead because smokers poison themselves; instead of nonsmokers subsidizing the evil habit of smokers, as antismoking activists so often claim, it's the smokers who subsidize nonsmokers.

Yes, you say, but cigarettes are addictive. They sure are. The tobacco industry can lie all they want to about this, but the record is shamefully clear on their control of nicotine levels and their attempts to conceal from the public the addictive (and other unhealthful) qualities of cigarettes. Unlike addiction to hard drugs, however, addiction to nicotine has consequences that are more personal than societal. Among other things, cigarette addiction has not resulted in the kind of violent crime so often associated with addiction to hard drugs. I've never heard of any "nicotine-crazed killers" loose on our streets. Or of anyone robbing a little old lady to get money for cigarettes. If anything, according to smokers, cigarettes relax them and diminish their feelings of stress and aggression. Moreover, cigarettes are legal and easily obtainable, and even with the steadily increasing taxes imposed on them, they also remain relatively cheap. All that would change if the antismoking zealots had their way.

I can see it now: in their determination to protect Americans from the dangers of cigarette smoking, the zealots band together under the umbrella organization Americans Stop Smoking Happily or Lose Everything Suddenly (ASSHOLES). They persuade the government to pass laws that prohibit growing tobacco or making, selling or advertising cigarettes. Supplies plummet. Demand soars. A black market quickly develops to fill the void. Prices skyrocket. As with Prohibition, people start making their own illicit cigarettes—growing small tobacco plants in the backyard or on isolated plots of vacant land not likely to be discovered by authorities. Some of the tobacco is grown—and some of the cigarettes made—under unsanitary conditions. People get sick—and die—from the toxic, bootleg product. Meanwhile, gangs fight for control of the small patches of suddenly coveted tobacco-growing land and for the increasingly valuable crops they produce. Kids—and adults—start stealing cigarettes and hijacking shipments of cigarettes. Latter-day Al Capones use modern terrorist tactics in a battle to control the illicit tobacco trade. Suddenly, Joe Camel looks pretty benign by comparison.

Even under this admittedly unlikely scenario, far fewer people would die than die now from the direct effects of smoking cigarettes. But an outright ban on cigarettes would not be the universally beneficent act that many of its proponents suggest. It would inevitably create some of the same conditions, including erosion of respect for all law, that was occasioned by Prohibition.

What about secondhand smoke, sidestream smoke? Isn't it worth banning cigarettes to save the lives and safeguard the comfort of the tens of millions of nonsmokers who don't want to be subjected to the ill effects of other people's bad habits? I can understand why some people might not wish to be exposed to other people's smoke—cigarette smoke, cigar smoke, pipe smoke, any tobacco smoke. I would absolutely defend their right to a smoke-free environment. So why not use the traditional American art of compromise? In offices, why can't we prohibit smoking in public spaces (hallways, elevators, rest rooms, cafeterias, open work areas) and have designated smoking areas—not cramped, fetid hovels, but reasonably comfortable, well-ventilated rooms in which nonsmokers need never appear? In restaurants, why can't we have smoking sections and nonsmoking sections, clearly separated (by walls or distance), with proper ventilation and with the smoking section limited to no more than 25 percent of the total space (that being the percentage of Americans who smoke)? Wouldn't these steps protect both the rights and health of the nonsmoker and the rights and pleasure of the smoker?

While I think nonsmokers have a right to a smoke-free environment, I do not think that we have to pass laws requiring that no one be allowed to smoke within twenty-five miles of any other living (or recently deceased) human being. But that seems to be the direction in which we are rapidly heading. On weekdays, throughout the country, you can see cigarette smokers huddled together outside office buildings, furtively and frantically puffing their cigarettes, like dope fiends fearful of imminent discovery and arrest. In Davis, California, you can't even smoke within twenty feet of the entrance to a building. Nor can you smoke at bus stops or in public parks (unless you walk while doing so).

I think the "smoking/no-smoking area" compromise would work if we were all reasonable—in part because I think much of the science on secondhand smoke has been greatly exaggerated. "Secondhand smoke"—technically "environmental tobacco smoke"—has joined the pantheon of words and phrases that invoke an automatically negative response, regardless of the facts. The journal *Risk Analysis* reported on a study a few years ago, for example, involving 1,461 epidemiologists, toxicologists, physicians and general scientists who were asked about the dangers of dioxin, radon and environmental tobacco smoke. Each participant was read a vignette designed to reflect the mainstream scientific thinking on each of the three substances. "For half of the participants . . . the substance was named," *Risk Analysis* said. "For the other half . . . the substance was not named but was identified only as Substance X, Y or Z." Of those participants who were told specifically that the substance in question was environmental tobacco smoke, 70 percent said it was a serious health hazard, and 85 percent said "background exposure" to it required public health intervention. Of those for whom secondhand smoke was identified solely as "Substance X," only 33 percent thought it posed a serious health hazard, and only 41 percent thought "background exposure" to it required public health intervention. These disparities were far greater than when the same experiment was performed with dioxin and radon, thus proving the totemic impact of the mere words "environmental tobacco smoke," even among supposedly learned and dispassionate scientists and physicians.

Interestingly, except for coverage of the U.S. surgeon general's landmark 1964 report and, to a lesser degree, follow-up reports in 1967, 1982 and 1986, the dangers of smoking did not receive widespread public or news media attention until recent years, when activists seized on the issue of secondhand smoke. In fact, many medical experts long complained that if the media had covered the hazards of smoking a fraction as thoroughly as they covered many other, lesser hazards, millions more smokers might have quit and tens of thousands of lives might have been saved.

But as Susan Okie of the *Washington Post* documented in 1985, most magazines ignored the smoking story, and some magazines actually censored stories that might have offended the tobacco companies, which accounted for about 9 percent of magazine advertising at the time. Newspapers, which drew only 1 percent of their advertising from tobacco companies, were not substantially better.

It may be significant that, until relatively recently, many journalists smoked; like most other smokers, they scoffed at the risks inherent in their habit. But today's better-educated journalists, like their better-educated readers, are much less likely to smoke. In contrast with previous generations of journalists—many of them hard-living, hard-drinking news hounds whose only exercise was using a dull knife to cut a tough steak—many journalists are now card-carrying members of the jogging, tofu-eating, Perrier-drinking, health club set, and they aggressively object to anyone smoking anywhere around them.

Reputable reporters try hard to prevent their personal feelings from unfairly influencing what they cover. But they're only human, and that's not always possible. As Timothy Noah, an environmental reporter for the *Wall Street Journal,* told me when I wrote about this issue for the *Los Angeles Times* in 1994, "The changing culture of the newsroom has probably affected the way the media cover" the smoking issue.

The growing sensitivity of many in the media to smoking has coincided with the development of secondhand smoke as a "hot" story. *Time* magazine was right in 1994 when it said that "nothing has galvanized today's anti-smoking activities as much as the Environmental Protection Agency report released a year ago that classified environmental tobacco smoke as a Class-A carcinogen."

That EPA report enabled antismoking activists—like AIDS activists before them—to say: "Everyone is at risk." No longer could smokers smugly say, "It's none of your business if I want to poison myself." Now, according to the EPA, everyone was being poisoned. The groundswell of opposition to smoking mushroomed, and the media moved in: Television specials. Front-page newspaper series. Newsmagazine cover stories *(Time:* "Is It All Over for Smokers?"; *U.S. News & World Report:* "Should Cigarettes Be Outlawed?"). The EPA report made smoking a political issue, not just a medical issue, and the media have always been more interested in politics than in medicine; the former almost invariably provides clear conflict and controversy while the latter is usually burdened by uncertain data.

The data in the 1993 EPA report on secondhand smoke, like

most other studies on this subject, seem especially uncertain . . .
and, not surprisingly in the current climate, especially political. As
Sheryl Stolberg of the *Los Angeles Times* noted in a comprehensive
1994 series on secondhand smoke, the campaign against secondhand smoke is "a little bit of science—still emerging, not all of it
conclusive—shaping a lot of public policy." Later, in an interview,
Stolberg told me that while she personally believed "secondhand
smoke is bad for your health," she thought that "if you really examine the overall body of evidence, you'll see that politics really
comes into play and that the medical evidence has been used to, in
essence, sell the notion to the public that secondhand smoke is bad
for you, and it may have led some people to think it's a lot worse for
the general public than it really is."

Clearly, Stolberg said, "the real health risk from tobacco
smoke is smoking." The issue of secondhand smoke is "more com-
plicated than most people believe."

That it is.

The most oft-cited studies on secondhand smoke generally involve the nonsmoking spouses of smokers. It is assumed, probably
correctly, that they are exposed to secondhand smoke in a more
constant and consistent pattern than are other nonsmokers. But it
also seems reasonable to assume that most husbands and wives
come to share certain activities and proclivities—those commonali-
ties often being part of what drew them together in the first place
and what keeps them together over time. In that context, it's worth
noting that most smokers have bad habits other than smoking. They
tend to have poorer nutrition than do most nonsmokers, consuming
more calories, more fat and more junk food. One study, published
in the *Journal of the American Dietetic Association,* said that
women smokers ate less fruits and vegetables and consumed less
iron, fiber and folate, as well as vitamins A and C, than did women
nonsmokers. Smokers of both sexes also tend to drink more alcohol
and more caffeine than do nonsmokers and to exercise less and go
less often to the doctor for routine physical examinations. In general, then, even apart from smoking itself, most smokers tend to lead
far less healthy lives than do nonsmokers. They also tend to be less
well educated: only 13 percent of college graduates smoke, com-

pared with 32 percent of high school dropouts. A cigarette smoker who isn't well educated, doesn't eat a well-balanced diet, doesn't exercise, drinks heavily and only goes to the doctor when he or she is very sick is likely to have a spouse who shares at least some of those unhealthful characteristics, even if said spouse doesn't smoke cigarettes. That would severely distort the findings of any study purporting to show the effects of secondhand smoke on the health and mortality of nonsmoking spouses. People who make careless or risky decisions on health, hygiene and lifestyle are likely to die prematurely, even if they don't smoke cigarettes. But most studies of secondhand smoke do not take that into account.

For this reason, among many others, critics in science, medicine and the Congressional Research Service have accused the EPA of distorting the findings in its 1993 report. They say the EPA ignored contrary studies, used unreliable methodology, failed to consider such "confounding factors" as diet, health care, poverty, heredity, cholesterol, weight, blood pressure, exercise and consumption of alcohol and caffeine and changed its statistical standards midstream to produce the politically desired result.

After a twenty-month study, the Congressional Research Office—an independent research arm of Congress—released a seventy-page report in November 1995 that said "statistical evidence does not appear to support a conclusion that there are substantial health effects of passive smoking."

Others in government also objected to the EPA's methodology.

"I am adamantly opposed to smoking; I completely agree about the magnitude of this health threat for people who smoke," Michael Gough, then senior associate in the congressional Office of Technology Assessment, told me in 1994. "But I think that the EPA played very fast and loose with its own rules in order to come to the conclusion that [secondhand] smoke is a carcinogen."

The EPA says it "absolutely stands by" its report, and it released an eight-page, point-by-point rebuttal of its critics' charges. The EPA and others in the antismoking movement also point out that most independent scientists agree that heavy exposure to secondhand smoke can exacerbate respiratory illnesses in nonsmokers, can cause death and disease in some healthy nonsmokers and can contribute to respiratory ailments in children. But just how much exposure is "heavy" and how great a contributor secondhand smoke is to death and disease—and to which diseases—are questions not incontrovertibly settled, many independent scientists say.

"There is a real problem estimating the quantitative effect of environmental tobacco smoke," says Sir Richard Doll of Oxford University, one of the world's preeminent epidemiologists.

Research on secondhand smoke and heart disease in particular is relatively new and incomplete at this time. Yet antismoking activists say 70 percent of the deaths linked to secondhand smoke—37,000 of the 53,000 annual deaths—come from heart disease. A far smaller number of deaths—3,000—are attributed to lung cancer. But because of the dread power of the word "cancer" and the long-established connection between smoking and lung cancer, it was lung cancer that the EPA emphasized in its report. The first major conclusion, listed at the top of the first page of its 137-page report, said secondhand smoke is "a human lung carcinogen, responsible for approximately 3,000 lung cancer deaths annually in U.S. non-smokers."

That statistic was the lead paragraph in virtually every major media story on the EPA report. And it is that linkage that has propelled the antismoking movement in this country from the fringes to center stage, turning smokers everywhere into pariahs and making virtually everyone else paranoid, convinced that one whiff of someone else's cigarette will turn their lungs into tumorous masses faster than you can say Lucky Strike.

Cigar smokers have become the most vilified pariahs of all—the one minority that it is still socially acceptable to persecute and to discriminate against, even though there have been no major studies on the effects on health of secondhand cigar smoke and even though it is secondhand cigarette smoke that is by far the most prevalent. (There are, after all, about 45 million cigarette smokers in the United States, compared with a mere 9 million cigar smokers, and—as already noted—most cigarette smokers tend to smoke more or less constantly while most cigar smokers do not.)

There is now a federal excise tax on cigars—almost 13 percent of the manufacturer's price. On top of that, forty states now impose their own taxes on cigars. I used to think the 33 percent tax on rental cars in France was confiscatory, but Oregon, Utah and Minnesota have cigar taxes of 35 percent of the wholesale price; in Hawaii and Idaho, it's 40 percent; in Washington, it's a staggering 74.9 percent. Increasingly, some cities and counties also tax cigars; in Alabama alone, forty-seven cities and counties have such taxes, according to the Cigar Association of America.

I suppose cigars could be considered a luxury, and those able to afford them should be willing to pay the government a price for this privilege. I suppose, too, that since some cigar smokers—a small minority really—are rude and inconsiderate, they should have to pay the price of obloquy and ostracism as well. Cigar-smoking boors deserve no sympathy—and no tolerance. They light up without asking anyone's permission, frequently in situations where it is obvious that the ventilation is inadequate. I've even seen men trying to light cigars on airplanes, where the close quarters and captive audience would seem to suggest to any rational human being that nothing stronger than salmon should be smoked. Some prominent cigar smokers demand—and receive—special treatment. When Hillcrest Country Club in Los Angeles posted a sign prohibiting cigar smoking a few years ago, longtime member George Burns, then ninety-five, protested. The next day, a new sign went up: "Cigar Smoking Prohibited for Anyone Under 95." At the Legal Seafood restaurant in Boston, the menu specifies "No pipe or cigar smoking in the dining room except for Red Auerbach," the former, longtime coach of the Boston Celtics.

Many cigar smokers are rich and powerful. Some are also arrogant. They're accustomed to getting their own way. When *Cigar Aficionado* conducted a survey of potential subscribers in 1992, it found that their average household income was $194,000. Average net worth was $1.5 million. More than 60 percent said they wore wristwatches that cost more than $500. Ninety percent had traveled abroad at least once in the previous year. A disproportionately large number were presidents, CEOs and possessors of advanced college degrees. In Hollywood, in particular, the image of the imperious mogul with a cigar in his hand has long been a staple—a stereotype. Such legendary movie giants as Jack Warner, Darryl Zanuck, Harry

Cohn, Sam Arkoff, Carl Laemmle and Ernst Lubitsch all smoked
cigars; even in the health-obsessed nineties, there are producers and
directors carrying on the tradition—smoking cigars and behaving
like despots.

Andrew Bergman, the director of *Honeymoon in Vegas* and
The Freshman, smokes cigars on the set, and he says he has no
problems with cast or crew.

"I'm the boss," he says. "Nobody bitches."

John Milius, the director of *Conan the Barbarian* and *The
Wind and the Lion* and the author of screenplays for *Jeremiah Johnson, The Life and Times of Judge Roy Bean* and *Geronimo,* says
anyone who complains about his cigars on the set can "get another
job."

"On my movies, everyone is told beforehand, 'This will be a
smoking set,' " Milius says.

Milius says he rarely hears complaints about his cigars, even in
his office—except from "the bunch of Disney pukes" who rent some
of the space at the Sony Studios where his office is located.

Ron Shelton, director of *Bull Durham, White Men Can't Jump*
and *Cobb,* says, "There are few ground rules for working with me;
one of them is that I'm going to smoke cigars."

What are the others?

"That's about it." He pauses. "No, there are two rules: if you
complain about my cigars, I'll never work with you again; if you lie
to me about anything, I'll kill you."

Once, Shelton says, he lit up on the set and an actor with a
small part complained. Shelton returned to his trailer and wrote the
actor out of the scene. End of complaint. End of job.

"I'm respectful of others in situations where I feel it's not my
privilege to dictate the environment," Shelton says. "I'll only smoke
in a restaurant where I know it's accepted and enjoyed. But on the
set, well—it's *my* set."

Moguls—movie or otherwise—tend to brandish their cigars as
symbols of their success, "batons of power," in the words of one
cigar merchant I know. Interestingly, cigars were first introduced to
the United States by an altogether different kind of mogul—a military mogul. In 1763 General Israel Putnam brought three cigar-

laden donkeys back from Cuba after fighting against the Spanish on behalf of the British army. Seven years later, the country's first cigar store opened in Lancaster, Pennsylvania. As settlers moved West, cigars were among the commodities shipped on Conestoga wagons—hence the word "stogie." But then, as now, western Europeans smoked far more cigars than did Americans, and it wasn't until the war with Mexico exposed many Americans to Spanish influence that the cigar's association with wealth, luxury and success became part of its image here. By the time of the Civil War, that association was so well rooted that Ulysses S. Grant, a heavy cigar smoker, received huge numbers of cigars from admirers eager to congratulate him on various battlefield victories—eleven thousand cigars after the battle at Fort Donelson, for example, and thirty thousand for winning at Appomattox. In the decade after the Civil War, cigars became "the dominant mode of tobacco use," as John Burnham puts it in *Bad Habits,* precisely because they were part of the conspicuous consumption of that period but also because they were "decisively masculine. . . . The cigarette started out in the nineteenth century as the smoke of fringe and deviant groups. No 'real man' would smoke a cigarette, and no one who could afford a cigar would have taken a cigarette." Cigar smoking increased more or less steadily in the United States from about the late 1860s onward, and by the turn of the century, elegant cigar stores resembled exclusive men's clubs. Many fashionable restaurants had large humidors, with hundreds of private-label cigars for their best customers. Mansions had private cigar rooms to which the gentlemen repaired after dinner. Railroads had cigar cars for the same purpose. Per capita cigar consumption among men reached its all-time peak of 202 cigars per year in the 1920s, as the cigar became another symbol of the success (and excess) of that tumultuous decade.

Smoking a good cigar was (and, in many quarters, remains) a symbolic, unmistakable way of saying to the world, "I've made it." The number of men who make that statement through their cigars, in a rude and supercilious manner, is relatively small, the imperious behavior of certain magnates in Hollywood and elsewhere notwithstanding. But the kind of material success that cigars have long represented to men has been historically (and unfairly) denied to most

women. That may help explain why it is generally women who object most strenuously—and act so pugnaciously—in the presence of
cigar smokers, even those cigar smokers who are polite and considerate. (This is not a new phenomenon. Queen Victoria of England
banned smoking from Windsor Castle; when she died, King Edward
VII lifted the ban, thus prompting an American tobacco company to
name a cigar after him.)

In Rudyard Kipling's early poem "The Betrothed," a woman
about to be married sends her almost-husband a letter in which she
tells him he must choose between her and his cigars. (You may be
able to divine the man's choice by noting one of the final lines of the
poem: "And a woman is only a woman, but a good cigar is a
Smoke.") Although that exchange set the tone for the gender cigar
wars to come, there was a time when women not only enjoyed
smoking cigars themselves, they did so with their doctors' blessings.
"The link between women and the healing power of cigars, it seems,
goes back hundreds of years and may have its earliest roots in pre-
Columbian society," *Cigar Aficionado* said last year. "In fourteenth-
century Aztec culture, for example, tobacco gourds and pouches
were the insignia of women doctors and midwives." In early-
seventeenth-century Paris, doctors often prescribed hand-rolled "cigars" for their women patients, *Cigar Aficionado* said, quoting Paul
de Reneaulme, in *Botanic Compendium,* as writing, "How many
women have I seen almost lifeless from headache or toothache or
catarrh restored to their former health by the use of this plant."

Cigar Aficionado is not, of course, an unbiased or scholarly
source on the curative power of cigars. Moreover, there are many
substances and practices that were once thought healthful that modern science has since proved hazardous. But contemporary accounts
do suggest that almost as many women as men smoked cigars in
eighteenth-century Europe, and through the years a number of famous women have continued to do so—Virginia Woolf, Amy Lowell, Marlene Dietrich and George Sand among them. It was Sand
herself who said, "The cigar numbs sorrow and fills the solitary
hours with a million gracious images." But the hostility of many
women toward cigars today is often so virulent and so unreason-
able—and some women are so eager to make spectacles of them-

selves in order to lodge their anticigar protests as dramatically as possible—that I'm convinced they're not motivated purely by dislike of the smell or by fear of the possible health hazard. Maybe there's something so symbolically, so resolutely masculine about cigars that the very sight of one enrages certain women and incites in them a certain Panatela envy; these women may see the cigar as emblematic of the abhorrently sexist discrimination, exploitation and exclusivity that many men have long practiced and that women have had to fight hard to overcome.

But is that any excuse for the kind of nastiness that so many cigar smokers encounter these days, even if they are not only polite and considerate but equal opportunity employers and vigorous feminists themselves? Remember the old advertising slogan "Should a Gentleman Offer a Tiparillo to a Lady?" Any gentleman who made such an offer today would probably find his Tiparillo stuffed down his trachea. I know that some cigars—cheap cigars—smell bad. Good cigars have a pungent odor, too—pleasantly pungent to some, *un*pleasantly pungent to others. (My own sister once insisted that if I wanted to light up, I would have to go outside . . . in the middle of winter . . . in Denver . . . where the temperature, as I recall, was sixteen degrees.) I think most cigar smokers realize that many people find their smoke offensive; most try to be considerate of those nearby. That doesn't seem to stop some critics—women in particular. Not all women, of course. My sister notwithstanding, I've known many women who enjoy the aroma of a good cigar—two wives and a half dozen friends among them—and I've known several women who actually enjoy smoking a cigar themselves. Although women represent only .1 percent of all cigar smokers, the number is increasing rapidly, especially in big cities. The Davidoff store in New York says women now represent 6 percent of its cigar buyers, double the number two years ago. In 1995, Davidoff sponsored a $95-a-head dinner "dedicated to women of the 90s"; the event was supposed to introduce women to cigars, but to the surprise of virtually everyone in attendance, it turned out that most of the women had been secret cigar smokers for years. In Los Angeles—hotbed of antismoking zealotry, site of hundreds of state-financed billboards calling cigarettes "One Weapon That Kills from Both Ends"—120 women belong to the George Sand Smoker Society. (A similar chapter meets—and smokes—in New York.) But these enlightened ladies are an exception. I've had women scream obscenities at me across two lanes of city traffic when I was smoking in the privacy of my own car, and virtually every cigar smoker I know has been similarly accosted by a woman at one time or another. Indoors or out, in a restaurant or an office, on a street corner or in your own home, cigar smoking is now made to seem somewhere between child molestation and gang rape on the scale of antisocial activities.

Two wrongs—two rudenesses—do not make a right, as everyone's mother probably said at one time or another. But human nature being what it is, it's not surprising that some cigar smokers react in kind. I know one guy who responds to complaints about his cigar by saying, with an air of innocence, "Why? Does the smoking bother your nose job?" Another cigar smoker of my acquaintance, having tolerated—without a murmur of criticism—two hours of crying, screaming, silverware-throwing and food fights among three young kids at an adjacent table in a restaurant, was stunned when the mother of the children demanded that he extinguish his cigar, which he had lit just after she and her battling brood had risen from the table and begun to walk toward the door. He glared right back at her and said, "As long as we're getting rid of nuisances, madam, how about your family?"

I'm not proud of it, but I have to admit that I can't help smiling secretly when I hear stories like that. Or like the one about the prominent attorney, having dinner in a Philadelphia restaurant, who listened to a woman's request that he put out his cigar, then said, "Madam, this cigar cost more than your entire meal." Or the man who had finished dinner in a Chicago restaurant and was so chagrined when a woman told him to "Go smoke that damn thing in the bathroom" that he said, "Go eat your dinner in the bathroom."

Just how bad is it for cigar smokers? How frenzied are the fulminations of the tobacco tyrants? I know of one man who was asked to extinguish his cigar late one night on the deck of a cruise ship, in the middle of the Caribbean, with, as he later put it, "several trillion cubic feet of air to dissipate my offending smoke." A tobacconist in New York told me that several of his customers have had their cigars literally snatched from their lips by irate women who happened to be standing or sitting nearby. A man in Los Angeles told me he'd been slapped in the face, without warning, by a woman who didn't like the smell of his cigar. A restaurateur in Houston told me that one of his best customers—"an elderly gentleman, the sweetest guy in the world"—was smoking a cigar after dinner late one night when a woman walked over from another table, picked up the glass of water on his table and poured it over his head.

Carl Doumani, the proprietor of Stag's Leap Winery in the Napa Valley, recalls a night a few years ago when he lit up a cigar in a restaurant after everyone was through eating, only to have a woman smack him in the head with her purse. Doumani is six foot two and weighs 220 pounds, but she hit him so hard that he toppled off his chair, onto the floor, and his glasses went flying across the room. What most bothered Doumani wasn't the blow, though; it was the woman's perfume. It was so potent that during dinner, it had overpowered everything on his plate and everything on his guests' plates. But he hadn't uttered a word of complaint—until dinner was over and he'd taken out his cigar and *she* had complained to the waiter. That's when Doumani replied, "Will you please tell the lady that when she gets rid of that perfume, I'll put my cigar out." That's when the woman hit him with her purse.

Of course, there are now people who want to outlaw perfume as well as cigars. ABC's *20/20* broadcasted a program on "the perfume wars" in 1995, in which perfume was blamed for migraine headaches, asthma attacks, nausea, dizziness and blocked sinuses. Pickets were shown carrying signs that said, "Perfume poisons the planet." A magazine editor on the program, who was attacked for including "scent strips" in her publication, said, "It seems like people are trying to control aesthetics in a very frightening way." Fashion designer Donna Karan reminded viewers that virtually everything in life has a scent, and she suggested that overly sensitive folks should "walk around with nose clips."

I wouldn't go that far. Some people *are* allergic to perfume—or to cigar and cigarette smoke. Or, as I've noted before, they just don't like the smell of tobacco smoke—not even the residual smell of tobacco smoke in clothing or draperies or carpets, hours or days after any smoker has been on the premises. That's why many hotels now have nonsmoking rooms and why some rental car firms now have nonsmoking cars. But antismoking zealots are behaving irrationally these days, prompted by what Russell Baker, writing in the *New York Times* a couple of years ago, called "the natural urge of the high-minded to rescue the rest of suffering and ignorant humanity from ignorance, squalor, godlessness and evil habits."

"The missionary impulse of people blessed with higher wisdom can be a terrifying force," Baker wrote, "but why has it focused all this fury on tobacco rather than the many other things that are killing us?"

The federal government has taken only the most minimal steps to control firearms, for example, but when the United States Postal Service issued a twenty-nine-cent stamp in 1994 honoring Robert Johnson, the legendary Delta bluesman, they made sure they removed the cigarette from his lips—a cigarette that was his trademark and that was present in the photograph on which their engraving was based. (Why does this remind me of the publishers of history books in Communist China, who used to remove cigarettes from photos of Mao Tse-tung? Why does it remind me of Adolf Hitler, a rabid antismoker before his time, who ordered cigarette smoke removed from a photo of Joseph Stalin shaking hands with Joachim von Ribbentrop, the Nazi foreign minister?)

For years, the Hudson River city of Hyde Park in upstate New York has used as its unofficial symbol the famous silhouette of a grinning President Franklin Delano Roosevelt with a cigarette holder clenched between his teeth. The silhouette has long appeared on city trucks, stationery and road signs as well as in countless commercial applications. Roosevelt is, after all, Hyde Park's most famous native son, and the silhouette of him with the cigarette holder is not only the most recognizable of all Roosevelt images, it also embodies the jaunty, optimistic FDR manner that played a crucial psychological role in leading America out of the Depression and on to victory in World War II. But when a Hyde Park city councilman suggested in 1995 that the FDR silhoutte be made the town's official seal, many opponents of smoking leaped into the fray. Such an official designation, they said, would glamorize and legitimize smoking. Better, they thought, to rewrite history.

Antismoking zealots are everywhere these days, becoming more extreme by the moment. They haven't yet proposed legislation requiring the nose-slittings and public whippings to which smokers in some countries were once subjected, but that could be the next pall on the mall. Some of today's antismoking fanatics remind me of Murad IV, the seventeenth-century Turkish ruler. Having outlawed tobacco, Murad would disguise himself and approach Istanbul merchants who were suspected of selling it anyway; he'd offer them huge cash premiums and a vow of silence in exchange for tobacco. If they succumbed and sold him some, he beheaded them instantly and left their bloody corpses in the street as a warning to other merchants.

We, of course, are more civilized. We resort to courts, not swords. Thus, civil court judges in California, Ohio and Georgia have held that exposing someone to secondhand smoke can constitute "battery." In New York, a couple sued the Rainbow Room for $1 million, claiming that while dining there on their honeymoon, smoke from a nearby table "upset their expected right to conjugal happiness." Meanwhile, in Missouri, David Daut and his wife, Angelique, and their two young children were on their way to a family wedding in Chicago when their minivan broke down at about 3:30 in the morning. Fortunately, the breakdown occurred right in front of both a service station and a hotel. Unfortunately, when Daut asked the clerk at the hotel if he could smoke a cigarette in his room, the clerk said that if he was a smoker, he could not have the room. Daut promised not to smoke and offered to leave all his cigarettes with the clerk. The clerk said he still couldn't have the room. Daut said he'd sleep in his car, despite temperatures in the forties, if his wife and children could sleep in the room. The general manager of the hotel, who had by that time been summoned to mediate the escalating dispute, flatly refused.

It seems to me that a little common sense and mutual courtesy could have easily resolved this dispute—and could resolve most others involving secondhand smoke, whether from cigars or cigarettes (or pipes, for that matter, although I have neither smoked nor re-

searched pipes so I can't really speak intelligently about them or
their detractors). To be fair, I have encountered (and, I hope, displayed) my fair share of both common sense and courtesy in the
great cigar struggle. Given the strong antismoking laws in California
(among many other states), it's now virtually impossible to smoke in
a restaurant unless you go to the bar or have a private room. I host a
wine and cigar lunch for eight good friends—men and women—
every three or four months, and that's what we do. Even so, we
don't light up our cigars until we've finished our multicourse meal,
by which time it's usually well past four o'clock in the afternoon and
all the other customers—and most of the wait staff—have gone
home.

On more routine restaurant visits, I only smoke a cigar if it's
late and no one else is around and the owner has assured me that my
doing so will not subject him to immediate imprisonment under the
Los Angeles and California antismoking ordinances. But even before
the no-smoking ordinances went into effect, I made every effort to
be polite and considerate. I never tried to smoke in small, crowded,
poorly ventilated restaurants or in delis, pizza parlors, hamburger
joints or other places not designed for lingering. I ate dinner on the
late side—8:00 or 8:30 P.M. or later—so that by the time I was
through eating my leisurely dinner and ready to smoke, virtually
everyone else was also through eating (and most were on their way
home). If anyone nearby looked as if he or she might object to my
cigar—and such stern-faced, tight-lipped, beady-eyed folks are de-
pressingly easy to spot—I asked if they minded. If they did, I didn't
light up. If anyone at a nearby table was still eating when I was
through, or if the adjacent table was jammed up against mine,
whether its occupants were still eating or not, I also asked if there
was any objection to my cigar. Again, if there was an objection—or
if I just sensed some ambivalence—I forsook my cigar, without a
whimper of protest (unless the complainant had been smoking cigarettes throughout his and my dinner. I've lost track of the number of
times I've seen or heard about people chain-smoking cigarettes from
the moment they sit down, then angrily objecting to someone at
another table smoking a cigar after everyone is through eating. That
seems to me the height of audacity—and hypocrisy).

Among the many reasons I look forward to my annual gastronomic pilgrimage to France is the realization that I will be able to leisurely smoke a cigar after dinner every night without having to worry about these problems. No one in France, or anywhere else in Europe, has ever raised the slightest objection to my cigar. I suspect that many people there still believe that, as one Frenchman told me, "If Churchill had put out his cigar, we'd all be speaking German today." In France in particular, a cigar is regarded as an integral part of dinner, like a fork or a glass of wine. The French speak of the postprandial "three Cs"—coffee, cognac and cigars—and at most of the better restaurants, waiters bring cigar humidors to the table after coffee is served. But in this country, despite a rich cigar-smoking tradition—Thomas Edison, Mark Twain, Orson Welles, John Kennedy and at least a half dozen other presidents were stogie aficionados—most of my cigar-smoking friends say they now encounter so much hostility that they've given up trying to smoke in restaurants. (Hell, President Clinton likes cigars, but he can't even smoke them at home; smoking is no longer permitted in the White House. When United States marines completed a daring rescue of downed pilot Scott O'Grady in Bosnia in 1995, President Clinton had to sneak out of the White House proper, onto the Truman Balcony, to smoke a celebratory cigar with Tony Lake, his national security adviser. Don't blame this all on Hillary, though, just because she banned smoking from the White House in 1993. Barbara Bush was so opposed to cigars that when her son and her husband's press secretary spotted her approaching as they puffed away during the 1992 Republican national convention, they immediately jammed their lit cigars into their pockets and left them there, smoldering, until she was out of both sight and sniffing range.)

Fortunately, until relatively recently, I personally encountered only occasional objections to my cigars in restaurants. Until they were emboldened by the current hysteria over secondhand smoke, those people who did object did so politely most of the time. When a group of women sweetly asked a friend and me not to smoke after lunch in an Italian restaurant several years ago, we took our cigars into the bar, for which they graciously thanked us; on their way out, they thanked us again. On another occasion, a man responded to

my "Will this bother you?" cigar question by saying, "We'd appreciate it if you'd wait until we finish our dessert." Ten minutes later,
still wiping the last crumbs of chocolate cake from his lips, the man
leaned over and said, "We're through now. Thank you for asking—
and for waiting. You can smoke now."

If everyone behaved as these folks did, we could all coexist,
smokers and nonsmokers, in a climate of civility *and* good health,
both mental and physical. But many people who think cigar smoking is a barbaric practice act like barbarians themselves, glaring malevolently and snarling at every cigar smoker as if he were Havana
the Hun.

In an effort to circumvent this hostility—and in response to the
veritable blizzard of antismoking regulations that have been passed
in recent years—more than two hundred restaurants and hotels
throughout the country have begun hosting and publicizing cigar-
only nights. On a given night, usually weekly or monthly, they have
special, multicourse dinners with fine wines and fine cigars, where
everyone knows beforehand that cigars are the raison d'être of the
evening and that no complaints will be tolerated. In 1995, there
were almost two thousand such events in more than thirty-five states
nationwide. Some events draw participants from that many states in
a single night. Virtually all sell out instantly. Cigar smokers respond
eagerly to invitations that include the assurance that, for one night
anyway, they will be able to smoke without any of the angry stares
and pseudo coughs they usually encounter.

Henry Schielein, then general manager of the Ritz-Carlton hotel in Laguna Niguel, on the Pacific Coast about two hours south of
Los Angeles, probably deserves much of the credit for the renaissance of the cigar dinner. Schielein, whose proposal of marriage
twenty-nine years ago was contingent on his fiancée agreeing to accept his cigars "for the rest of our lives," was annoyed one night in
1983 when he noticed that people were scowling at him as he lit up
a cigar in the dining room at the Ritz-Carlton in Boston. Schielein
had just taken over as general manager of the hotel, and he made
two quick decisions that night: he'd sponsor a dinner for cigar
smokers once a year and he'd turn the ladies' tearoom into a cigar
smokers' lounge every night.

When Schielein moved to Laguna Niguel in 1989, he started having annual cigar dinners there, too. Ritz-Carltons in various other cities—Philadelphia, San Francisco, Marina del Rey (Los Angeles) and Washington, D.C. among them—have since followed suit. In general, all adhere to the Schielein formula of black tie, multicourse, multiwine dinners followed by cigars, cognac, Armagnac and vintage port. Cigar retailers and distributors often provide a large selection of complimentary cigars for these events, and there are few sights more amusing than watching a hundred tuxedo-clad men, most of them quite wealthy, scrambling like so many hyperkinetic penguins to stuff their pockets with as many free cigars as they can grab.

In 1995 the Chicago-based Arnie Morton's steak house chain sponsored a series of cigar dinners at its twenty-three restaurants nationwide. Other restaurants and other hotels have hosted their own cigar extravaganzas. Some have a dozen guests; some have several hundred. Some are formal; some are casual. Some serve a set menu; some let diners choose from the regular menu. Some provide complimentary cigars, courtesy of local tobacconists or national distributors; others expect guests to provide their own cigars. Some attendees smoke throughout the meal—on occasion a different cigar for every course; others just smoke when dinner is through. Prices for the events range from $40 to $250 per person. All have one thing in common: cigar smokers clinging together with an odd blend of relief, desperation and joy.

The sudden proliferation of special cigar dinners is evidence that cigars—especially premium cigars, those priced at one dollar or more—are making a comeback, despite the present paranoia about smoke. Total cigar sales in this country actually reached a peak, slightly more than 9 billion, in 1964, when they increased a whopping 25 percent over the previous year. The big jump was spurred by the surgeon general's report on smoking, which targeted cigarettes specifically and which thus sent many cigarette smokers scurrying to their local cigar stores for a replacement fix. But cigar sales decreased virtually every year thereafter, by about 5 percent a year. By 1972, sales had dropped back below pre-1964 levels, and in 1993 total cigar sales were down to slightly more than 2 billion, a 78 percent drop from 1964; per capita cigar consumption among men was down to about twenty-six a year, a drop of 87 percent since the Roaring Twenties. Cigar sales finally turned around again in 1994, increasing about 7 percent. Imports of premium cigars, which account for only about 6 percent of total cigar sales but about 27 percent of total cigar dollars, have increased even more dramatically, up 27 percent from 1992 to 1994 and up another 30 percent from 1994 to 1995. The demand for premium cigars has been so great that for the past three years the industry hasn't been able to keep up with the consumers' orders; in mid-1995 back orders totaled almost 25 million cigars—and these numbers don't include Cuban cigars, which are illegal but which many serious cigar aficionados smuggle into this country anyway. (Anyone returning directly to the United States from Cuba is permitted to bring in up to one hundred cigars. But visas for legal travel to Cuba are usually issued only to journalists and academics, so relatively few Cuban cigars come in legally. Men who can afford high-priced Havanas tend to travel, though—or to have friends or business associates who travel—and bringing Havanas in from Canada, Mexico, the Caribbean and western Europe, past this country's notoriously lax customs agents, is generally no more difficult or risky than bringing in an ugly necktie. An estimated 6 million Cuban cigars find their way into this country annually. A few Cohibas—my favorite Cuban cigar now that Davidoff no longer makes cigars there—even find their way into my humidor on occasion.)

Thus, while social opprobrium and antismoking ordinances make it impossible for most people to smoke as many cigars as they might like—offices, restaurants and most other public spaces now being out of bounds—when people do smoke, they generally smoke better cigars. Many carriage-trade wine stores have begun selling premium cigars, too, and many tobacconists who specialize in such cigars have begun providing their own "cigar lounges" or private "cigar clubs" to attract customers and give them a place to enjoy their costly purchases. (Although the average cigar costs only twenty-two cents, today's upscale smoker generally spends an average of three to five dollars apiece, and cigars costing six to ten dollars are common; a few cost as much as twenty-five dollars each.)

Antismoking fever runs particularly high in Los Angeles, especially among the tofumongers on the yuppie Westside, but in spite of this—or, more likely, *because* of it—there are now more than a dozen cigar lounges and clubs in that area alone, half of them in Beverly Hills. One is combined with a wine bar owned by George Hamilton, the actor; another, the Grand Havana Room, has an unlisted telephone number and what is alleged to be the world's largest humidor. Nazareth Guluzian, proprietor of the Beverly Hills cigar store that bears *his* name, originally had just a couple of armchairs in his store for customers, then found the demand for sitting and smoking so great that he put in sofas, added cognac and an espresso machine and turned the shop into a private cigar club; he leased another, smaller store a few yards away to accommodate the actual retail business. Three blocks away, on Via Rodeo, the *faux* avenue that looks like what Hollywood thinks Avenue Victor Hugo in Paris should look like, the Davidoff cigar store has a similar smoking club (they call it a keep). There, for a mere $2,500 a year ($2,000 of which is redeemable in Davidoff merchandise), smokers can relax and indulge themselves without fear that someone will break into a splenetic rage at the mere sight of a stogie. (In New York, a few restaurants are making similar, if less luxe, accommodations for cigarette smokers in the wake of 1995's draconian antismoking regulations. Jimmy Duke cut the seating capacity of his restaurant Drake's Drum in half to bring it below the thirty-five-seat limit at which the smoking ordinance applies. His "smokeeasy" has been renamed "Drake's Drum—The Smoke Inn.")

Cigar smoking actually began to make a tentative comeback in the United States in the mid-1980s, in part because of the doubling of federal excise taxes on cigarettes, which triggered a replay of the reaction that cigarette smokers had had to the 1964 surgeon general's report. But this time money, not health, was the impetus for change. Also, the economy was booming in the 1980s, and boom times always boost cigar sales. But the biggest reason for the boost was another kind of boom, the coming of age of the baby boomers: the largest group of men in history had reached the age of thirty-five, and that seems to be "the magical age when men traditionally start to smoke cigars," as *Time* magazine observed in 1984. Without question, however, the single biggest reason for the surge in the consumption of premium cigars—and for the veritable explosion in cigar dinners and private cigar clubs—is *Cigar Aficionado,* which published its first issue in September 1992. Cigar smokers and cigar retailers and wholesalers, both here and abroad, say that by tapping into a wellspring of resentment among the nation's cigar smokers, *Cigar Aficionado* has legitimized the pleasure for countless thousands of closet smokers, would-be smokers and simple curiosity-seekers.

Founded by Marvin Shanken, who also publishes the *Wine Spectator* magazine, *Cigar Aficionado* is a thick, slick, advertising-fat, quarterly journal that serves as both forum and clearinghouse for cigar information, entertainment, evaluations and anecdotes. Because it began publishing amid the antismoking frenzy of the 1990s—and during a recession—*Cigar Aficionado* was initially dismissed as a pipe dream (so to speak), an unrealistic ego trip for Shanken. But it immediately became a stunning success, reaching a circulation of almost two hundred thousand, spinning off a monthly cigar newsletter and attracting more than two million dollars in advertising in a single, bulging (404-page) issue in December 1995. The magazine's letters-to-the-editor "column" runs at least five pages every issue, and it's filled with (a) tales of smokers grievously wronged and (b) paeans of praise for Shanken, who unabashedly basks in tributes that would embarrass even Donald Trump and Rush Limbaugh. But with these letters and with its stories about famous, successful men who smoke cigars and its 100-point rating system for cigars and its articles and photographs on cigar accoutrements and cigar-friendly environments, *Cigar Aficionado* has provided a rallying point for the upscale downtrodden. Suddenly, cigar smokers across the land are breaking free of their shackles and greeting each other with the equivalent of fraternal handshakes and proclamations that they are "Free at last, free at last, thank Marv almighty, free at last."

5

G O D
A N D   M A N —
A N D
W O M A N

Scientists trace sexual activity among animals back more than a billion and a half years. Of course, what *they* mean by "sex"—the fusing of cells by organisms known as protists—involved none of the passionate pawing, snorting, moaning and groaning that we have come to associate with sex in more developed mammals, human and otherwise. Lynn Margulis, a biologist at the University of Massachusetts, Amherst, has suggested that during times of starvation, protists ate each other, and that if one did not entirely digest another, the nuclei of the two fused. Since this ensured survival, Margulis theorizes that this process of "sexual" union was passed on to future generations through evolution. As J. Madeleine Nash wrote in *Time* magazine in 1992, "From this vantage point, human sexuality seems little more than a wondrous accident, born of a kind of original sin among protozoa. Most population biologists, however, believe sex was maintained over evolutionary time because it somehow enhanced survival.

"The mixing and matching of parental genes, they argue, provide organisms with a novel mechanism for generating genetically different offspring, thereby increasing the odds that their progeny could exploit new niches in a changing environment and, by virtue of their diversity, have a better chance of surviving the assaults of bacteria and other tiny germs that rapidly evolve tricks for eluding their hosts' defenses."

When I was at Pepperdine, I had a professor—Professor Thompson—who taught both philosophy and the history of Western civilization. His favorite topic in both classes was evolution, and he often ended his lectures by telling the class, "Evolutionists can trace life back only as far as a stagnant pond . . . but they don't tell you Who created that stagnant pond." Then he would slowly raise his right arm, index finger extended, until it was pointed straight up, to the heavens, while he gradually tilted his head back so that his eyes were also directed heavenward. His movements were so exaggerated that on several occasions, I was sure he was going to topple over backward, and I always thought he took it as a personal affront that God never took visible note of this performance in His name, if only with a thunderclap or a lightning bolt to serve as an exclamation point to the lecture.

Given my experience with Professor Thompson, among others, at Pepperdine, I suspect it's no coincidence that the people who are the most outspoken about sex-as-sin are also those who most haughtily reject the theory of evolution. To them, evolution is blasphemy—and sex is Divine. Or at least it should be. Indeed, they want to have it both ways: yes, sex—like everything else—was created by God, but, no, you shouldn't engage in it for fear of offending God.

Huh?

I've often thought that the people who are the most aggressive in their depiction of human sexuality as basically immoral are trying to deny both pleasure and reality. They don't want others to have pleasure because they think pleasure is intrinsically wrong. Hemingway once said, "Moral is what you feel good after"; our bluenosed brethren think that anything you feel good after must, by definition, be *im*moral. In their view, man wasn't put on earth to have a good time but to do good works, and the two are mutually exclusive. Since sex is the most fun—the most intense pleasure—one can have, it is also the pleasure most often and most roundly condemned and proscribed. Moreover, the most altruistic members of our society would argue that as long as one person is suffering, anywhere in the world, it's wrong for anyone else to be happy. I do not doubt either the sincerity or the generosity of spirit that motivates many who hold such noble thoughts. But I do believe that they are, at times, misguided. I doubt that even Mother Teresa would suggest that I could somehow alleviate the pain and suffering of the starving untouchables of Calcutta by choosing not to get laid tonight. Besides, I think that many of those who seek to suppress sexuality in our society are prompted more by their own suffering than by the suffering of others. Misery does indeed love company; people who aren't having any fun don't want anyone else to have any fun either, sexual or otherwise.

When I read all those stories in late 1994 about the exhaustive study *Sex in America,* based on surveys by the National Opinion Research Center at the University of Chicago, I couldn't help wondering if the media's huge, collective sigh of relief about how sexually "normal" (i.e., dull) most of us are was somehow a reflection of this neurotic desire to keep others from having too much fun. Was media coverage of the study simply an expression of how most journalists feel about their own sex lives? Or was it a projection of how journalists think their readers and viewers feel about *their* sex lives? Probably both. Regardless, journalists who reported on the study were positively giddy in their desire to assure Americans that no matter how lackluster or infrequent their own sexual activity, everyone else's sex life was just as bad. Or worse.

Time magazine got right to the point: "Is there a living, breathing adult who hasn't at times felt the nagging suspicion that in bedrooms across the country, on kitchen tables, in limos and other venues too scintillating to mention, other folks are having more sex, livelier sex, better sex? Maybe even that quiet couple next door is having more fun in bed."

Not to worry, *Time* said. The overall impression of the study was that "the sex lives of most Americans are about as exciting as a peanut-butter-and-jelly sandwich." The *Los Angeles Times* said the study showed the average American's sex life to be about as exciting as "a bowl of warm oatmeal." (See? What did I tell you about the intriguing nexus among the palate, the penis and the pudenda in our language?)

Although much of this survey rings true—especially in an era of AIDS-inspired caution—I'm not certain that it's the Rolls-Royce of reliability in every area. After all, I saw a study nine months later that said some people make love so vigorously that their blood pressure skyrockets, bursting tiny blood vessels and tearing tissues in the eye, causing blurred vision, even blindness, that can last for months. I was tempted to call my broker and ask him to get me heavily into ophthalmology stocks immediately except that (1) I'm sure these people are rare exceptions and (2) I don't have a stockbroker. Still, I'm a bit wary of some of the University of Chicago findings. If that study is correct that most married couples don't have sex very frequently, don't have oral sex, don't cheat and yet are quite satisfied with their sex lives, why is the divorce rate almost 50 percent? The implication is that maybe sex is not really so important—which is exactly what those who aren't getting much (and who don't want anyone else to get much) would like us all to think. Another explanation for the survey findings may be that the people answering the survey didn't necessarily tell the truth on certain questions, in part because most folks are not terribly comfortable talking about their sex lives and in part because the survey-takers asked their questions in person, often with the respondent's spouse present. (If a stranger—a "middle-aged woman," as the authors of the study described their surveyors—came into your home, plopped down on your leather sofa and asked, "Have you been faithful for the past year?" how likely would you be to smile at your mate and answer, "No. Just last Tuesday, when Cathy was helping our children with their homework, I stayed late at the office and boffed my secretary"?)

The average person, the University of Chicago study said, has sex six times a month—less than twice a week. Thirty percent have sex only a few times a year—or not at all. More than 80 percent had only one sexual partner or no partner at all in the past year. Married couples and people living together had the most sex. Most married people are faithful.

I agree that marital fidelity is a good thing. Marital vows should be taken seriously. People who cheat on their spouses are behaving dishonestly—and foolishly; they risk disease, out-of-wedlock childbirth, the pain of damaging or destroying their marriages and hurting their spouses, children and lovers. I recognize the societal and public policy implications in broken homes and abandoned children, but still, isn't this largely a private matter, between husband and wife? Unless your neighbor or officemate—or anyone else, for that matter—is having an affair with *your* spouse, why should you care if anyone else is unfaithful? And yet, Americans have always been imperiously judgmental about such behavior. Is that our latent Puritanism rearing its meddlesome head once again? Or is it envy? (I believe it was H. L. Mencken who defined puritanism as "the haunting fear that someone, somewhere, may be happy.")

Nowhere does the matter of other people's infidelities figure more prominently (or more pruriently) than in our national breast-beating the past few years about the sex lives of our presidential candidates.

Franklin Delano Roosevelt had a mistress. John F. Kennedy apparently had several. Lyndon Johnson's pursuit of various women was "no secret in the White House press corps," says Larry Sabato in *Feeding Frenzy*. But none of these sexcapades was reported in the media at the time. Starting with Gary Hart and continuing—with a vengeance—in Bill Clinton's 1992 campaign, all that changed. Suddenly, what a presidential candidate did in the bedroom was Important News.

Why?

The sexual revolution that began in the 1960s made public discussion of sex commonplace by the 1980s. At the same time, belated disclosures about President Kennedy's dalliances embarrassed many in the press corps who knew about them—or should have known about them—but didn't share that knowledge with their readers; reporters covering Hart, Clinton and other presidential candidates were determined not to be similarly embarrassed. The heightened skepticism and censoriousness of this post-Vietnam, post-Watergate press corps has also contributed to the scrutiny of candidates' sex lives, as has the assignment, after generations of discrimination and neglect, of a significant number of women to the political press corps. The very presence of women reporters—and the feminist manifesto, "the personal *is* the political"—have helped to shatter the good old boys' conspiracy of silence and to broaden the definition of "news" itself.

To repeat, I am not contending that infidelity is either good or harmless. It is neither. It is reprehensible. Nor do I agree with Camille Paglia, the feminist other feminists love to hate, when she says, "I'm for a high libido president! I applaud him if he goes out and picks up women." I don't applaud any married man who goes out and picks up women (or any married woman who goes out and picks up men, for that matter). Given the ineluctable implication of the "pick up" construct—seeking out someone solely for one's own sexual pleasure—I don't applaud single people who do it either (unless the desire for a purely sexual relationship is mutual). But withholding applause—approval—is one thing; casting stones—and ballots—based exclusively on a candidate's sexual proclivities is quite another. One's sex life—marital, premarital, extramarital, nonmarital—is, it seems to me, a private, not a public, matter. I don't think a candidate's sex life is anyone's business other than the candidate's, his or her spouse's, the lover's and the children, if any, of those involved. Surveys have repeatedly shown that the American public agrees. The self-appointed morals squad in the American media and in society at large has decided, however, that marital infidelity is a test of presidential "character." I know all the arguments advanced to justify this position: If the candidate lies to (and cheats on) his wife, might he not lie to (and cheat on) the voting, taxpaying public? If he shows bad judgment in his personal life, might he be guilty of bad judgment in his political life? If he's addicted to risky behavior in the bedroom, might he be given to risky behavior in the Oval Office? If he neglects or mistreats his wife, might he neglect or mistreat all women, in everything from executive appointments to legislative goals?

Depending on the individual candidate, the answer to all those questions may well be yes. But I have a better, one-word answer: Nixon. I don't recall ever hearing any stories about Richard Nixon cheating on his wife. But he may have been the most immoral man ever to inhabit the White House.

If a politician has any of the flaws that the bedroom snoops insist are revealed by infidelity, I think those flaws will manifest themselves somewhere outside the bedroom as well; a politician's shortcomings should be apparent in his public policies and personnel choices—as, God knows, they were with Nixon. (Would you rather have a president responsible for the Peace Corps and the peaceful settlement of the Cuban missile crisis or one responsible for Watergate and the bombing of Cambodia?) If a candidate's only serious shortcoming is that he can't keep his fly zipped, that shouldn't automatically disqualify him from higher office—especially not these days, when most candidates for president tend to be moral and/or intellectual pygmies, and we need any decent candidate we can persuade to enter the lists. Gary Hart may have been a philanderer, but it's worth noting that *Ms.* magazine gave him a 95 percent approval rating for his votes in the Senate on issues affecting women.

By and large, however, we know only what the media tell us about our candidates, and competition from tabloid television, the supermarket tabloids, CNN and a host of television "magazine" shows have put a premium on speed and titillation, even in the most reputable news organizations. I don't mean to suggest that the news media ignored the sex lives of political figures until the moment in 1987 when Gary Hart and Donna Rice did (or did not) perform their notorious nocturnal version of Miami vice. It was, after all, almost a century earlier, in 1896, that two prominent legal scholars—Louis Brandeis, later a Supreme Court justice, and Samuel Warren—wrote that to "satisfy a prurient taste the details of sexual relations are spread . . . in the columns of the daily papers."

Mitchell Stephens, in his book *A History of News,* says the first newspaper printed in the United States, in 1690, "discussed a report that the king of France 'used to lie with his "Son's Wife." ' " Newspapers of the 1830s contained similar material, often not so delicately phrased, and newspapers in the mid-1870s were filled with lustily detailed accounts of various sex scandals of the day. The

New York Sun branded Grover Cleveland, the president-to-be, "a coarse debauchee who might bring his harlots to Washington . . . a man leprous with immorality." Milton Rugoff, in his book *America's Gilded Age,* says many newspapers in the late nineteenth century "paraded intimate details of private life with as much zest as any paper of our day; they seized even more hungrily on sexual scandals. . . ."

One explanation for the earlier sexual excesses in the American press is that most of the press then just wasn't very professional—or very responsible. Most newspapers in the United States were little more than attack dogs for their political patrons. As such, they cared more about embarrassing their political opponents than about good taste, Puritan traditions *or* journalistic principles.

In recent decades, as politically motivated newspaper editors and publishers have increasingly given way to responsible, professional journalists, many have "got religion" and now insist on applying their standards of honesty and integrity in government not only to issues of corruption, payoffs and conflict of interest but to the private lives of public figures as well. Although some editors have asked if it's fair to discuss the private behavior of public officials unless that behavior affects their public performance, most editors have been forced to worry more about competition than about conscience in this era of media conglomerates and public stockholders. It's fine to be responsible and high-minded, but what if that stance costs your newspaper both prestige and readers when editors at rival papers are not similarly inclined?

The journalistic contretemps about the sex lives of political candidates here baffles journalists—and readers—in Europe, Asia and many other areas of the world. Many western European leaders are known to have mistresses, but no one seems to care. Historically, Asians have also tended to ignore the sexual peccadilloes of their politicians, in part because women have traditionally been relegated to a lower position in the social order. But there's a religious explanation as well: some Eastern religions don't have the same kinds of sexual strictures found in Christianity. Several years ago, in the aftermath of disclosures that Japanese Prime Minister Sosuke Uno had had an affair with a geisha four years earlier, Uno's ruling

Liberal Democratic Party suffered a humiliating defeat at the polls; Uno himself resigned. Although other factors were involved, a key issue was that Uno had paid the geisha, Mitsuko Nakanishi, "only" $21,000 during their five-month affair; when the relationship ended, Uno did not provide consolation money in "adequate" sums. To the Japanese public, it was not so much a matter of Uno having behaved immorally by cheating on his wife sexually as it was a matter of his having behaved unfairly by not compensating his mistress economically.

In the United States, in large measure because of our Puritan/ Christian heritage and our journalists' perspective, Uno would have been pilloried as an unprincipled philanderer, regardless of how much he paid his mistress (and if he had paid her a considerable sum of money, he would have been pilloried further). Although the sexually liberated 1960s were the formative years for many of today's most influential American journalists, a growing number of these journalists find their belief in individual sexual freedom at odds with their resentment of the moral bankruptcy they see in many people in power. The latter attitude is increasingly resonant with a general public that seems more and more disenchanted with all authority figures and institutions. I don't want to overstate my point, but I do think that many people resent the power and glamour a presidential candidate enjoys and they just don't want him to have all that (illicit) fun, too. It's bad enough the lying scumbag will break all his campaign promises and get rich off unethical, if not illegal, political payoffs; we don't want him romping naked through the Elysian fields with some leggy, bosomy blonde as well.

The denial of reality by bluenoses and other members of their ilk lodge is every bit as strong as their denial of pleasure. They seem to think that hormones and testosterone are simply biological commodities, not real life forces. After survival, water and food, sex is the most basic—and the strongest—human instinct. Given the high suicide rate and the growing number of anorexics among us, it might be argued that only our need for water is stronger than our sex drive. The pleasure police seem to deny the very existence of the sex drive, except as some malicious, malevolent force fiendishly implanted in the human psyche by The Devil. They would even like to believe that teenagers don't—or shouldn't—masturbate. Look at the firestorm they kicked up in 1994 when Dr. Joycelyn Elders, then the surgeon general of the United States, dared to mention that "perhaps" information on masturbation should be included in schools' sex education curriculum. Never mind that studies have shown that 90 percent of teenage boys and 65 percent to 70 percent of teenage girls masturbate; the Bible says that Onan was "evil in the sight of Jehovah" because he spilled his seed on the ground, so that makes masturbation, ipso facto, a sin. (Personally, I always thought it just made Onan a particularly maladroit member of the Jerusalem 4-H Club, but in consulting biblical scholars while researching this book, I found that even here, masturbation has gotten a bum rap. God didn't kill Onan because he had masturbated, but because he had withdrawn prematurely during intercourse with Tamar, his late brother's wife, thus disobeying God, who had ordered him to impregnate her, in keeping with Jewish tradition.)

During the Elders controversy, Gina Kolata wrote in the *New York Times* about a Swiss doctor, Simon André Tissot, whose mid-eighteenth-century pamphlet *Onanism, or a Treatise on the Disorders of Masturbation* ignited the Western world's antimasturbation fixation. As Kolata recounted, the enormous success of that work—it was translated into several languages and frequently reprinted—triggered a groundswell of moralizing and misinformation. Dr. Tissot argued that masturbation drained the body of vital fluids and caused various neuroses as well as tuberculosis. Americans—never comfortable with sex anyway—later seized on this thesis and expanded it to include warnings that masturbation caused epilepsy, blindness, amnesia, acne, bed-wetting, nail-biting and shyness, among several dozen other physical and social maladies. J. H. Kellogg—our old friend, the therapeutic enema maven from Battle Creek, Michigan—wrote a best-selling book in 1888 that said parents could prevent their children from masturbating if they tied their hands or bandaged their genitals. As a further deterrent, Kellogg recommended having boys circumcised without anesthetic—and pouring carbolic acid on a girl's clitoris. Another nineteenth-century entrepreneur, Sylvester Graham, the inventor of the graham cracker, insisted in his 1834 book *A Lecture to Young Men on Chastity,* that any teenage boy who masturbated would become "a confirmed and degraded idiot . . . a blighted body—and a ruined soul." Graham proposed a preventive regimen that included—surprise—regular consumption of the product he invented. Other antimasturbation crusaders in the nineteenth century developed genital alarms that rang anytime the wearer had an erection. (This was, I suppose, history's first alarm cock.)

Given this enlightened tradition, one shouldn't have been shocked when some people got so upset by Dr. Elders's seemingly innocuous comment on masturbation that she was forced to resign, almost immediately. But what did she say, exactly? Well, after her speech to a World AIDS Day conference at the United Nations, Dr. Rob Clark, a member of the Society for the Psychological Study of Social Issues, rose from the audience to ask her a question. Noting that "the campaign against AIDS has already destroyed many taboos about discussion of sex in public," Dr. Clark asked what Dr. Elders thought of the prospects for "a more explicit discussion" of masturbation.

Dr. Elders responded by restating her strong advocacy of a "comprehensive . . . age-appropriate" health education program in the schools; she then offered the perfectly reasonable observation that "In regard to masturbation, I think that that is something that's a part of human sexuality and it is a part of something that perhaps should be taught."

Dr. Elders did not suggest that children be taught *how* to masturbate or that they be urged *to* masturbate. (As if anyone has to be told either. Like most baby boys, my son, Lucas, found his penis—his *paloma*, as he came to call it—before he found his voice; he realized instantly that touching it felt good. When his hormones kick in, I don't think he'll need a road map to find it again—or a teacher to tell him what to do or how to do it.) All Dr. Elders said, in essence, was that teenagers should be told how masturbation fits into overall human sexuality, presumably (although she didn't say this) without guilt and with the assurance that masturbation will not make them go blind, go insane or grow warts on their hands. In theory, conservatives and other members of the Christian Right should favor the mention of masturbation in a class on sex education. Masturbation avoids the alleged "sin" of fornication as well as the risk of disease, pregnancy and premature emotional entanglements. Masturbation is also, however, pleasurable, and that's what really outraged Dr. Elders's critics. The idea that children would hear in school anything other than a condemnation of any form of sexual pleasure enraged those who cling tenaciously to the belief that sex is dirty, evil—only (and barely) tolerable as a biological necessity. They grew terrified that if information on masturbation were included in the school curriculum, kids might spend too much time doing their homework.

The religious Right was also in the forefront of the battle against a health handbook that publisher Holt, Rinehart and Winston tried to sell to high schools in Texas a couple of years ago. By the time the various lobbying groups were through, the Texas Board of Education demanded so many revisions that Holt withdrew its book from the Texas market. Critics of the proposed text wanted the deletion of a number of clinical illustrations, including one showing a self-examination for testicular cancer; they also insisted on the deletion of telephone numbers for teenage suicide prevention groups and for gay and lesbian groups. Holt decided that making all the requested changes, exclusively for the Texas market, would not be economically feasible. Moreover, William Talkington, the president of Holt, said in a letter to the Texas commissioner of education, "Some of the mandated revisions are in opposition to the fundamental philosophy of our program and are potentially injurious to the students of Texas." Holt would refuse to publish a high school textbook that "does not provide children with adequate instruction on life-threatening issues," Talkington said.

People who are very religious are not the only ones who want to tell us what should and should not be done in our own bedrooms and in our children's classrooms. But through the ages, they have generally been the most persistent, the most organized and the most self-righteous. For Fundamentalist Christians and other true-believing biblical literalists, the theory of the Immaculate Conception is crucial proof of the rectitude of their position; if the event they regard as the most important in the history of the world—the birth of Christ—took place without benefit of sex, then surely sex cannot be intrinsically good. It may be indulged in for the sole purpose of procreation, and even then, they seem to feel, no pleasure should be taken from the act itself. (I often think how much better this world would be if the second chapter of Genesis said, "And on the seventh day, God got laid.")

Perhaps because I'm not religious myself, I've never fully understood why so many of the very religious—worshipers of God in virtually any form, from Mecca to Memphis—are so determined to deny and denounce the legitimate pleasures of the flesh, the unparalleled joys of sex. One explanation, I suppose, is that they think any pleasure so great should be reserved for the hereafter—that earthbound man is unworthy of such joy. The Calvinists preached a variation on that theme—that the more diligent one is about rejecting temporary pleasure in this life, the more likely one is to be rewarded with everlasting pleasure in the next. By extension, that means any earthly pleasure must be followed by punishment, in order to absolve the pleasure-taker of his sin and render him, once more, potentially fit for celestial pleasure after death. Richard Steere, the American poet, offered yet another variation on this theme three centuries ago, when he said that all temporal pleasures and rewards, "in comparison . . . [with] heavenly joys . . . are not worthy of the least esteem but rather are to be scornfully despised."

These teachings bear a depressing similarity to that of the Puritans who first settled this country and who are ultimately responsible for the anhedonia and erotophobia that have always lain just beneath the surface—and often, as now, right on the surface—of American life. Although we have had to contend, from time to time, with a kind of secularized puritanism in this country, the original Puritans were a sect of strictly religious lineage, Protestants in England dedicated to "purifying" the Church of England in the second half of the sixteenth century and the first half of the seventeenth century. They were biblical literalists, insistent that society be governed by the word and spirit of the New Testament; they were committed to the eradication of anything in church liturgy and individual behavior that could not be traced to a specific biblical text. (That meant eliminating everything from religious vestments to the celebration of Christmas itself.) Today's Church of England was born of a compromise—blessed by the royal family—between the Catholic Church and radical British Protestants, and this turned the Puritans into renegades—enemies of the state. Like many religious zealots, the Puritans resisted bitterly, went to war, seized power and executed their most powerful enemies—in their case, King Charles I and the archbishop of Canterbury. The linear descendants of these Puritans were the pioneers and Pilgrims who sailed to Plymouth Rock in 1620—"the purest of the purifiers" in the words of one scholar.

John Philip Jenkins, a professor of religious studies and history at Pennsylvania State University, has said of the Puritans in both seventeenth-century England and colonial America, "If a given society was attempting to live up to the role of God's new Israel, then it was justifiable to enforce appropriate standards on every individual in that community." The pernicious influence of these Puritans has lasted more than three centuries and, if anything, is increasing today.

"It's impossible . . . to dismiss the continuing, subliminal impact of the very first European ideas that came to this continent," writes Samuel Eliot Morison, the distinguished historian. "New England differed from the other English colonies in that it was founded largely for the purpose of trying an experiment in Christian living. . . . A new City of God was their aim." Interestingly, Puritanism was essentially a middle-class phenomenon—"far too exigent in its moral demands ever to be popular with earthy-minded peasants, or with the nobility and the very rich, who saw no point in having money if you could not do what you liked with it," Morison notes. The Puritans, he says, were utterly devoted to the concept that "Religion should permeate every phase of living. Man belonged to God alone; his only purpose in life was to enhance God's glory and do God's will; and every variety of human activity, every sort of human conduct, presumably unpleasing to God, must be discouraged if not suppressed."

Thus, Morison says, Puritanism was "an enemy to that genial glorification of the natural man, with all his instincts and appetites, that characterized the Renaissance, and the great Elizabethans." Ultimately, Puritanism "taught that natural man was wholly vile, corrupt and prone to evil." Sex, being the most "natural" of acts, then, not only is vile but warrants punishment. This means not only that one avoids sex but that, in the spirit of Christian evangelism and community, one tries to persuade others to do likewise.

To me, all this is as foreign—as nonsensical, as inhuman—as arguing that love itself is evil. To me, making love to a woman I love is, without question, the greatest, most exciting, most satisfying, even (yea) the most spiritual pleasure on earth. (To be perfectly honest, I remember thinking more than once when I was young, single and horny that sex with someone I didn't love was probably the second greatest pleasure on earth—and that sex with someone I didn't even like all that much was somewhere between the third and sixth greatest pleasure, depending on when I'd last eaten a great meal or read a great book . . . and on how well the Dodgers were playing that week.) Maybe it's precisely because sex is so overpowering, so all-consuming, so capable of not only overwhelming but of obliterating all else, that the extreme religionists among us are so opposed to it and so appalled by it. In their view, the only all-consuming passion should be passion for God. Any pleasure that appears to rival or supplant one's devotion to God, even for a brief, ecstatic moment, is blasphemous. Besides, sex is about losing control, about abandoning oneself to the moment (and to another). Most very religious people seem to think that the only "Other" to Whom one should ever abandon oneself is God—and that losing control is tantamount to losing sight of God, to rendering oneself vulnerable to sin and temptation in every form. The early Christian moralists, writes British philosopher Roger Scruton, "repudiated" sexual desire and arousal as "a falling away from our spiritual fulfilment, a dangerous toying on the threshold of perdition"; to them, "the melting of the flesh in sexual excitement is a premonition of our final melting in death."

Fears—perhaps subconscious fears—about loss of control and the imminence of death may help explain why the pleasure police often seem the most strident as the millennium approaches. It happened with the Victorians near the end of the nineteenth century, and it's happening across an even broader range of human activity with American bluenoses and alarmists as we approach the end of the twentieth century. The onset of a new millennium does strange things to some people. Historian Hillel Schwartz has written of the *fin de siècle* syndrome, with its "desires for purification and rejuvenation at century's turn," and *Newsweek* magazine, in a 1994 cover story on "America's Quest for Spiritual Meaning," suggested that "anxiety over the coming millennium" may explain why "millions of Americans are embarking on a search for the sacred in their lives."

Writing in the *Washington Post* last year, Liesl Schillinger said that with the imminence of the millennium, "thoughts of eternity and death joust in the collective unconscious, emerging in art, politics, religion, music, dress and social behavior. . . . People start believing in psychics, joining cults, dressing in black, piercing their flesh, killing themselves and writing songs about Heaven, Hell, Satan and the Madonna."

Michelle Stacey, in her book *Consumed,* says, "There is something apocalyptic about the nineties—certainly about the turn of the millennium that we are approaching—something that calls up thoughts of mortality, of endings, of historic and even religious shifts that are so large as to be out of our control." Anxiety about loss of control on so cosmic a level could exacerbate fears about loss of control on a more personal level, especially among religious Christians, for whom the millennium—the two-thousandth anniversary of the birth of Christ—holds special significance (and special problems: How can they possibly fit two thousand candles on His birthday cake? And: Would He really prefer carob to chocolate?).

In his fascinating book *The Red Queen: Sex and the Evolution of Human Nature,* Matt Ridley, a British zoologist-turned-journalist, offers a much more pragmatic explanation for scornful religious attitudes toward sex. The church became "obsessed with matters of sex" very early on, he says, because "It recognized sexual competition to be one of the principal causes of murder and mayhem.

"The gradual synonymy of sex and sin in Christendom," Ridley argues, "is surely based more on the fact that sex often leads to trouble [i.e., violence] rather than that there is something inherently sinful about sex."

Ridley examines this syndrome in animals—man's forebears, the chimpanzee foremost among them—and he suggests that as man evolved, he began to use "wealth, power and violence as a means to sexual ends. . . ." Like the animals that went before them, he says, early, pre-Christian tribes most often waged war over sexual rights, not over territorial rights or the rights to scarce material resources, as is traditionally taught in school, where livestock and agricultural land are more commonly seen as the prizes that warriors sought and defended. Anthropologist Napoleon Chagnon agrees. After studying the Yanomamo tribes in Venezuela, he concluded, "These people were not fighting over what I was trained to believe they were fighting over. . . . They were fighting over women." Chagnon was ridiculed for his findings, which prompted him to observe, "You are allowed to admit the stomach as a source of war but not the gonads."

Ridley cites the Pitcairn Islanders as a particularly striking example of the violence born of sex—and of the religious strictures on sex, born of that violence.

"In 1790, nine mutineers from HMS *Bounty* landed on Pitcairn along with six male and thirteen female Polynesians," Ridley writes. "Thousands of miles from the nearest inhabitants, unknown to the world, they set about building a life on the little island. . . . When the colony was discovered eighteen years later, ten of the women had survived and only one of the men. Of the other men, one had committed suicide, one had died [presumably of natural causes] and twelve had been murdered. The survivor was simply the last man left standing in an orgy of violence motivated entirely by sexual competition. He promptly underwent a conversion to Christianity and prescribed monogamy for [the previously polygamous] Pitcairn society."

The very religious—and some of the not-so-very religious as well—are wont to cite scripture to support their position on sin, temptation and every specific sexual activity from masturbation to fornication to homosexuality. This is the basic approach that underlies the "Sex Respect" movement, a coalition of gay-bashing, anti-abortion Christian Fundamentalists who want schools to force children to take a class that preaches abstinence and chastity and that teaches that French kissing can cause AIDS. Sex Respect is a twelve-week course based on a textbook written by Coleen Kelly Mast, a woman in Golf, Illinois. Mrs. Mast, an antiabortion activist, developed her text with the help of a $300,000 grant that the Reagan administration awarded to the Committee on the Status of Woman in 1986. (The committee was stripped of its federal funding a year later after settlement of a lawsuit in which the federal government was accused of violating the constitutional separation of church and state by using tax money to finance programs that were more religious than educational.)

Sex Respect, the book, is essentially a moralistic tome, arguing against promiscuity and premarital sex, emphasizing chastity and largely avoiding the standard sex education fare of anatomy, reproduction and birth control. Much like Sally Cline's book for adults, *Women, Passion and Celibacy,* which suggests that women's gardening and piano-playing skills would improve if only they would abandon the foolishness of sex, the teacher's manual for Sex Respect includes a list of recommended alternatives to sex on a date—playing Monopoly, riding a bicycle and baking cookies among them. (Needless to say, masturbation is not proposed as an alternative—a foolish oversight, it seems to me; masturbating may not be as uplifting as playing Monopoly or baking cookies, but it is both quicker and cheaper.)

Sex Respect is now used in more than fifteen hundred school districts. It has triggered a nationwide movement, complete with bumper stickers: "control your urgin'—be a virgin." It has also sparked a series of courtroom challenges and a number of nasty school board election campaigns between candidates from the Christian Right who advocate Sex Respect instruction and members of Planned Parenthood and others who vigorously oppose it. Thirty percent of the parents in Beaufort, South Carolina, withdrew their children from Sex Respect classes, and 2,500 parents, students and educators signed petitions attacking the program. School officials in Enfield, Connecticut, launched a pilot Sex Respect course, then canceled it when parents complained that it taught children "fear, guilt and shame."

Sex Respect is one of more than a dozen programs now available that teach teens the evils of premarital sex. Ironically, California—erstwhile leader of the sexual freedom movement in the

1960s—is also a pioneer in the abstinence-makes-the-heart-grow-fonder movement in the 1990s. The state has approved a three-year, $5-million program to demonstrate to teenagers the pleasure of postponing pleasure—to persuade them that chastity can be more fun than sex, drugs and rock and roll. The Baptists have a similar program nationwide under the banner "True Love Waits."

The mass media, ever on the alert for new trends, have picked up on the chastity movement. The *New York Times* headlined "Proud to Be a Virgin: Nowadays, you can be respected even if you don't do it." The *Washington Post* described chastity as a new teenage counterculture. *Mademoiselle* magazine published "The New Chastity," which it branded "the latest stage in the sexual revolution." Creators of television situation comedies, always attuned to demands from viewers for the latest novelty—and to pressure from sponsors to "keep it clean"—have found a bonanza in chastity.

In this era of AIDS and unwanted teenage pregnancy, I would be the last to encourage promiscuity or to denigrate chastity. I'll have more to say on AIDS shortly, but I know the statistics on teenage pregnancy—and on sexually transmitted diseases other than AIDS. The United States has the highest teen pregnancy rate of any developed nation. Every year, more than 1 million teenagers here get pregnant; that's one in nine girls aged fifteen to nineteen. One-fourth of all U.S. teenagers contract some kind of venereal disease; one-third of the 20 million cases of sexually transmitted diseases reported annually in the United States occur among teenagers. Even many of the girls who don't get pregnant—and those boys *and* girls who don't get a sexually transmitted disease—have sex too early, too often and with too many different partners. About a third of fifteen-year-old boys have already had sex; so have 27 percent of fifteen-year-old girls. The average male has his first sexual experience at sixteen, the average female at seventeen. About 75 percent of young Americans have sex before they turn twenty. Among sexually active teenage girls, according to one survey, an astounding 61 percent have had multiple partners—up dramatically from 38 percent in 1971.

The reasons for this sexual explosion among the young are fairly evident. To begin with, as I—and many others before me—

have already noted, the let-it-all-hang-out, do-your-own-thing ethos of the 1960s free-love revolution brought sex out of the closet. That reversal of our puritanical, sex-as-a-dirty-little-secret tradition was long overdue. Many people and many relationships are much healthier today because sex is no longer in the closet. Although it's no longer popular to say so, I would argue that, despite some excesses, society at large is also better off. But the sexual revolution helped create a climate in which many young people got the wrong message—or at least a mixed message. No, sex is not dirty. Neither, however, is it an activity to be engaged in as casually as chewing a piece of gum.

The increasingly explicit sexual nature of advertising and other mass media and pop culture messages today have underscored the availability and desirability of sex—anytime, anywhere, for or with anyone. In addition, the growing number of working mothers and the diminished availability of after-school programs in school districts ravaged by recession and taxpayer rebellions have left many teens with too little supervision and too much free time. Sex flourishes in just such a vacuum.

Most teenagers, especially young teenagers, aren't ready for the emotional responsibility of sex. Most don't practice sound birth control. They risk disease, pregnancy and emotional distress. I don't think, however, that the solution is to teach teens that sex is wicked and dangerous and that abstinence is the only rational and moral course of action until you get married, at which point—depending on who's doing the teaching—sex is magically transformed into either an officially sanctioned pleasure or a necessary means to achieve the very end (parenthood) that you've spent your entire adolescence taking cold showers and baking cookies in an effort to avoid. As the sex educator Sol Gordon once said, "There's something wrong with a country that says, 'Sex is dirty; save it for someone you love.'"

Sex education should certainly include information—and warnings—on the dangers of disease and pregnancy. It should also include a discussion of abstinence and chastity. But the content shouldn't be limited to that, and the tone shouldn't be alarmist and moralistic. Anatomy, reproduction and birth control should not be ignored, and most important of all, teenagers should be told, in school and at home alike, that sex—as exciting and wonderful as it can be—is ultimately, ideally, only one factor in a very large equation, a key element in building lasting relationships founded on genuine love, mutual respect and individual dignity and responsibility. By teaching instead of preaching, by telling teenagers *all* about sex— the emotional as well as the physical, the undeniable pleasure as well as the potential pain—one may well encourage them, especially the youngest among them, to wait, if not until marriage, at least until they're old enough, mature enough, to consider the consequences of their actions.

This is essentially the approach taken by Dr. Henry Foster, Jr., the obstetrician-gynecologist from Meharry Medical College in Nashville, whom President Clinton nominated in 1995 to succeed Dr. Joycelyn Elders as United States surgeon general. In 1987 Dr. Foster created a program called "I Have a Future," which combines sex education, family planning, medical services and job training, all in an effort to persuade teenagers to postpone sex and parenthood while they mature personally, develop socially and begin their careers. Many graduates of Dr. Foster's program—and many experts who have worked in it, observed it or evaluated it—say that its pragmatic, commonsense approach, combined with tangible, attainable incentives, is a far more effective deterrent to teen sex, promiscuity and pregnancy than are the sin- and fear-based programs that simply preach abstinence. Of course, the Republicans filibustered Foster's nomination to death in the Senate. Although his initial understatement of the number of abortions he had performed as an obstetrician gave his opponents a powerful weapon to use against him, he ultimately fell victim to both presidential politics and the antiabortion lobby.

Sex education in the United States began, tentatively, in the 1940s, driven largely by fear about the spiraling rate of syphilis. By the 1960s the John Birch Society and other right-wing extremists were demanding the removal of sex education from the public school curriculum. Fundamentalist Christians joined the holy war in the 1970s, and by the middle of that decade, legislatures in more than twenty states had been persuaded to restrict or abolish sex education.

The most logical and persuasive argument against sex education in the classroom has long been that sex is very intimate, a matter of personal and family values, and thus any teaching about it should take place in the home, not the school. I agree completely. Or I would agree if I thought parents *would* tell their children about sex—all about sex, the good and the bad. Most—the vast majority, my own parents included—have not. I was so determined to avoid that mistake with my own children that I probably went overboard. When my stepdaughter, Jordan, was eleven or twelve, she asked me what a French kiss was. By the time I was through answering, I think I had damn near drawn a verbal diagram explaining oral sex. But Jordy either didn't care or didn't understand; either way, she didn't say much at the time, and I saw no aftereffects of my gratuitous lecture on human sexual relationships. My openness about matters sexual must have registered at least subconsciously, though. Almost a decade later, when a young man asked Jordy to go to bed with him—it would have been her first sexual experience—she came directly to me to discuss it, before she did anything. I have the same kind of relationship with Jordy's brother, Christopher; I was out of town when he had his first sexual experience—he was in his early twenties, as I recall—but I can still remember his having me paged in the St. Louis airport the next morning to discuss it. He didn't want to brag. He just wanted to share his happiness and, more important, to ask several questions. As my son, Lucas, grows older, I hope I'll be able to convey to him the right information and attitudes about sex—and to let him know that he, too, can ask me any question without fear of avoidance or disapproval. As with alcohol, I think that parents who are open and who avoid making sex seem evil and forbidden are far more likely than their puritanical counterparts to have children who develop a healthy attitude about it and don't indulge too soon or too much.

Most parents, I fear, are too timid or too uncomfortable to discuss sex openly and honestly with their children. So the schools have to do the job. Driven largely by the fear of AIDS, many have started doing just that in recent years. Since 1987, twenty-two state legislatures have mandated the inclusion of some form of sex education in the schools. But this time around, unfortunately, the aim seems less education than intimidation, more a narrow (and narrow-minded) moralistic agenda than a broad-based public policy.

Because the Sex Respect curriculum largely eschews any form of sex education other than abstinence, it attracted the critical attention of men like Michael Gotlieb, a rabbi in the small Southern California community of Vista, when the program was implemented there by right-wing members of the school board (who were subsequently voted out of office by angry parents). Rabbi Gotlieb says it's programs like Sex Respect, rather than the acts they seek to prevent, that are "both immoral and sinful."

"We do render a terrible disservice to our children by withholding vital information on sexuality from them," Rabbi Gotlieb wrote in the *Los Angeles Times*. Not that Gotlieb opposes the teaching of abstinence. "Abstinence until marriage is an ideal and the basic approach to sexuality that I would advocate as a rabbi," he says. "It is not only by far the best form of birth control [and disease prevention], it elevates sexuality and makes it sacred." But Gotlieb says he does not want people who engage in premarital sex to "think that they are committing a grave sin." Premarital sex between consenting adults is "not immoral," he says; it is merely "unholy."

"The difference between the two is significant."

Indeed it is. Sex—premarital or otherwise—becomes a moral issue when deceit, violence or exploitation is employed. Incest, rape and philandering are immoral. Sex itself is not. I've already said that I am not a religious Jew, and I neither want to pretend to any expertise on Judaism nor to exalt it above other religions. But I do think it noteworthy that just as Judaism is less condemnatory of alcohol than are many other religions, so Judaism seems less condemnatory of (and more open to) human sexuality than are most of the world's other religions, especially Western religions. Some Eastern religions celebrate eroticism as a kind of divine sensibility—*vide* the *Kama Sutra*—but others require a renunciation of sex, either because of the earthly pleasure it provides or the emotional attachment it involves. Christianity has never seemed altogether comfortable with sex. I've always had a fairly superficial explanation for the difference between (most) Jews and (many) Christians on the issue of sexual behavior: the pain and persecution born of anti-Semitism have historically forced Jews to worry about their own survival, individually and collectively, thus leaving them less time to waste fretting about who was doing what to whom between the sheets. But upon further examination, I've found that the explanation is more complex than that.

To begin with, Judaism is more embracing of pleasure in general than are most other religions. Jews certainly believe in heaven and hell, but they don't believe that man should forgo all pleasure on earth in order to ensure happiness in heaven; they don't regard life as a spartan dress rehearsal for death. There is a passage in the Talmud, the holy book of Jewish civil and religious law, that says, "A person will be called to account on judgment day for every permissible thing that he might have enjoyed but did not."

As Andrew Sullivan, a gay Catholic, wrote last year in his thought-provoking book *Virtually Normal,* Jewish scriptural regulations governing sex have "less to do with personal morality, as we would understand it today, and more to do with what is owed to the community at large, the protection of children, and the maintenance of stable family ties."

Like all religions, Judaism has its official prohibitions on pleasure seeking—some aspects of sex specifically included. But most of these restrictions are observed, if at all, only by Orthodox Jews, many of whom, for example, follow ancient rules that forbid sex during a woman's menstrual period and for five days thereafter. Orthodox Jews also believe that the Torah condemns homosexuality, and they believe that women should cover themselves from head to foot so as not to "tempt" men other than their husbands; in Orthodox temples, men and women sit apart for the same reason. But in many instances, Orthodox Jews are not following the Bible or the Talmud so much as the *Shulkhan Arukh,* a code of Jewish law written during the sixteenth century, when Judaism in Europe began to absorb some of the sex-as-sin approach of the surrounding Protestant and Catholic cultures. Orthodox Jews are in a small minority today in the United States; mainstream, modern American Judaism—Conservative and Reform Judaism—believes in "a balance between extremes," says the *Encyclopedia Judaica*. "It insists on a stern discipline of moral restraints and yet avoids excessive prudery or asceticism. . . . It rejects the notion of considering the sex instinct as intrinsically sinful or shameful." One Jewish scholar characterizes this balancing act as a rejection of both the "uncontrolled sexual expression that paganism preaches" and "the Christian reaction to the excesses of paganism"—the Christian identification of sex with original sin.

Marjorie Suchocki, the dean of the School of Theology at Claremont in Southern California and the author of *The Fall to Violence: Original Sin in Relational Theology,* says that while Judaism has historically viewed human sexuality through an anthropological prism—"the interrelatedness of body and soul"—Christianity "draws its models from the Greco-Roman world, with its hierarchy of mind *over* body. Clearly, sexuality is the one place where the body overwhelms reason. Therefore, sexuality is a clear and present danger."

Dean Suchocki argues that this view of sex is responsible for both the "ideal" of celibacy and the opposition to birth control that are central to some religions and sects. Although religions that demand celibacy from their clergy profess to do so on the grounds that celibacy frees man for a higher form of love—love of God and of His holy instrument, the Church—Dean Suchocki suggests, "The whole notion behind the celibacy of the clergy is that they are supposedly in such control of their bodies that they no longer need sex." By secular extension, the requirement that lay people have sex only under circumstances that make procreation possible circumscribes sex "totally within the realm of reason," she says—sex at a specific time, for a specific (approved) purpose.

The Catholic Church is the primary Western advocate both of celibacy and of sex that must always be open to procreation. But the former has been practiced in at least some Protestant sects as well, deriving its impetus in part from Paul's First Epistle to the Corinthians, in which he writes that he wishes all men were celibate, "as I am. . . . It is good for a man not to touch a woman." In contrast,

Judaism virtually insists that its rabbis be married, and while rabbis and lay Jews alike are expected to "go forth and multiply," sexual relations between husband and wife are encouraged, whether procreation is possible or not. Judaism takes both a more hedonistic and a more practical view of the human sex drive than do most other religions.

"With considerable realism," says Rabbi Joseph Telushkin, in *Jewish Wisdom,* "the Rabbis saw sexual thoughts as omnipresent. . . . The Talmud never associated saintliness with a dormant libido." Sex is perceived as an integral and important part of everyday married life in Judaism—a pleasure, a binding agent and a means of communication as well as procreation. The prayer book for the Jewish Sabbath includes the entire Song of Songs from the Old Testament, in part because its vivid, quasi-erotic imagery is intended to so arouse a man that he will make love to his wife that very night. (Where in the New Testament or the Koran or any similar scriptural writing can one find such frankly sexual language as "Thy rounded thighs are like jewels. . . . Thy two breasts are like two fawns. . . . Let thy breasts be as clusters of the vine, and the smell of thy breath like apples, and thy mouth like the best wine"?)

According to the Talmud, scholars in particular are supposed to make love to their wives every Sabbath, an obligation so rigorously fulfilled that Jewish lore tells the story of a scholar named Judah, who was "so attracted by his subject of study" that he forgot to return home one Sabbath evening, whereupon his father-in-law initiated a formal sign of mourning; he assumed that Judah must have died, "for had Judah been alive, he would not have neglected the performance of his marital duties." The Talmud actually prescribes minimum schedules of sexual relations for married couples, based on the husband's work (i.e., his availability): "For men of independent means, every day. For laborers, twice weekly. For donkey drivers, once a week. For camel drivers, once every thirty days. For sailors, once every six months."

Modern-day employers grumble about the difficulties of moving their workers to new cities because of the complications of two-career households, but under ancient Jewish laws, any man who

wanted to take a new job farther from home than his old one could
be overruled by his wife, "on the grounds that their sexual relations
would become less frequent." (Much of Jewish law and custom on
sex is largely attuned to the man's sexual needs and desires, and
Orthodox Judaism in particular, like many Eastern religions, often
relegates women to second-class status. But Jewish law and custom
do officially acknowledge a woman's sexual needs and rights, an
acknowledgment unknown to most religions and most cultures,
which implicitly assume that a woman merely tolerates sex in order
to have children, please her husband and assure her own marital
security. Thus, Jewish law says that a woman may divorce her husband if he "forbids himself by vow from having intercourse" with
her for two weeks at a time. Some interpretations say the courts may
compel a divorce after just *one* week of connubial neglect.)

Judaism disapproves of adultery as thoroughly as does Christianity. ("Thou shalt not commit adultery" *is* the Seventh Com-
mandment.) Judaism is pragmatic here, too, though. "If a man sees
that his evil impulse is conquering him," the Talmud says, "let him
go to a place where he is unknown, put on black clothes, wrap
himself in a black cloak, and do what his heart desires. . . ." In
other words: Don't do it. But if you have to do it, at least go far
away and wear a disguise and don't embarrass your wife.

Contrast this view with that of Jesus, as reported by Matthew
in the New Testament—and made famous 1,976 years later by another humble Christian, Jimmy Carter, as reported by Robert Scheer
in *Playboy:* "Everyone who looks at a woman lustfully has already
committed adultery with her in his heart."

In non-Orthodox Jewish circles, there is even discussion about
whether nonmarital sex—fornication—is at least implicitly sanctioned by the Talmud. Many rabbis say it is. "Non-marital sex is a
legitimate possibility in Judaism," one rabbi wrote to the Jewish
magazine *Moment* during a discussion of this issue in 1994. (Perhaps that's why 64 percent of Jews questioned by the National
Opinion Research Center at the University of Chicago reported
more than five sex partners since the age of eighteen, substantially
more than the 37 percent to 43 percent reported by members of

other religions.) To the best of my knowledge, the "legitimate possibility" of nonmarital sex is not entertained by any other major, organized Western religion.

Leo Rosten, in his hugely entertaining book *The Joys of Yiddish,* perhaps best captures the Jewish sexual ethos when he recounts the tale of a Mr. Berkowitz, a man who died without having committed "even one little sin" in his entire life.

"You performed nothing but *mitzvahs* [good deeds]?" the chief admitting angel says when Berkowitz gets to heaven. "We can't let you in. . . . You must be like other men—fallible, subject to temptation . . . at least *once.* So I will send you back to earth for twenty-four hours, during which time you must commit a sin—*one little sin.* Then appear before us again, at least *human."*

Back on earth, Berkowitz didn't know what to do until "a buxom woman gave him a wink. . . . Mr. Berkowitz responded with alacrity. The lady was neither young nor beautiful—but she was willing." Late that night, having made love with this willing stranger, convinced that he had finally sinned, Berkowitz is getting dressed, counting the minutes before he is to be whisked back to heaven, when his blood froze as the old maid in the bed sighed, "Oh, Mr. Berkowitz, what a *mitzvah* you performed this night!"

I'm perfectly willing to acknowledge that as a Jew myself— even, essentially, a nonpracticing Jew—I'm not without bias on the subject of Jews and sex. I realize that Jewish law is filled with sexual prohibitions, large and small, and that the Orthodox Jews who follow those laws are probably as disinclined as Fundamentalist Christians or devout Catholics toward wanton pleasures of the flesh. But even the most Orthodox Jews don't generally try to force others to play by their rules. I know of no organized Jewish battalion in the moral militia. I wish I could say the same for the Roman Catholic Church.

I do not want, in the process of condemning intolerance, to seem intolerant myself. In the course of this book, I criticize racists, sexists and gay-bashers, among others; I do not want to be a Catholic-basher. I know that many Catholic theologians are fond of saying that anti-Catholicism is "the anti-Semitism of the intellectuals."

What I think they mean is that opinion makers seem more willing these days to express (or at least to tolerate) anti-Catholic views than anti-black/Latino/Asian/Jewish/female/gay views. There is clearly an element of truth in this. But I think it is also difficult to dispute the charge that the Catholic Church—the Vatican hierarchy, *not* the rank-and-file church membership—has long played a significant role in the assault on pleasure, especially sexual pleasure.

Some critics of the church oversimplify—distort—its position on sex to suggest that official church doctrine condemns, indeed forbids, all sex that does not end in conception. What the church really teaches is that every sexual act must occur within the bonds of marriage and must be open to the *possibility* of conception—i.e., that no "artificial" birth control can be used. Sexual pleasure taken in the course of such sex acts is officially approved by the church as a worthy step in a spiritual journey, even if conception itself does not take place. But in reality, the ban on birth control injects an element of anxiety into any act of sexual intercourse in which the participants do not want to conceive a child. Unless one wishes to marry early and have a child every nine months or so for the rest of one's married, childbearing years, that means a truly faithful Catholic will have to engage in many sex acts burdened by that anxiety. Sure, one could practice the rhythm method of birth control, which the Catholic Church, in 1951—in the pontificate of Pope Pius XII— finally conceded does not violate church teaching. But as my father used to joke, "There's a name for people who practice the rhythm method. 'Parents.' " Even if you do practice it, you necessarily limit the days when you can have intercourse. This, combined with the aforementioned anxiety—and the ban on premarital sex—inevitably means less sex. Less pleasure.

I suppose it is no surprise that a hierarchical institution that's been led by (presumably) celibate males for more than twelve hundred years would have considerable difficulty coming to grips, so to speak, with sex. Thanks, in part, to the mass media, it sometimes seems as if the Catholic Church—the leaders of the church anyway—think and speak of nothing but sex, thus confirming what a friend of mine once said in another context: "Sex? Why do it when you can talk about it." These church leaders—in their role as a powerful sociopolitical force, not just spiritual authorities—often seem obsessed with sex and with the effects and implications of sexuality in the modern world. Look at all the church strictures that involve sex in one way or another. No sex outside marriage. No sex that is not open to procreation. No homosexuality. No abortion. Catholics who divorce and remarry are not allowed to receive communion unless they either get an annulment or abstain from sex with their new partners. Priests are not allowed to have sex or marry.

Pope John Paul II is a formidably intelligent and courageous man. In his outspoken support for poor people and immigrants, he has taken bold and highly moral stands that shame many American politicians. In his support for human rights, his opposition to communism and his unprecedented rapprochement with Jews after centuries of Catholic Church anti-Semitism, he has established himself as one of the most important leaders of the twentieth century. One would think that such a man might recognize the wisdom in the old jest "He no play-a the game, he no make-a the rules." But, no, JPII—the travelingest pope in history—jets from continent to continent, bemoaning, among many other things, the decline of morality in the West, as best (worst?) evidenced by all those fornicating fools in the bad old U.S. of A.

Before he became pope—when he was simply Bishop Karol Wojtyla—John Paul startled some high-ranking Catholic conservatives by actually discussing sex and orgasm in his 1969 book *Love and Responsibility*. He wrote movingly about sex as an almost mystical experience. Having been an actor, a writer, a philosopher and a quarry worker, among other things, before entering an underground seminary at the age of twenty-two, Wojtyla seemed cut from a distinctly different bolt of secular cloth than were most of his predecessors. Some Catholics dared hope that he might loosen the church's restrictive approach to sexuality. But as pope, he has made it clear that what he calls the "pure value of the body and of sex" is in making more Catholic babies.

The pope's positions on contraception, homosexual acts and sterilization are all essentially the same—that sex involving any such behavior is "literally insignificant," in the words of Joaquin Navarro-Valls, his official spokesman. "Only sexual activity that has potential consequences in the conception of a child has any political importance," Navarro says. In other words, sex purely for its own sake—for the pleasure it provides, for the intimacy it involves—is politically "insignificant." I realize that a sex act may, on occasion, have political consequences, but the idea that all sex acts should be looked at in those terms is appalling to me.

Andrew Greeley, the controversial Catholic priest and best-selling author, says the pope just doesn't understand either the power or the importance of sex in marriage.

I don't mean to grant Greeley, who deals primarily in popular social science, a standing comparable to that rightfully enjoyed by Pope John Paul II, a classic intellectual, an eminent philosopher and theologian and the revered leader of one of the world's great religions. But Greeley does represent a point of view held by many Catholics, and his reasoning is often persuasive, if not necessarily transcendental.

"It is now beyond any reasonable doubt in such disciplines as evolutionary biology and comparative primatology that what is distinctive and unique about human sexuality in comparison to all other higher primates is its function as a bonding mechanism between man and woman," Greeley says. "Unlike all other primates, the human infant requires the care and attention of adults for many years after birth . . . before it can survive without them. Thus, evolution selected for those characteristics that would bind the man and the woman permanently (or quasi-permanently).

"Much of what is unique about human sexuality has no counterpart in other species. . . . lovemaking in private, secondary sexual characteristics (only in humans do breasts develop before the first birth) . . . constant availability for and interest in sex, the duration of the sexual interlude, the intensity of the pleasure, intercourse after the end of fertility. None of these specifically human dimensions of sex are required for reproduction; all are required for bonding."

Scientist Jared Diamond has written, in his book *The Third Chimpanzee*, "In no species besides humans has the purpose of copulation become so unrelated to conception." Thus, Greeley argues, "Must not one say that it is natural and in most circumstances necessary for humans to make love often to sustain the bonding between them?"

When Pope John Paul II issued his 1993 encyclical *Veritatis Splendor,* a dense, complex, tightly reasoned assault on situational ethics and moral relativism, he included artificial contraception along with homicide, genocide, torture and mutilation as an "intrinsically evil" act. Relishing the irony of turning the pope's words back on him, Greeley now asks, "Might not one go so far as to say that it is a violation of nature and thus *intrinsically evil* to attempt to prevent such exchanges of marital love?"

Unfortunately, Greeley says, "Church leaders either do not listen to those who are exploring the sexual nature of humans or contemptuously dismiss them as wrong."

Many Catholics sincerely believe in the teachings of the church on birth control and other sexual issues. They see these as matters of fundamental faith, not opinion or interpretation. Many of them have arrived at this position not through faith alone, but through their own careful consideration of the moral issues involved. The pope himself has argued that he has no right to change the church's teachings, that he is bound by the Bible, by church tradition and by the practices of Christ. But many Catholics—in the United States, probably most Catholics—routinely ignore the Vatican's pontif-ications on artificial birth control, even though they may both accept and admire the life-affirming spirit that motivates the ban.

"One of the great strengths of the Catholic Church is its infinite capacity for hypocrisy," says Roberto Suro, a Catholic himself, who covered the Vatican in the latter half of the 1980s for *Time* magazine and the *New York Times.* "The Church can lay down rules on things like birth control, divorce, homosexuality and sex outside of marriage while ignoring the fact that many of its faithful, even its priests, break those rules, and this has been going on for centuries."

According to a 1994 *New York Times*–CBS News poll, 88 percent of American Catholics think someone who practices artificial birth control can still be a good Catholic. Another poll, taken by *Time* and CNN, found that only 14 percent of American Catholics believe they should always obey the Vatican's moral teachings; the overwhelming majority said their personal morality was their own business. In Mexico, which is 93 percent Catholic, 88 percent of those surveyed by the Gallup organization said a decision on having an abortion should be made by the couple involved or by the woman alone. Even on the pope's home turf, Italy, abortion is legal during the first three months of pregnancy. Italy has the lowest birthrate in the world; Spain, another overwhelmingly Catholic country, is a close second. In fact, it could be argued that the stern dictates of the Catholic Church notwithstanding, people in predominantly Catholic countries—certainly the predominantly Catholic countries of western Europe (France, Italy, Spain, Ireland)—are considerably more tolerant of, indeed more likely to indulge in, pleasures of all kinds than are the denizens of Protestant-dominated Germany, England and Switzerland. (Whether this difference is ultimately rooted in religion, culture, temperament or weather, I'll leave to social anthropologists to determine. But it may be worth noting that Victorianism was a Protestant, not a Catholic, phenomenon.)

In the United States, according to the 1994 *Sex in America* study conducted by the National Opinion Research Center, there is no significant difference in basic sexual activities among adherents of different religions. Andrew Greeley's own research, also based in part on surveys taken by the National Opinion Research Center, suggests that Catholics are actually more sexually active—and more sexually playful—than are non-Catholics and are more likely to enjoy sex than are non-Catholics.

Greeley's book *Sex: The Catholic Experience*—which some might see as an oxymoron—is based on NORC surveys of 4,400 people from 1989 to 1991, as well as on surveys of more than 1,300 people for his own study of marriage in the early 1990s. Among the findings:

- Sixty-eight percent of Catholics have sex at least once a week, compared to 56 percent of non-Catholics.

- Sixty-four percent of Catholic women scored high on a "sexual playfulness" scale that includes such activities as undressing your husband, showering, bathing or swimming nude with your husband and experimenting with various sexual techniques; sexual playfulness among non-Catholics: 42 percent.
- Thirty percent of Catholics have purchased erotic underwear, compared with 20 percent of non-Catholics.
- Only 17 percent of Catholics polled said they disapproved of premarital sex, while almost twice as many non-Catholics—33 percent—said they disapproved.

The Roman Catholic Church has long been the largest single religious denomination by far in the United States—about 59 million strong today—but a great many of them are obviously indifferent to the sexual fiats of their leader, even as public opinion polls show that they continue to love and respect him. Sixty-nine percent of those Catholics who attend mass weekly say the pope's position on a particular social or political issue "has no bearing on how they view that issue themselves," a *New York Times*–CBS News poll reported in October 1995. The same poll showed that 67 percent of U.S. Catholics "hold favorable opinions of the Pope, while a mere two percent feel unfavorably disposed." Those seemingly contradictory findings are easily explained, says Peter Steinfels, longtime religion writer for the *New York Times*. To most Catholics, he says, the pope is "not a leader whose marching orders they await but a repository of what they value and hope for." E. J. Dionne of the *Washington Post,* who formerly covered the Vatican for the *New York Times,* agrees and suggests that while many Catholics disagree with the pope on specific issues, they welcome his "moral challenge." The pope, Dionne wrote in the fall of 1995, "is not peddling cheap grace. He makes all of us feel a little uncomfortable. That's the task of all serious moral teachers."

One further explanation for the divergence of many Catholics from both papal preaching and public perception may lie in the Catholic sacrament known officially as Reconciliation—what is commonly called Confession. In principle, the granting of absolution is contingent upon the penitent's commitment to sin no more. But in practice, if one may do anything one wishes and then confess that "sin" to a priest and be forgiven by God—and then, if one is so inclined, "sin" again, confess again and be forgiven again—the incentive to ignore one's own desires and avoid "sin" in the first place is, shall we say, greatly reduced.

The irresistible lure of forbidden fruit may also be a factor in the active sex lives that many Catholics seem to enjoy. So may the attitudes implicit in a survey I saw that asked people to pinpoint their image of God on a seven-point scale between "master" and "spouse." Catholics, on average, placed God much closer to the "spouse" end of the spectrum than did non-Catholics. Unless one is deeply into bondage, it stands to reason that a spousal image of God is more likely to lead to the indulgence in (and the enjoyment of) sex than is an image of God as a stern and unforgiving taskmaster. Of potentially greater consequence, Greeley says Catholics see sex as a "gift from God," which strongly suggests that it is "meant to be enjoyed." Some Catholics argue that it is precisely because sex is a gift from God that each sex act should be seen not simply as an occasion for casual pleasure but as a spiritual event, an opportunity (with a concurrent obligation) to rededicate oneself to God, preferably by creating life out of the act.

Whatever the interpretation of sex as "a gift from God," I like the sound of the phrase—and the concept itself. Hell, I've often thanked God—cried out appreciatively to God—at critical moments of sexual union. Sex as a gift from God certainly makes a lot more sense than sex as a sin for which God will punish you. If God created everything—sex and stagnant ponds included—He must have had a reason. And if God is good, as people of all faiths believe, why would He create something so beautiful and so powerful—and then say it's bad?

Religious scholars suggest that Saint Augustine was originally responsible for the dark view the Catholic Church officially takes of sexual activity not conducted within the bonds of marriage and not open to the possibility of procreation. He argued that sex was justified *only* for the purpose of procreation and that it was sinful even then because it required one to lose control. Saint Augustine saw in sexual arousal "the sign of original sin," writes Roger Scruton. Saint Augustine was not alone in his dour, guilt-plagued approach to life, of course. Just as many revered Catholics who came after him superseded or modified or rejected his views, so many prominent Protestant figures of an ascetic or even misogynistic bent have made Protestantism, at various times, even less hospitable than Catholicism to libidinous pleasures.

For much of this country's existence, the sex-as-sin teachings and beliefs of the various religious groups—from Puritans to Papists to Pentecostals—were reinforced by the basic demographics of the country and by basic human nature. We were largely a rural society, a nation of farms and villages and small towns. In 1800 only 5 percent of the nation's population lived in places with more than 2,500 population. Everyone knew who his neighbor was and what his neighbor did. Philandering, homosexual behavior, group sex, kinky sex, public nudity, illegitimate birth—any departure from the norm was easily detected and its perpetrator quickly embarrassed, sometimes ostracized. This long acted as a brake on some of man's more adventurous sexual instincts. But by 1950, 65 percent of the nation's population lived in places with more than 2,500 population; the figure is now 75 percent. As our society became increasingly urbanized—and increasingly anonymous—socially induced inhibitions began to fade. It's ironic that the 1950s—long scorned as the boring decade, the decade of the dreary man in the gray flannel suit and the equally dreary woman in the gray suburban kitchen—became, in retrospect, the hothouse in which the sexual flowering of America began.

Urbanization was perhaps the first, albeit most gradual, of the forces that took root in those unlikely years of Dwight Eisenhower, Joe McCarthy and Ozzie and Harriet. Penicillin, the Pill and *Playboy* also played key roles in the revolution. Just as urbanization greatly reduced the potential for neighborly disapproval of some forms of sexual activity, so the introduction of penicillin as a treatment for venereal disease greatly reduced the medical and social penalties one might pay for such activity. Penicillin, though discovered in 1929 and used in the armed forces in World War II, didn't come into widespread use in the general public until the early 1950s. The first widely successful tests of the birth control pill took place around the same time, and by 1962 the Pill was being used by more than 1 million women. Suddenly, the biggest deterrent to non-procreative sex was gone.

Into the breach, proclaiming sex-as-pleasure to be the true American birthright, stepped one Hugh Marston Hefner, the twenty-seven-year-old grandson of midwestern puritans—churchgoing Nebraska farmers who prohibited smoking, drinking and swearing. Hefner published the first issue of *Playboy* magazine in December 1953, but he was so uncertain about its future that he didn't put the date on the cover. Within a year, his blend of glossy, airbrushed nudes, racy cartoons, short fiction and an unabashedly hedonistic philosophy was selling 100,000 copies a month. Circulation climbed into the millions before the end of the decade, and Hefner created a complete line of *Playboy* merchandise and a chain of Playboy Clubs. The prime attraction of the clubs were the Playboy Bunnies—waitresses with rabbit ears—shapely young women whose ample chests were artfully cantilevered for maximum legal exposure as they waited on panting young men striving to emulate Hefner's own urbane, pseudo-sophistication. Thus was a whole generation of young men introduced to both the consumer society—advice on buying everything from a sport coat to a sports car to a stereo—and the celebration of sex as neither sinful nor shameful, but as guilt-free fun.

"The spectacular rise of *Playboy* reflected the postwar decline of Calvinism and puritanism in America," says David Halberstam in his massive and wonderfully insightful pop chronicle *The Fifties*. "If religion existed only as a negative force, Hefner was saying, if it spoke only of the denial of pleasure and made people feel furtive about what was natural, then it was in trouble. He preached pleasure. He touched the right chord at precisely the right moment."

There was much that was wrong about Hefner's message, too, of course, ranging from his emphasis on shallow materialism to the blatant sexism inherent in his treatment of women as sex objects.

Feminists, campus radicals and environmentalists would begin to address those grievous flaws in the next decade. But at the time, those most outraged by Hefner's photos and his philosophy were the religious and secular puritans who wanted sex to stay in the closet, where it had always been. They saw Hefner as the devil incarnate, and they wanted *Playboy* banned from newsstands, the mail and virtually any other public display or availability.

Hefner, however, was exploiting the increased affluence of the average American, which provided the resources and the mind-set that enabled ordinary young men to lust after not only the material possessions but also the personal freedoms previously enjoyed only by the rich. The simultaneous unleashing of the libido and the pocketbook made the puritans' task doubly daunting. Hefner was also able to capitalize on the work done by a man he had idolized— Alfred Kinsey.

Kinsey's landmark studies of human sexuality were published in 1948 *(Sexual Behavior in the Human Male)* and 1953 *(Sexual Behavior in the Human Female)*. Both became instant best-sellers. Kinsey's books pointed out that infidelity and homosexuality were much more widespread than generally thought. They also pointed out that premarital sex often led to better marriages. And that good sex often meant a good marriage. And that masturbation wouldn't make one go insane. Hefner thought Kinsey's views validated his own, and that helped give him the confidence necessary to start *Playboy* and to aggressively challenge those in society who hypocritically insisted on a self-righteous, punitive approach toward sex. Self-appointed guardians of public morality bitterly assailed both Kinsey and Hefner. Hefner was the easier target—a bunny-come-lately, an *Esquire* magazine reject trying to make money by selling "dirty" pictures. He had no real standing in society. But Kinsey was a Serious Scientist, a university professor, an entomologist and zoologist by training, and his work was based on several thousand personal interviews (although serious questions have been raised in recent years about his methodology, especially on homosexuality and childhood sexuality). Like Hefner, Kinsey was a midwesterner, but unlike Hefner—who was divorced—Kinsey stayed married to the same woman, the first woman he ever dated, his entire adult life.

None of this prevented his detractors from accusing him of the academic equivalent of "writing dirty words on fences," as one said.

When Kinsey's second book was published, Billy Graham, the country's unofficial First Preacher, said, "It is impossible to estimate the damage this book will do to the already deteriorating morals of America." Other critics "furiously disagreed with almost everything," Halberstam wrote, "above all his failure to condemn what he had found. Not only had he angered the traditional conservative bastions of social mores—the Protestant churches on the right and the Catholic Church—but to his surprise, he had enraged the most powerful voices in the liberal Protestant clergy as well." Within months after publication of Kinsey's second book, the Rockefeller Foundation, the most important financial underwriter of his research, withdrew its support.

But it was too late. Kinsey had already made sex a subject that people could begin to talk about. He helped create the environment in which Hefner could publish foldout photographs of pneumatic nymphets, naked except for the staples in their navels—and in which such revolutionary 1950s icons as Marilyn Monroe, Marlon Brando, James Dean and Elvis Presley could flaunt their raw sexuality to an adoring public.

Self-appointed moral arbiters objected to all four—and to their many, equally smoldering if less talented imitators—but it was Elvis who aroused the most frenzied response, from fans and critics alike. Elvis was a rebel—in the way he looked, in the way he dressed, in the way he wore his hair, in the way he blended white country music with what was then called "Negro rhythm and blues." He seemed a threat to everything many Americans held dear. His primary threat—his primal threat—was, however, neither musical nor racial, neither sartorial nor tonsorial. It was sexual. When he began pounding his guitar and grinding his hips, alarmed parents everywhere saw him as the Pied Piper of pubescent temptation.

"Elvis was assailed all through his first big year by a chorus of newspaper writers, pulpit preachers, high-school teachers, police officials and local politicians," writes Albert Goldman in his 1981 biography *Elvis*. "Some of his assailants demanded that action be taken either to curb Elvis's performances or to run him out of town." When Elvis made his now-legendary appearance on *The Ed Sullivan Show*, cameramen were instructed not to let their lenses drift below his waist, lest a single shot of his pulsating pelvis drive an entire generation of American youth into immediate and permanent sexual depravity.

As it turned out, Elvis—the churchgoing mama's boy—was but a mild precursor to the raucous sexuality of the 1960s and '70s rock music scene. As Dave Marsh, the rock critic, wrote of that scene, ". . . everyone I know got involved in all of this—rock and roll—to get laid, centrally."

The sexual revolution in America had countless ramifications that enraged many parents and social commentators: A devaluation of chastity, fidelity and marriage—and, at times, of sex itself. A spread of sexually transmitted diseases. An upsurge in out-of-wedlock childbirths. A coarsening of the public dialogue. But no single facet of sexual liberation so enraged and so discomfited so many as the aggressive movement of gays, out of the closet and into the mainstream.

Historically, most gays in this country—like most blacks, before Martin Luther King—"knew their place": societal pressures had forced them to be discreet about their sexual orientation, and most Americans had been discreet about how appalled they were by that orientation and all that it implied.

But when blacks, Latinos, women and college students began demanding their rights—when others began agitating for the rights of whales, trees and obscure worms with unpronounceable names— gays rightly figured that they, too, were entitled to the full protection of the law. Like comedian Rodney Dangerfield, they wanted respect; like Rosa Parks, they wanted equal opportunity. Like all Americans, they wanted to be allowed the pursuit of happiness, without fear of persecution or prosecution, without being ridiculed or marginalized. Middle America would have none of it. Gay-bashing—literally and figuratively—became a blood sport in some cities. In others, special ordinances were passed to guarantee that gay rights would *not* be guaranteed by the force of law. Until 1973, the American Psychiatric Association classified homosexuality as a mental illness. Only recently has science begun to suggest what many gays have long insisted on—that homosexuality is an orientation, dictated by biology, not a matter of individual choice or preference.

For many years now, public opinion surveys have shown that most people think there should be laws protecting the basic civil rights of gays. But people don't always tell the truth to pollsters on sensitive matters, not when there are perceived "right" and "wrong" answers. The polls notwithstanding, resentment of and violence against gays continue. In Los Angeles County—long one of the country's more gay-friendly, or at least gay-tolerant, jurisdictions—more hate crimes were committed against gays in 1993 than against blacks, Jews or any other identifiable group. It was the first time in the fifteen years that the county Commission on Human Relations has been keeping hate-crime statistics that gays were victimized more often than blacks. (The numbers of gay victims is probably even higher than reported; studies have shown that many gays don't tell authorities about attacks on them for fear of "secondary victimization": they know that many police officers are rabidly antigay, so they fear further physical abuse by them. They also fear public disclosure of their sexual orientation.)

Interestingly, the Catholic Church, while officially calling it "deplorable that homosexual persons have been and are the object of violent malice in speech or in action," seems to blame gay rights advocates for that violence. The Vatican's Congregation for the Propagation of the Doctrine of the Faith has said, "When civil legislation is introduced to protect behavior to which no one has any conceivable right, neither the church nor society at large should be surprised when other distorted notions and practices gain ground, and irrational and violent reactions increase." This is in keeping with the Vatican's new and oddly ambivalent approach to homosexuality in general. In theory at least, the Catholic Church has taken a somewhat more enlightened, or at least less condemnatory, stance toward homosexuality in recent years; it has opposed discrimination against gays and it has "profoundly deepened its understanding of the involuntariness of homosexuality, the need to understand it, the need to care for homosexual persons, the dignity of the people who were constitutively homosexual," Andrew Sullivan writes in *Virtually Normal*. But Sullivan points out that the church has simultaneously "deepened and strengthened its condemnation of any homosexual activity." Church teachings that prohibit any possible approval of homosexual sexual acts are now "far more categorical" than they were before. Thus, Sullivan says, the church has moved in "two simultaneous and opposite directions: a deeper respect for and understanding of homosexual persons and a sterner rejection of almost anything those persons might do to express themselves sexually." The individual homosexual is blameless, the Vatican says, but "if this blameless condition was acted upon, it would be always and everywhere evil." In other words, you can be gay; just don't have sex.

Why are so many people antigay? Why should anyone care whether his neighbor or colleague goes to bed with someone of the same sex rather than the opposite sex? (I remember the night a friend announced he was gay and looked at me as if he expected me to be critical or judgmental. I told him I was surprised he didn't know me well enough to realize that as long as he was happy, I didn't care if he got that way fucking guys, girls or Great Danes.)

Not surprisingly, as with all matters sexual, religious extremists have been in the forefront of the drive to suppress and stigmatize gays, to condemn homosexuality as "a hideous affliction which affected heterosexuals, which should always be resisted and which could be cured," as Sullivan puts it. According to several studies by Gregory Herek, a social psychologist at the University of California at Davis, "High religiosity or membership in a conservative or fundamentalist denomination" are the primary characteristics of "greater hostility" toward gays. One relatively benign explanation for the correlation between religiosity and homophobia is the emphasis in most religions on what Herek calls "the inherent virtue of committed marital relationships through which children are conceived and raised in the faith." Since a gay couple cannot conceive a child, gays are excluded from the primary purpose of a virtuous life.

This is certainly a key factor in the Catholic Church's position on homosexuality. Homosexual feelings are "ordered toward an intrinsic moral evil," in the words of the Vatican's Congregation for the Propagation of the Doctrine of the Faith.

Religious extremists are often among those who say that the Bible brands homosexuality a sin. To them, homosexuality is also an implicit repudiation of God's grand design for humankind—an "observable offense against God and the natural order," in the words of that apostle of enlightenment Robert Dornan, the right-wing Republican congressman from Southern California. Specifically, many of these gay-bashers regard homosexuality as a violation of the principle of "complementarity," the ordered differentiation that God intended when he created man and woman as the essential complementary parts of the universe.

But the very religious, while often among the most virulent in their condemnation of gays, are by no means alone. Regardless of their degree of religiosity, people with very conservative political views also tend to be more hostile toward gays, Herek's studies show. Many political moderates and even some liberals seem to feel threatened by homosexuality, too, though. This seems to be a special problem for men in our macho society. Studies by Herek and others consistently show that women are generally less hostile to gays than are most men. In part, this may be because women generally seem more accepting than do men about a whole range of "different" human behavior. The larger explanation, however, may be that women are more secure in their own sexual identity than men are—and that for many women, sexual identity may be a smaller and less volatile component of an overall sense of self than is the case for most men. Thus, women feel less threatened by homosexuality. Nor do they seem to worry that they may be latent homosexuals themselves. Men also seem more likely to be bullies, to feel the need to define and proclaim their own superiority ("We're Number One!") by defining and proclaiming the inferiority of others.

The maternal instinct notwithstanding, many fathers actually seem more worried than mothers that a gay will proselytize their children—that every gay male is just itching to get his horny hands on their prepubescent sons. Studies have repeatedly shown that gays are no more likely than heterosexuals to molest children, but the countervailing public perception is "a manifestation of a general cultural tendency to portray disliked minority groups (e.g., Jews, blacks) as threats to the dominant society's most vulnerable members," says Gregory Herek.

Within the nuclear family, a significant portion of the child-molestation cases these days involves adult daughters charging their fathers with incest, ten or twenty or thirty years after the (alleged) fact, often with the aid of hypnotically induced memories. I don't believe in capital punishment, but if there were any crime that might make me reconsider, it's child abuse—sexual or otherwise—by a parent. Parenthood is a sacred trust; those who abuse it in this way should probably be lobotomized and strung up by their pubic hairs, preferably over a shallow pool filled with starving piranha. But not everyone accused of molesting his child is guilty. There is considerable skepticism in scientific circles about "recovered memory"; a False Memory Syndrome group in Philadelphia has investigated many cases in which the "memory" was not "recovered" but induced, either innocently or intentionally, by therapists who range from the well-meaning to the misguided to the publicity-hungry.

"Many of us believe we have another Salem-type witch-hunt situation," says Dr. Paul McHugh, the head of the psychiatry department at the Johns Hopkins School of Medicine.

Where child molestation is concerned, there is often an unfair presumption of guilt, no matter how unlikely the accusation or the accuser. Look at how much attention was paid a couple of years ago to a thirty-four-year-old Philadelphia man's accusations that Cardinal Joseph Bernardin of Chicago, one of the most respected figures in the Catholic Church, had molested him seventeen years earlier. The case seemed wobbly from the outset, and the man ultimately recanted, but not before Cardinal Bernardin had been subjected to an excruciating public humiliation.

The McMartin Pre-School molestation case, which ate up $15 million in taxpayers' money and riveted media and public attention in Southern California for almost the entire decade of the eighties, was a tragic example of how moralists who see sexual perversion behind every bush can callously ruin human lives. I hate to keep entering what should be unnecessary disclaimers, but I don't want my position to be misunderstood: People who molest children are the lowest scum on earth. They deserve the most severe penalties the law allows. But, again, not everyone accused of child molestation is guilty. In the McMartin case, frantic parents, an overeager social worker, an overzealous prosecutorial force and a gullible and complicitous news media combined to make life a living hell for innocent little children and the entire staff of the McMartin school. In the end—after two trials based on the most lurid, heinous charges imaginable—not one person was convicted. But the frenzy ignited by McMartin triggered similar child-molestation scares across the country.

The McMartin and Bernardin cases would not be possible were it not for the pleasure police and their efforts to stigmatize sex—and especially gay sex.

I've often thought that many people are made uncomfortable by gays simply because homosexuality is different, something they haven't personally experienced and don't—can't—understand. Proximity conquers prejudice; firsthand experience prevails over ignorance. For gays, this is a catch-22 situation: because so many people are hostile toward gays, most gays have remained in the closet; but because they're in the closet, their heterosexual relatives, friends, neighbors and colleagues don't have the opportunity to know that they're homosexuals and to see firsthand that, for the most part, they're no different from heterosexuals. Far more gays have "come out" in recent years, but they have often been disproportionately—inevitably, given the circumstances—the more strident or flamboyant gays, and in many quarters, this has exacerbated the prevailing homophobia. Some of our more prominent—and more odious—gay-bashers (Patrick Buchanan among them) have even suggested that AIDS is simply divine retribution for sinful behavior and that gays are now paying with their lives for their promiscuous lifestyle.

In its early stages in particular, the AIDS epidemic drove painfully home to most gays just how hostile—or how murderously indifferent—heterosexual America was to them. The Reagan administration made no line recommendations for AIDS research funding until the epidemic was three years old. President Reagan didn't make his first speech entirely devoted to AIDS until the epidemic

was six years old—by which time 36,058 Americans had been diagnosed with the disease and 20,849 had died from it. With very few
exceptions, the presumably far more liberal news media didn't do
appreciably better. The AIDS epidemic was two years old before the
first AIDS story appeared on the front page of the *New York Times*.

"It was a goddamn disgrace . . . outrageous" that most
newspapers "essentially ignored" the AIDS story in the early years,
Donald Drake, the medical writer for the *Philadelphia Inquirer* told
me several years later. "There is a homophobia on the part of the
American press. . . . If it [AIDS] had involved any other group of
people, they [the media] would have been all over it."

Drake did do some early AIDS stories himself, and his editors
published them, prominently. But Jerry Bishop, medical writer for
the *Wall Street Journal,* found his early AIDS stories cut, buried or
rejected outright by editors unable or unwilling to wrap such disqui-
eting information around the *Journal*'s sacrosanct stock market tables.

"As long as it seemed to be a disease affecting only homosexual males, neither the editors nor the readers felt like it was a threat
. . . to the general population . . . which made it of not much
concern," Bishop told me.

Ironically, it took a homosexual male—Rock Hudson—to dramatically change that.

More than twelve thousand people were suffering from AIDS
and more than six thousand had died of the disease before Hudson
was diagnosed with it, but just five days before that diagnosis, Marlene Cimons, a reporter in the Washington bureau of the *Los Angeles Times,* says one of her editors in Washington questioned her use
of the word "epidemic" in a story on AIDS funding.

"Couldn't we call it an 'outbreak'?" he asked. "I don't know
anyone who has this disease, do you?"

When Hudson died, in October 1985, *USA Today* published
an editorial that said, "With Hudson's death, many of us are realizing that AIDS is not a 'gay plague' but everybody's problem."

Although Hudson was gay himself, that was not widely known
outside Hollywood, and his long film career, especially his roles as

Doris Day's male love interest, had made him both familiar to millions and prototypically (if ultimately, fraudulently) heterosexual.

"Prior to Rock Hudson's death . . . U.S. policy-makers and the public could have concluded from mass media coverage [in general] that AIDS was perversely fascinating but, overall, not very important as a national issue," say James Dearing and Everett Rogers of the Annenberg School for Communication at the University of Southern California in their study "The Agenda-Setting Process for the Issue of AIDS." But after Hudson's death—beginning, really, with his diagnosis for AIDS—AIDS was suddenly front-page news, cover story news, network news. Everywhere. AIDS stories in the major print media more than tripled in the first six months after the announcement of Hudson's diagnosis. Government funding for AIDS research skyrocketed accordingly. Gradually, however, long-overdue public awareness became greatly overstated public anxiety. Words like "terror," "nightmare" and "fear" began showing up in the nation's news media as the "gay plague" became the heterosexual panic. Everyone was said to be "at risk."

Time magazine published a cover story on "How heterosexuals are coping with a disease that can make sex deadly." Oprah Winfrey warned viewers, "AIDS has both sexes running scared. Research studies now project that one in five . . . heterosexuals could be dead of AIDS in the next three years." HBO broadcast a special program, *Talking Sex: Making Love in the '90s,* in which assorted young men and women took turns rhapsodizing about how their fear of AIDS had prompted them to abandon such mundane pursuits as intercourse and oral sex, in favor of the unparalleled pleasures of "outercourse," talking dirty on the telephone, touching each other's earlobes and rubbing each other's genitals with—I kid you not—vegetable scrubbers.

Sex—if any of this can be called sex—is "easier and more fun now," one woman insisted.

Trilled another: "I love all of the foreplay. The actual penetration is—pfft! thanks a lot."

Apart from the obvious personal question—what kind of sex life (and what kind of lovers) did these folks have *before* AIDS if they now prefer vegetable scrubbers to vaginal sex?—there is a larger public policy question involved here: how in hell did average, heterosexual, suburban Joe and Jane America come to be terrified of a disease that is still overwhelmingly confined to gays, bisexuals, intravenous drug users and those who have sex with gays, bisexuals and intravenous drug users?

AIDS has wreaked horrible devastation in the last dozen-plus years. It is a shattering global tragedy that warrants human compassion, scientific research, massive government action and public and private funding. The delayed response of the government, the media and society at large was shameful and unforgivable. But statistics from the Centers for Disease Control make it clear that the news media and assorted, far-from-disinterested parties have greatly overstated the AIDS threat in the general heterosexual community.

Although the number and percentage of heterosexual AIDS deaths have increased considerably in recent years—especially among women—the Centers for Disease Control says that only 6 percent of all adult and adolescent AIDS cases have involved heterosexual contact, and two-thirds of those involved people who had sex with someone who already had (or was in a known risk group for) HIV infection. Only 2.2 percent of AIDS cases have involved heterosexuals with no other known risk factor.

"We are convinced that there is not and very unlikely ever will be a heterosexual AIDS epidemic in this country," say the authors of *Sex in America.*

Why should the United States be different from Africa, where there *is* a heterosexual AIDS epidemic? Several reasons: The widespread use in Africa of unsterilized needles. The lack of careful screening of the African blood supply. The high level in Africa of other sexually transmitted diseases and the concomitant presence of many open genital sores and ulcers that facilitate the transmission of AIDS. The chronically weakened immune system of many Africans because of poverty, hunger, poor hygiene and inadequate medical care. The polygamy and promiscuity prevalent in many areas of Africa, occasioned in part by tradition and in part by the transition from subsistence farming in villages to a cash economy in cities, a shift that suddenly made it possible for many men to afford several

sexual partners. There are also primitive tribal practices still observed in some parts of Africa that render heterosexuals more vulnerable to AIDS than they would be elsewhere. But the United States
is not Africa, and AIDS is not presently a serious threat to the non-
promiscuous, non-intravenous-drug-using, North American heterosexual who doesn't patronize prostitutes or take other foolish risks.
AIDS is deadly, but as diseases go, it's relatively hard for otherwise
healthy people to acquire through ordinary vaginal intercourse.
Studies estimate that the transmission rate is less than 1 percent
during each sex act between an infected man and an uninfected
woman.

That doesn't make AIDS any less worthy of our dollars, our
efforts, our sympathy and our prayers. It should go without saying
that gay lives are every bit as important as heterosexual lives. But
let's fight the war we have, not the one we don't.

Should all Americans—homosexual and heterosexual alike—
take AIDS into consideration when they contemplate sex with someone other than a longtime, monogamous partner? Absolutely.
Young people in particular should be taught about the dangers of
AIDS and how to avoid those dangers. The young are prone to both
carelessness and cocky misperceptions about their own immortality.
(One study showed that 58 percent of young girls still refuse to use
contraception during their first act of sexual intercourse.) But prudence is the watchword—prudence, not panic. America has panicked. A 1992 Gallup poll showed that Americans thought AIDS the
single greatest health threat to the country; AIDS was actually the
eleventh ranked killer that year, claiming only a tiny fraction of the
lives snuffed out by the perennial top killers, heart disease and cancer, and also far behind stroke, chronic diseases of the liver and
lungs, pneumonia and diabetes, among other ailments.

So why the panic?

The answers lie in the independent efforts and contradictory
philosophies of a most unlikely alliance. On the one hand, you have
gay leaders, other AIDS activists and their supporters. Having seen
so many young, gay men die of AIDS—while an uncaring, heterosexual America looked on, smugly certain that it could only happen
to "them"—the activists learned the hard way that the only way to

get government funding, scientific research and media attention was to make AIDS seem a serious threat to heterosexuals as well. If AIDS could be democratized—if the power structure could be made to view AIDS as "our" disease, not just "their" disease—a huge outpouring of financial, emotional and medical support would be forthcoming. As we have seen, that's exactly what happened after Rock Hudson's death. Beginning in about 1985, the face of AIDS, as depicted in both the news media and official government public health messages, became heterosexual, white, attractive and middle-class—the girl or boy next door (if you happened to live in the right neighborhood). The implicit message was not only racist, not only cruel and unfair to gays *("You* don't matter"), but counterproductive as well. The more money spent on a broad-based education campaign, the less money is available for education of those most likely to get the disease.

The leaders of the AIDS-is-gonna-kill-us-all brigade were aided and abetted in their efforts by the all-purpose alarmists increasingly among us, people who—whether because of genetics, parental influence or some exotic blend of masochism and *Schadenfreude*—see doom everywhere they look. There is, I am convinced, a certain self-loathing buried deeply (or perhaps not so deeply) in the very souls of these individuals. They fear life because, at some level—conscious? subconscious?—they don't think they're worthy of the joys life has to offer.

"We *should* dislike much about ourselves," Richard John Neuhaus, the neoconservative theologian, told *Newsweek* magazine in 1995, "because there is much about ourselves that is not only profoundly dislikable but odious." Well, shit, Richard, speak for yourself. God knows, I'm not perfect. Far—disconcertingly far, embarrassingly far—from it. Like everyone I know, I have many flaws, large and small—characteristics I would love to change in an effort to make myself a better person. But odious? All of us? I sure hope not.

More important—but with an agenda diametrically opposed to that of the AIDS activists—are the nation's homophobes, Christian Fundamentalists, right-wing conservatives and puritans of assorted stripes, all of whom seized on AIDS as an opportunity to hammer anew at their longtime theme of sex-as-sin. Only this time, these members of the moral militia had an unprecedentedly potent weapon in their arsenal: death itself. In effect, "Abstain or die" became their battle cry.

These are the same kind of people who first tried to convince us to give up sex to avoid the inevitable brain damage caused by syphilis. When penicillin largely removed that threat, they had to resort to other arguments until herpes struck. That, too, was seen as an incurable disease, a proper punishment for promiscuity—and another reason to abandon sex. As historian Martin Duberman says, "The powers that be have always used epidemics in order to reinforce moral lessons. And epidemics, because they involve so much terror, are very good enforcers of the code."

Scaring people is generally more effective than simply preaching to them. That's why cardiologists often warn patients that sexual excitement could lead to a heart attack. But in 1993 Dr. James Muller, a Harvard Medical School researcher, studied 1,172 men and women recovering from heart attacks and found that while only 1 percent of the heart attacks were triggered by sex, 10 percent were triggered by the patient's simply waking up in the morning. I'm surprised that the nation's bedroom monitors didn't immediately call for a constitutional amendment to ban sleep. Or alarm clocks.

The hypocrisy and moral bankruptcy of the armies of abstention are demonstrated anew virtually every time the subject of condoms comes up. The United States has the highest teen pregnancy rate of any developed nation, not necessarily because our teens may be more active sexually, but because birth control is more available in many other countries. Yes, absention is, without question, the single best way to avoid pregnancy, AIDS and other sexually transmitted diseases. But human nature being what it is, many people choose not to abstain. The second best way to avoid the potentially negative consequences of sex is to use a condom. Responsible gay activists know this and promote it. But the moralists who rail about skyrocketing teen pregnancy rates and the threat of AIDS to heterosexuals continue to fight condoms, in the air, on land and sea. They oppose condom ads on television. They don't want condoms shown in movies. They don't want government public service messages on condoms broadcast anywhere, at any time. They don't want condoms given out—or talked about—in schools, even though the American Academy of Pediatrics, which represents more than forty thousand doctors nationwide, recommended in 1995 that condoms be distributed as part of high school sex education programs.

"We favor abstinence," says the academy's Dr. Victor Strasburger, "but we know kids may not abstain till they're married or thirty-five or whatever."

The pleasure police were quick to respond to the academy's eminently reasonable stance.

Beverly LaHaye of Concerned Women for America said she was "outraged" by the pediatricians' proposal.

"Sending a mixed message to teens—promoting condoms while giving lip service to abstinence—is destructive to young people's lives and undermines parents," she said.

Outrage was also immediate when the United States Health and Human Services Department unveiled several public service announcements advocating condom use. Gary Bauer, a White House domestic policy aide during the Reagan administration and now president of the Family Research Council, accused the Clinton administration of pushing a "political agenda." Instead of condom ads, Bauer said, the federal government should "be creative in telling Americans that abstinence outside of marriage is the best way to prevent transmission." The Catholic Church was even more strident in its reaction. Monsignor Robert Lynch, general secretary of the National Conference of Catholic Bishops and the United States Catholic Conference, said the condom ads would promote "a dangerous myth . . . promote promiscuity and a false sense of security."

Translation: "Just when we thought we'd found a way to scare people into abstaining from sex, here comes the federal government, trying to let people screw anew."

6
---

*D*onald Symons, an anthropologist at the University of California at Santa Barbara, has an intriguing theory to explain the promiscuity of gay males. Symons says that gay males are promiscuous because they're male, not because they're gay. He notes that male homosexuals not only have considerably more sex partners than do male (or female) heterosexuals but also tend to have considerably more sex partners than do female homosexuals. Gay men may well want to establish intimate, monogamous, long-term relationships, Symons says, but this desire is undermined to some extent by both "the male desire for sexual variety [and] the unprecedented opportunity to satisfy this desire in the world of men." (Such was the case before AIDS anyway, and in some gay quarters it is still—or again—the case.)

"I am suggesting," Symons says, "that heterosexual men would be as likely as homosexual men to have sex most often with strangers, to participate in anonymous orgies in public baths and to stop off in public rest rooms for five minutes of fellatio on the way home from work if women were interested in these activities."

Symons probably overstates his case somewhat, but studies— not to mention personal experience and common sense—strongly confirm his view that men, heterosexual *and* homosexual, are generally more eager for more sex, more often, with a greater variety of partners than are most women. Prostitutes, call girls and escort services exist almost exclusively because of this imbalance. (Quick: Name the male equivalent of Heidi Fleiss or the Mayflower Madam.) Operators of computer bulletin boards say that 98.9 percent of the consumers of on-line pornography are men. The University of Chicago *Sex in America* study found that the median number of sex partners for a man in his lifetime is eleven, for a woman three. The same survey found that while 54 percent of men thought about sex at least once a day, only 19 percent of women did so.

It is not fashionable these days to speak in these terms. Men and women are now presumed to be not only equal (which they clearly are) but *The Same,* in all matters, sex included (which they demonstrably are not). But in the words of Charles Darwin, "No one disputes that the bull differs in disposition from the cow, the wild boar from the sow, the stallion from the mare," so why not the man from the woman? As Matt Ridley points out in *The Red Queen,* "evolutionary history" shows that it isn't just socially induced machismo that makes men promiscuous. Man descended from apes, and among apes, Ridley says, there were always "great rewards" for males who aggressively sought mating opportunities. Early in human history, men who capitalized on sexual opportunities obviously left more descendants than those who did not; since we are then, by definition, "descended from prolific ancestors," as Ridley puts it, "it is a fair bet that modern men possess a streak of sexual opportunism. . . . This is not to say that men are irredeemably promiscuous or that every man is a potential rapist, it is just that men are more likely to be tempted by an opportunity for casual sex than [are] women."

Many men enjoy sex that is purely physical, even impersonal—recreational sex, "sport fucking." Evolutionary, social and familial pressures have led to a different sexual mind-set for most women.

"Having sex with a stranger not only encumbered a Pleistocene woman with a possible pregnancy before she had won the man's commitment to help rear the child," Ridley says, "but it also exposed her to probable revenge from her husband if she had one and to possible spinsterhood if she did not. These enormous risks were offset by no great reward," so most women chose not to have casual sex; the descendants of these women, Ridley theorizes, are likely to have inherited this disinclination toward casual sex.

This seems a bit glib to me, but whether for reasons of evolutionary psychobiology or some more contemporary emotional development—or a complex interweaving of the two—most women do seem to prefer sex that involves an intense emotional connection over sex that is simply a random romp in the hay with a relative stranger, however skillful that stranger may be. Men and women *are* different in many ways, and it's foolish to argue that those differences are purely superficial.

Yes, men have long used the differences, real and imagined, between men and women to discriminate against women, to deprive them of the right to vote, to work, to become bosses, doctors, lawyers, baseball players and combat soldiers, even to deny that they have the capacity to reason. Racists in America have used similar arguments to brand African Americans as genetically inferior and to deny them their rightful opportunity in the workplace, in academe and virtually everywhere else. What Barbara Ehrenreich has written—"Few areas of science are as littered with intellectual rubbish as the study of innate mental differences between the sexes"—could also be applied to most claims of innate differences among the races. Just as many reputable studies have shown that there are far more similarities than differences between blacks and whites, so Carol Tavris, a social psychologist and the author of *The Mismeasure of Woman: Why Women Are Not the Better Sex, the Inferior Sex, or the Opposite Sex,* has argued eloquently that there are more similarities than differences between men and women. Anne Fausto-Sterling, a biologist, an expert in gender studies and the author of *Myths of Gender: Biological Theories About Men and Women,* has made similar arguments. But the exaggeration or outright invention of some gender differences doesn't mean there are no legitimate gender differences (just as there are *some* differences between races—skin color, for example).

When compared to women, men are—on average—deficient in writing skills and reading comprehension; on average, women score very poorly in mathematics and science when compared to men. Although many studies have been unable to determine whether such differences are truly genetic or merely the product of socialization and other environmental factors, an increasing number of studies do show differences that can only be genetic—organic—in origin. This is where the analogy between race and gender begins to break down. After all, there *are* clear, observable, incontrovertible differences between men and women, beginning with childbearing and all the physiological and psychological characteristics involved therein. No perceived difference between the races, not even skin color, is as momentous. It would be difficult to overstate the potential implications of this one difference. Many recent studies have also shown several differences between the brains of men and women, starting with the simple fact that women's brains are, on average, smaller than men's but that women's brains contain an average of about 11 percent more brain cells. This strongly suggests that women's brains work more efficiently. Male and female brains function differently even when performing the same tasks, and as the *Los Angeles Times* pointed out in 1995, "It has become increasingly clear that men and women do not think alike."

A 1995 article in the journal *Science,* based on six studies conducted over the past thirty-two years, reported that while the average man and the average woman have about the same level of intelligence, there are a disproportionately large number of men at both ends of the intelligence spectrum. Men account for seven of every eight people in the top 1 percent on IQ tests and about the same percentage in the bottom 1 percent. Another study published in *Science* reported on the use of magnetic resonance imaging to examine the metabolic activity of the brains of young men and women at rest. Men showed more activity in the portion of the brain that governs action, whereas women showed more activity in the portion of the brain that governs symbolic action; the difference between the two is the difference between hitting someone and merely glaring angrily at someone.

Several studies have shown that the corpus callosum, the large band of nerve fibers through which information passes between the left and right sides of the brain, is larger in women, which may enable the two halves of a woman's brain to function together more effectively. Thus, behavioral scientists trying to determine the organic basis for reading disorders found that when given a series of word-rhyming tasks, women use both sides of their brains, whereas men use only a small portion of the left side of their brains. Dr. Sally Shaywitz at the Yale University School of Medicine, a principal author of the study, took pains to point out that since the men and women in her study sounded out words equally well, her findings didn't mean that either method of doing so was superior. The female brain is not necessarily better than the male brain, or vice versa. The study, she told the *New York Times,* simply demonstrated that "the brain has a lot of different ways to get to the same result." In other words, different doesn't necessarily mean better or worse or unequal. Different means different—and with the sexes, different starts very early.

Although the media made much of a 1995 study suggesting that it's too little testosterone, rather than too much, that makes men aggressive, the study involved only fifty-four men, hardly enough for any definitive judgments. Nor did the study employ a conventional control group provided with dummy medication instead of the real testosterone administered to the test subjects. Earlier studies have suggested that it is testosterone that, in many ways, makes a man a man, and even if the results of the new study are ultimately confirmed, it won't change the basic fact that the effects of testosterone, whether too much or too little, mark a clear difference between men and women.

The very presence of testosterone makes a baby boy "different from a baby girl from its first day on the planet," writes Matt Ridley. "Boys are instantly obsessed with dismantling, assembling, destroying, possessing, and coveting things. Girls are fascinated by people and treat their toys as surrogate people. Hence, to suit their mentalities, we have invented toys that suit each sex. We give boys tractors and girls dolls. We are reinforcing the stereotypical obsessions that they already have, but we are not creating them."

The boy-girl distinctions do not apply in every case, but they are valid as a general rule, and most parents can confirm them from firsthand observation. My son, Lucas, and his friend Sarah were

born exactly a month apart and they both live in progressive households, with parents whose personal philosophies, daily behavior and
domestic roles are determinedly nonsexist. But Lucas does everything aggressively, and small metal cars were the first toys that attracted him, after which he graduated to swordplay, Batman and
baseball; Sarah loves dolls and playing dress-up, wants to wear
dresses rather than pants, invites only girls to her birthday parties
and, if there's a piñata at other kids' birthday parties, she is so much
"the pacifist" (as her mother puts it) that she refuses to hit it.

Some of the seeming distinctions between boys and girls are
actually just the manifestations of developmental stages that all children go through—often at different rates—and they fade with time,
as boys and girls become socialized and more similar to each other.
Given the still-rampant sexism in our society, they also, however,
become more *different* through the process of socialization. But sexism and socialization notwithstanding, boys and girls *are* inherently
different in some ways; so why are we surprised—why do we
deny—that little boys grow up to be men who are in many ways
very different from the women who were once their little-girl play-
mates?

There are some exceptions, of course. Sexually and in other
ways as well, some men have characteristics generally thought to be
predominantly female, and some women have characteristics generally thought to be predominantly male. (I'm *not* talking about gay
men and women.) In extreme cases, there is a clinical name for this,
congenital adrenal hyperplasia (CAH): one pregnancy in ten thousand results in the accidental exposure of the female fetus to the
male hormone androgen; the resultant babies are born female, but
tests show that they often have male attitudes and interests—among
them playing with boys' toys.

But one need not look to genetic defects to see such gender
reversals. To reverse the most obvious clichés: Some women are very
aggressive or good at tuning automobile engines; some men are sensitive and good at making dinner. Some men have very low sex
drives and/or very little inclination to stray; some women have very
strong sex drives and a considerable inclination to stray. I've always
had a number of characteristics generally (if stereotypically) thought

to be "feminine." In every intimate relationship I've had with a woman, I've been the more romantic and sentimental, the one more likely to make a big deal of birthdays and anniversaries, to arrange our social life and to be more attentive to household details. Although my wife, Lucy, is a devoted and loving mother, I am also the one who almost invariably takes Lucas to the doctor, dentist and barber, makes his breakfast and lunch and plays with him for an hour or so before dinner most weekday evenings (in part because of the pressures and hours of Lucy's job). Throughout my life, I've had more close female than male friends, and just as I wasn't interested in playing with trucks and tractors as a boy, so I've never been interested in cars, hunting, fishing, home repair projects or a night out with the boys (apart from Lucas) as an adult. Although I have a strong sex drive—I begin to get irritable after three or four days of "celibacy"—I have also been a practitioner of serial monogamy for most of my mature adult life. I haven't generally found impersonal sex or promiscuity terribly appealing (although there was one six-month period of delayed adolescence when I was thirty-one, between wives and so randy that—as a bemused friend said at the time—"You'd stick your dick in a woodpile and hope a snake would bite it"). Like most women, I prefer sex with an emotional connection.

In this modern, liberated age, it's entirely possible that there are far more women than I realize who enjoy purely recreational sex. I've actually known a few myself over the years. I've also been fortunate enough to know two or three women who were endowed with overpowering sex drives, including one—call her Sharon—who thought I was neglecting her if we didn't make love six or eight times a day. Needless to say, Sharon and I got along quite nicely. (I thought I was in love with her.) But even I was a bit taken aback once when she insisted on making love standing up in the ladies' room of a fancy Paris restaurant after a long, late lunch because she didn't think we could get back to our hotel room in time to make love before the Jewish High Holy Day of Yom Kippur began at sundown and made sex, among other things, verboten. As I've already said, I'm not a religious Jew and I didn't even know about the Yom Kippur ban on sex. But we'd already made love two or three times before coming to lunch, so when Sharon mentioned the Yom Kippur prohibition to me, I did not think I would leave the restaurant feeling sexually deprived if we did not fuck to beat the ban. But I am an accommodating sort, so off to the ladies' loo we strolled.

I think Sharon was most unusual in her appetite—and I don't mean just because she was a vegetarian. At the other end of the female sexual spectrum are the feminist extremists who argue that virtually all sex (at least all heterosexual sex) is evil. Their reasoning is different from that of the sex-hating religious extremists, of course; these feminists don't consider sex sinful, merely exploitive—an intimate extension of male domination.

The purest—or, rather, most impure—manifestation of male-dominated exploitive sex is prostitution. Prostitutes are often exploited twice: by the customers who pay them and by the pimps who may brutalize them, manipulate them into drug addiction (and dependency) and force them to surrender any shred of self-respect. Given my own feelings about love and sex, romance and sex, intimacy and sex, personal connection and sex, I've never been able to understand why anyone would go to a prostitute. Turning sex into a commercial transaction with a stranger is even more incomprehensible to me than voting Republican, eating at McDonald's or rooting for the Yankees. But having said all that, I still think that feminists and bluenoses alike should get out of the bedroom—even if that bedroom is in a cheap motel. Prostitution should be legal—legal and clean. In an ideal world, prostitution would not be necessary. All women who want to work would make a decent wage at jobs that were uplifting, not demeaning, and all men *and* women would have lifetime partners whose sexual appetites and inclinations perfectly matched their own. But in case you haven't noticed, we do not live in an ideal world. I don't see utopia on the street where I live. Nor do I see it on the streets where the streetwalkers walk. So if some men want to patronize prostitutes and some women want to rent their bodies to such men, I say *laissez le bons temps roulez*. But *roulez* safely. If prostitution is a business, let's treat it like one. Prostitutes should be monitored, taxed and subjected to regular health checks. That would go a long way toward eliminating the truly sinful behavior involved in prostitution—the violence, drugs, disease, exploitation and organized crime ties that so often accompany it.

I think most feminists who object to prostitution do so on wholly legitimate grounds—because it's exploitive and because only the women are punished, by social stigma and by the law. The men—the johns—get off scot-free. But I don't think you rectify that blatant inequity by punishing both the men *and* the women. I think you rectify it by punishing neither, and I am convinced that some radical feminists and bluenoses don't want that because what really bothers them most about prostitution is the sex itself.

Rush Limbaugh, the portly, self-important talk show host, calls feminists "femi-Nazis." Limbaugh is a simpleminded Neanderthal whose ugly, quasi-Fascist views have helped poison the political well in America, and as a feminist myself—a man who supported women's rights in word and deed before he ever heard of Betty Friedan—I bitterly resent his typically vicious and wantonly inaccurate characterization of all feminists. The vast majority of feminists have fought against insuperable odds and centuries of deeply entrenched male tradition and domination to begin a drive for long-overdue equality. Men like Limbaugh have resisted and derided them every agonizing step of the way, and I have only admiration for the women and nothing but contempt for Limbaugh and his sexist colleagues. But I do think that, as in all legitimate protest movements, there is a small, albeit very vocal and very visible fringe among the feminists who take absurdly extremist positions.

I'm speaking of the Andrea Dworkins of the world, the women who argue that sex with a man is immoral and that virtually any woman who has sex with a man is a traitor to the feminist cause. Such women use the term "pro-sex feminist" as "an epithet against women like me," Nadine Strossen, the president of the American Civil Liberties Union, complained during a roundtable discussion published in *Esquire* magazine in 1995. These radical feminists insist that a woman can't be "a true feminist," Strossen said, "if you don't attack men . . . if you also say 'Gee, men are decent people, too' . . . if you actually see something wonderful about men and about sex."

Strossen is not alone in her rejection of this narrow definition of feminism. Many other mainstream and progressive feminists have also criticized some of the positions taken by their extremist sisters. But it's the extremists—a tiny albeit very vocal minority—who get the most media attention, and in some of their proclamations, they have had surprising support—as in their insistence not only that Lorena Bobbitt was justified in cutting off her husband's penis but that she is a feminist hero whose act was the feminist equivalent of the Boston Tea Party, in the words of Camille Paglia.

Rape is a heinous crime, ignored or minimized for far too long in a criminal justice system run by and for men. Had Lorena Bobbitt wielded her knife in self-defense to prevent a rape—or in the heat of the moment, while the actual rape was being attempted or perpetrated, or even in the immediate aftermath of rape—I would wholeheartedly support what she did. In such a situation, I think that she—or any woman—would be justified in cutting off her attacker's cock *and* his balls—and cutting out his heart as well. But Lorena Bobbitt cut her husband's penis off as he lay sleeping in their marital bed. Then she claimed temporary insanity.

Bullshit.

Unfortunately, the gleeful reaction of some feminists to Bobbitt's impromptu surgery seemed of a piece with Marilyn French's proclamation in *The Women's Room,* that "All men are rapists, and that's all they are." (Susan McClary, a musicologist at the University of Minnesota, has managed to detect in the first movement of Beethoven's Ninth Symphony "the throttling, murderous rage of a rapist incapable of attaining release.") Or as Catharine MacKinnon writes on the first page of her book *Only Words,* "You grow up with your father holding you down and covering your mouth so another man can make a horrible searing pain between your legs. . . . When you are older, your husband ties you to the bed and drops hot wax on your nipples and brings in other men to watch and makes you smile through it."

Whew! No wonder MacKinnon is living with Jeffrey Masson. They truly deserve each other. But the language of the most radical feminists makes it easy for some men to dismiss all feminists as joyless, shrewish "sex-haters" and, worse, "man-haters"—or lesbians. The reasons advanced for this hatred—advanced by some women as well as men—are truly repugnant.

"There are a lot of homely women in women's studies," says Christina Hoff Sommers, the self-styled "feminist" and the author of *Who Stole Feminism.* "Preaching these anti-male, anti-sex sermons is a way for them to compensate for various heartaches—they're just mad at the beautiful girls."

That may be worse than Rush Limbaugh's "Feminism was established so that . . . ugly broads could have easier access to the mainstream."

In other words, according to this "reasoning," feminists are angry because they're ugly; they hate men because men reject them in favor of their more beautiful sisters (whom they also hate, not only because they're beautiful but because they consort [i.e., co-habit] with the enemy).

It's a nice, neat theory. I just don't happen to buy it. It's the theory that's ugly, not the women. Sure, there are some women who hate men, just as there are some men who hate women. There are also, it's clear, some feminists who are unattractive or lesbian (or both), just as there are some male chauvinists who are unattractive or gay (or both). But one look at Gloria Steinem should have demolished thirty years ago the canard that all feminists are ugly dykes—not that any fair-minded person, male or female, could ever have seriously considered that repellent, *ad hominem* argument anyway. To do so cheapens the discourse and vitiates legitimate objections to the extreme feminist positions on men and sex.

Perhaps I'm naive but I think most women who hate men—and I don't think there are really that many of them—do so because men have mistreated them and other women they know. Men have not raped them necessarily—not in a literal, physical sense anyway—but they have denigrated them, discriminated against them, stripped them of their self-respect, treated them as sex objects, violated their individual dignity and sense of self. No, all men are *not* rapists. Most men—the vast, overwhelming majority of men—are not rapists. But even in the theoretically enlightened 1990s, most men are not sensitive, thoughtful or egalitarian either, certainly not

where women are concerned. Over the years, single women in particular have told me story after story about the callous, solipsistic,
exploitive manner in which various men have treated them. I did not
think then and do not think now that they were lying or exaggerating or imagining things. I think women have every right to be critical
and suspicious of men. But it's one thing to be critical and suspicious; it's another thing entirely to assume that all men are rapists,
that men (and sex) are evil, that rape is "nothing more or less than a
conscious process by which *all men* keep *all women* in a state of
fear" (Susan Brownmiller) and that "the hurting of women is . . .
basic to the sexual pleasure of men" (Andrea Dworkin). Some men
are rapists. Many more brutalize and subjugate women in thousands
of subtle (and not-so-subtle) ways. But extrapolating from the appalling pathology of some men to stigmatize the entire gender is not
only faulty reasoning, it's destructive behavior. Just as it's wrong to
treat all young, African American males as muggers or gangbangers
just because some are, so it is wrong to treat all men as rapists and
brutalizers just because some are. Unfortunately, the gender ter-
rorists do precisely that, and in the process, they seek to deny, and
to destroy, the genuine pleasure of sex and of romance as well.

As I said earlier, I'm a romantic. On the Valentine's Day before
Lucy and I were married—when she was living in New York and I in
Los Angeles—I had three separate floral arrangements, from three
different florists, sent to her office . . . followed by a solid chocolate telephone with my phone number written on the dial in white
chocolate. Much as I enjoy buying Lucy presents and taking her to
dinner on special occasions, I especially enjoy doing so just for the
hell of it, no special occasion required. But according to Dworkin,
that just makes me a flirtatious rapist. "Romance," she has written,
"is rape embellished with meaningful looks."

In her 1987 book *Intercourse,* Dworkin terms the act for
which her book is named "the pure, sterile, formal expression of
man's contempt for women." "The hatred of women is a source of
sexual pleasure for men in its own right," she says, and sexual intercourse is "the essential sexual experience of power and potency and
possession," the equivalent of "wartime invasion." During intercourse, she says, women are "occupied [territory] . . . even if there

has been no resistance, no force, even if the occupied person said yes please, yes hurry, yes more." Such women—Molly Bloom presumably included—are "more base in their collaboration than other collaborators have ever been," in Dworkin's jaundiced eyes.

What she is saying, in effect, is that women have only two choices in life: lesbianism or celibacy.

But what if a heterosexual woman—could this possibly be?—truly enjoys sex? Any such (imagined?) pleasure, Dworkin insists, comes not from warmth, intimacy, love, excitement, not even from the release/relief/rejoicing of physical orgasm. No, according to Dworkin, it comes exclusively from the woman's enjoyment of her own "inferiority . . . a tragedy beyond the power of language to convey."

Gee, you coulda fooled me.

I don't mean to set myself up as some kind of sexual superman, more powerful than a locomotive, able to satisfy all women with a single thrust. I am sure that any number of women would be willing to testify to my inadequacies, in bed and elsewhere. But I also think that one would not need the FBI, Scotland Yard or the Royal Canadian Mounted Police to find women who would say they have derived genuine pleasure from sex with men (perhaps even, on occasion, with me) and that their pleasure came not from their inferiority but from their equality—a shared intimacy. At times, I would wager, most women have felt a sense of superiority in sex; they have truly enjoyed taking and giving pleasure to a loved one who at that moment deeply, perhaps desperately, wanted and needed that precise kind of intimacy with them. Such pleasure may well have been—often is, probably should be—"beyond the power of language to convey." But it is most definitely not a "tragedy"—unless you regard love as a tragedy (in which case, you have only my uncomprehending sympathy).

To use Dworkin's term, some men—*sacré bleu* balls—"collaborate" in this sad perception. They beat up on men as vigorously as some women do. "Manhood," says John Stoltenberg in *The End of Manhood*, is "the paradigm of injustice." But the view of man—rather than money—as the root of all evil requires one to take an almost equally dim view of women. In this construct—in which men are bad and sex is worse (or is it the other way around?)—women are absolved, indeed robbed, of the need to be responsible for themselves. They are reduced to mindless toys, to the Barbie-cum-Barbarella dolls of Hugh Hefner's wet dreams. They are victims, helpless to help themselves. Helen Reddy's feminist anthem "I am woman, I am strong" somehow becomes "I am woman, I am weak." The image of the justifiably angry woman is reduced to that of the scared little girl. Women who have struggled valiantly to achieve equality are dismissed as mere passive vessels.

Oddly, the most radical feminists want to have it both ways: on the one hand, women are equal to men, the same as men, only better; on the other, they're helpless victims, easily exploited and brutalized by men. In what seems a willful distortion of the findings of Matt Ridley and other scientists, Camille Paglia, the antifeminist feminist, argues that aggression and eroticism are "deeply intertwined" in men and that "Hunt, pursuit and capture are biologically programmed into male sexuality. Generation after generation, men must be educated, refined and ethically persuaded away from their tendency toward anarchy and brutishness." As usual, Paglia exaggerates; it is her preferred polemical mode. That's why she is both the feminist that other feminists love to hate and the feminist that talk show hosts love to book. "The minute you go out with a man . . . there is a risk," Paglia says. "You have to accept the fact that part of the sizzle of sex comes from the danger of sex. You can be overpowered."

To some extent, I realize, there is an element of metaphor in this analysis. But Paglia goes so far as to urge women to "take the risk, take the challenge—if you get raped, if you get beat up in a dark alley . . . it's okay. That was part of the risk of freedom, that's part of what we've demanded as women."

I suppose there are a few women who like to be overpowered—truly, physically, not just metaphorically—but I think this is far more male fantasy than female desire. Bondage magazines and S&M clubs notwithstanding, I don't think that many men really want to overpower and enslave women either. Do some men feel that way? Sure. The National Opinion Research Center found that about 3 percent of all men found forced sex "appealing." Even assuming that some men lied and that the real number is double—or triple—that, the Dworkin/MacKinnon argument that for pornography to "work sexually" for heterosexual men, "it must show sex and subordinate a woman at the same time" seems preposterous to me. I just can't believe that most normal men want to "subordinate" a woman sexually, however much they might wish to enchant and beguile her so that she would eagerly provide sex on demand. I realize that just as some women might see intercourse as man's "invasion" of woman—to use Andrea Dworkin's construct—so some women feel that the very position assumed by the man in traditional intercourse—on top—is an intrinsic subordination of women. But I've heard many men rhapsodize about making love with the woman on top. They don't feel subordinated. They feel transported, enraptured. Amen!

Paglia's suggestion that it's "okay" for a woman to get raped—that rape is a routine risk that women assume when they seek equality—is as preposterous as it is appalling. It's an odious thought that is more likely to allow men to justify their brutish behavior than anything Rush Limbaugh says. But Paglia is onto something, however egregiously she twists it to suit her own rhetorical fancy. Some of the most extreme feminists do mislead women into thinking they don't have to be careful to avoid sexual danger in many situations. I wish women could wear whatever they want and go wherever they want and do whatever they want, without having to worry about unwanted sexual attention—or worse. But in our violent, often sick, largely male-dominated society, that, alas, is unrealistic.

The duality of the extreme feminist position—woman-as-equal, woman-as-victim—results in a dishonest and ultimately self-defeating strategy that is perhaps best evidenced in what is, at once, one of the silliest and yet one of the most significant and most symbolic events in the current gender wars: the enactment of the "Sexual Offense Policy" at Antioch University and the subsequent adoption of similar codes of sexual conduct at a number of other colleges and universities.

This now-infamous sex code requires every student to seek and obtain specific verbal approval from any would-be partner for each step he or she proposes to take along the sexual highway. "Obtaining consent is an on-going process in any sexual interaction," the nine-page Antioch policy says. "Verbal consent should be obtained with each new level of physical and/or sexual contact/conduct in any given interaction, regardless of who initiates it. Asking 'Do you want to have sex with me?' is not enough. The request for consent must be specific to each act." Thus: May I kiss you? May I take off your bra? May I touch your right breast? Your left breast? Your nipple?

What happens if, having obtained official approval to remove, say, a young woman's panties, the young man—nervous, eager, anxious, excited, impassioned, clumsy—inadvertently brushes his fingers against her pubic hair, which step he has not yet sought permission for? He could be disciplined—expelled from school—for violating school policy. Ah-ha, you say, surely any young man smart enough to be admitted to a school with Antioch's lofty academic standards would be smart enough to take this possibility into account when he made his initial requests. Instead of making each one individually, *seriatim,* he would make them in pairs, where appropriate: "May I remove your bra *and* touch your breasts?"—just in case either his enthusiasm or his awkwardness leads him to unintentionally (and improperly) do the latter while intentionally (and properly) doing the former.

Some critics of the Antioch sex code—and of the trend toward like-minded policies and practices elsewhere in society—object on the grounds that these strictures deprive both sexes of the pleasure of seduction. I'm sure there are many men and women who agree with that criticism, and I am saddened that the pleasure police are so eager to stamp out fun wherever and whenever they find it that seduction is yet another of their casualties. Speaking strictly for myself, though, I've never found the seduction "game" much fun. Maybe that's because I've never been sure exactly how to play it. Or because I've been afraid of rejection. Or because my basic approach to life is to be direct. I've never wanted to Antioch a woman—"After you've swallowed that last bite of chocolate cake, may I please put my tongue in your mouth?"—but I have wanted to be reasonably certain that what I wanted to do was what the woman wanted, not just what I might have talked her or tricked her into thinking she wanted to do or had to do.

Obviously, seduction can be mutual, a reciprocal mating dance that delights both parties as they move—tentatively but teasingly— toward the inevitable consummation. But those who most often invoke the alleged (and "endangered") charms of seduction to justify their opposition to sexual behavior codes seem to mean something very different, something quite devious and one-sided. Norman Podhoretz, for example, has noted approvingly that "overcoming a woman's resistance by 'verbal and psychological' means has in the past been universally known as seduction." That positions the man as the clever, cunning hunter-warrior stalking and outsmarting the passive, helpless, uninterested woman. But I want a partner, not a prey, in sex, and I am by no means disappointed when the woman takes the initiative. I do not feel that I have been deprived of the challenge and excitement of the hunt, the thrill of the chase, the joy of conquest. Quite the contrary. I am delighted. In my single days, I was more than delighted; I was both relieved and thrilled. It's the sex that I enjoy—the shared intimacy and the physical sensation— not the pursuit. I still get a frisson of excitement when I recall the night, more than twenty years ago, when I was sitting on the sofa in my apartment alongside a beautiful woman, uncertain what to do next until she said, "You know, Shaw, if you walked into the bedroom, chances are I'd follow."

I did. She did. We did. And we subsequently got married.

A decade later—widowed—I met another woman on a blind date. (Let's call her Elizabeth.) It was a Saturday night, and we ate and drank and talked (but no more) until five o'clock in the morning, then agreed to have dinner again Monday night. After we'd ordered food and wine on that second date, I turned to Elizabeth and asked, "So, how did you spend your Sunday?" Not very clever or original, I'll admit, but—hey—it was early, and I'd only met the woman forty-eight hours ago.

Elizabeth smiled, looked right at me and said, "Having sexual fantasies about you."

I wish I could say that I came back with something snappy like, "Waiter—check, please," but I have no recollection of my re-

sponse. I think I was left speechless, stunned that this gorgeous creature—not only pretty and sexy but smart and sensitive and sophisticated—seemed so eager to go to bed with me that she was
volunteering, before the hors d'oeuvres arrived, that she'd been
fantasizing about me within hours of meeting me. Was I being
cheated of the opportunity to seduce Elizabeth? No. I'd much rather
strike it rich by winning the lottery than by embezzling a new acquaintance. Was Elizabeth seducing *me?* I don't think so. Seduction
is subtle and indirect; I thought she was being damned (and delightfully) direct, and I can still recall the excitement and the heightened
sense of anticipation I felt throughout that meal, knowing what rapture lay ahead. (In fairness, I should point out that several years
later, in a discussion about that evening, Elizabeth said she *had* been
seducing me. "I probably didn't realize it consciously at the time,"
she said, "but that kind of directness was the kind of seduction that
was right for you.")

Although I am not, knowingly, a devotee of seduction, I am a
wildly enthusiastic fan of the pleasures of both spontaneity and anticipation in all matters and, above all, in matters sexual. Sex—the
best sex—combines both anticipation *and* spontaneity; both are destroyed by the explicit, step-by-step approach embodied in the Antioch code and its libido-shackling progeny.

Sex, as I said earlier, is at least in part about losing control; it's
about uncertainty, about not being sure just what's going to happen
next. The delicious surprise of the unexpected is a crucial element in
the excitement of sex. Should I kiss her lips first or gently nibble her
earlobe? Would she like me to touch her breast through her blouse
and bra? Or not touch her body at all until she's completely naked?
Half-naked? Many of these thoughts aren't even thoughts, just instincts. You grope your way together toward the answers, sometimes making a mistake or two along the way. But you also wind up
feeling, "Oh, I can't wait to see what she [or he] will do next" and
"Oh, God, I've never been touched like that before."

Would it be better to ask—to avoid all mistakes and all sur-
prises, tactile and tactical alike?

No.

Contrary to what the sexual incrementalists would have you

believe, women (and men) have been letting their partners know
what they want and when they want (or don't want) it for thousands of years, without the bedroom equivalent of a legal deposi-
tion. Few women may be as direct as Elizabeth was on that lovely,
long-ago Monday night, but most know how to communicate their
interest, clearly and without ambiguity.

What about the potential for misunderstanding—and missed
opportunity? What of the "No" that means "Yes" or "Maybe"?
What of the vigorously resistant "No! Please! Don't! Stop!!" that
becomes the impassioned "No, please don't stop"? In the epic poem
Don Juan, Byron says that Julia, "whispering 'I will ne'er consent,'—consented." Catharine MacKinnon sees this as a male fantasy, what she described in a *New York Times* interview as the "pos-
itive-outcome rape scenario"—a woman, "aggressed against,"
resisting, resisting, resisting until, in the face of escalating aggression, "she begins to get into it. Finally she is shown to be ecstatically
consenting and having a wonderful time. . . . Not consenting is
itself the turn-on, saying no is part of meaning yes."

But Byron wasn't talking about aggression or rape and neither
am I. Nor am I talking about the conscious withholding-with-the-
intent-of-succumbing,   the   why-don't-you-see-if-you-can-talk-me-
into-it approach that has titillated and frustrated both sexes since (I
assume) Adam and Eve. Camille Paglia contends that this " 'No' has
always been, and always will be, part of the dangerous, alluring
courtship ritual of sex and seduction." But what I'm talking about
are the normal, genuine uncertainty and anxiety, the tantalizing and
intoxicating moments, the steps, half-steps and missteps that are
often a necessary, exciting and mutually pleasurable prelude to the
sex act, especially the first sex act between two people. Again, whatever the exact words, I think most men can tell the difference between a woman who—regardless of the exact words—is saying,
"I'm not sure yet that I want to do this; let's take it slowly and see
how I feel," and a women who—regardless of the exact words—is
saying, "If you touch me once more, you creep, I'll call the cops."

The Antioch code and its various imitators presuppose that
male students cannot make that distinction and that female students
cannot convey their desires (or lack thereof) without what amounts

to a verbal contract, with renewable options every twenty or thirty seconds (or longer, depending on the individual rhythms of the party of the first part and the party of the second part).

I suppose one should be grateful that the requests and the consents at Antioch can be verbal, that no written affidavits (witnessed? notarized?) are required to conform to school policy. But the whole process is ridiculous. It would be laughable if it were not so revealing of the damage being done to intimacy and romance in the name of—what? Equality? Sensitivity? Rape prevention?

I have already said that I think rape is a heinous crime. And I don't just mean the kind of vicious, clear-cut rape that everyone wants punished: strange man breaks into woman's house, punches her in the face and forces her, at gunpoint, to have sex with him. Date rape and acquaintance rape may, in some ways, be even worse; in these situations, the woman already knows the man, trusts him to some extent, has some legitimate level of expectation about him and his behavior and their relationship. This is especially true in the case of marital rape. If the man in any of these situations takes advantage of the woman in any way, violently or not, if he forces her or induces her to have sex when she doesn't really want to, he is violating her trust, betraying their relationship. Betrayal can often be more painful than physical injury.

But it seems to me that we are fast approaching a time when we will have as many different kinds of "rape" as there are Eskimo words for snow. Seduction is not rape. To categorize it as such trivializes the suffering of real rape victims and gives unwarranted aid and comfort to those who wrongly insist that there is no such thing as date rape or acquaintance rape or marital rape.

If a woman willingly has sex with a man and then decides—the next morning, the next week, the next year—that she wishes she hadn't done it, that's regret, not rape. Some feminists say that 25 percent of all women have been raped, most of them by dates or acquaintances. Catharine MacKinnon says "nearly half are victims of rape or attempted rape at least once in our lives, many more than once," and she says that 24 percent are raped in their marriages. Official rape statistics are notoriously unreliable—in large part because the blame-the-victim stigma associated with both the crime and its juridical aftermath discourages many women from reporting rape. Still, it's difficult to escape the conclusion that the one-in-four figure seems unreasonably high. Without attempting to minimize either the prevalence or the pain of rape, I would suggest that some of this exaggeration is deliberate, much as statistics on battered women, child molestation and the threat of heterosexual AIDS have been exaggerated, in an effort to arouse public sympathy and support for just causes.

Professor Margaret Gordon of the University of Washington says that when she conducted her own rape study, she "felt pressure" to produce statistics that would make rape seem "as prevalent as possible."

"I'm a pretty strong feminist," Gordon said, "but one of the things I was fighting was that the really avid feminists were trying to get me to say that things were worse than they really are."

Gordon found that one in fifty women has been raped in her lifetime. Other seemingly reliable studies have put the numbers at, variously, one in eight, one in seventeen and one in thirty-three. If reputable scholars can arrive at such disparate results, it's clear that we don't yet have a means of accurately measuring the incidence of rape in our society. What we do know, however, is that regardless of the specific numbers, rape is prevalent and rape is wrong; people are doing an injustice to rape victims—and to the cause of rape prevention—when they inflate rape statistics, no matter how praiseworthy their objective, whether they do so intentionally or simply by the misguided inclusion of all those women who suffered regret or remorse, not rape. For generations, defense attorneys have tried to win acquittals for men accused of rape by trying the victim, not the defendant. Typically, these attorneys try to depict the accusers of their clients as either promiscuous or unstable—sluts or nuts. As many feminists have rightly pointed out, that amounts to a second rape—a public rape—of the victim. But it's equally unfair to try to depict as a rapist a man who was doing something he had every reason to believe, at the time, the woman also wanted to do.

"The pendulum has really swung," Rikki Klieman, a prosecutor-turned-defense-attorney-turned-*Court TV*-anchor, told John Leo of *U.S. News & World Report* a couple of years ago. "In many cases, young men are now the victims." Klieman made her comment after having defended a male student accused of rape by a woman who had brought her toothbrush on the night in question, planned to spend the night and was "seen having a quiet breakfast with the man the morning after," as Leo reported.

Susan Estrich related a still more alarming tale around the same time in *USA Today*. Estrich, the campaign chief for Michael Dukakis's 1988 Democratic presidential campaign, is a professor of law and political science at the University of Southern California. More important, in this context, she is an outspoken feminist, the author of *Real Rape* and a rape victim herself. Estrich's May 26, 1994, *USA Today* column told the story of a freshman at Pomona College in the Los Angeles suburb of Claremont. The freshman's version of what happened, as related by Estrich, is that she and a male acquaintance, a sophomore, got drunk together at a party and went to his room. After kissing on the bed, she took her jacket off and he then took the rest of her clothes off. Although she felt uncomfortable lying naked on his bed, she didn't complain.

"At one point," Estrich writes, "when she was lying on top of him, she remembers that he pushed her head down to give him oral sex, which she [says] she did not feel comfortable refusing to do." So she did it. Then he got on top of her and they kissed some more and he said, "I should get a condom."

She shook her head no and said "uh-uh," which he apparently took to mean that she either didn't need or didn't want protection. They then had intercourse.

Two and a half years later, the woman accused the man of raping her, and the school scheduled a disciplinary hearing. Like Antioch, Pomona College has a campus code providing that "consent requires a clear, explicit agreement to engage in a specific [sexual] activity." The woman student claims she gave no such consent.

But the woman concedes that no force was used and that she never said no, clearly and explicitly. The absence of "no" doesn't necessarily mean "yes" any more than the absence of force necessarily means love. But surely it's standing reason on its head to suggest that a man should be punished for inferring consent when a woman comes to his room, lies on his bed, lets him undress her and gives him a blow job.

Doesn't the woman bear some responsibility? This was a gradual process, not a violent street-corner rape. There were many steps along the way, and she could have stopped at any one of them. She could have stayed sober, stayed out of his room, stayed dressed. She could have kept her mouth closed and her legs together. She could have just said "No!"

Drinking and dating can be every bit as volatile a mixture as drinking and driving. If a woman is so drunk that she cannot resist, a man cannot then invoke her implied consent to justify what amounts to forced intercourse. As Mary Koss, a professor of psychology at the University of Arizona and the author of several scholarly studies of rape, puts it, "The law punishes the drunk driver who kills a pedestrian. And likewise, the law needs to be here to protect the drunk woman from the driver of the penis." But in the Pomona College case, the woman said no force was used; to extend the drunk-driving analogy, she seems—by her own testimony—to have willingly prostrated herself in front of the car and willingly wrapped her lips around its hood ornament.

"I have spent my entire professional life trying to persuade prosecutors, police, judges and administrators to treat date rape as real rape," Estrich wrote. "This case makes me feel like the mother of Frankenstein. . . . A young man's life may be ruined unfairly."

Pomona College authorities ultimately dropped disciplinary proceedings against the man, but Estrich's point remains: "Feminism should not be a substitute for personal responsibility."

In their zeal to restrain and to stigmatize the male libido—and, by extension, to paint all men as rapists—the most radical feminists are making precisely that substitution.

I see a similarly unfortunate extremism in the rapidly escalating battle against sexual harassment, especially in the workplace. As with rape, let me be clear about my own feelings: sexual harassment is wrong. As with rape, it has been ignored or minimized for far too

long. I'm glad that society has finally decided to do something about
it. Sexual harassment should not be tolerated—not in the workplace, not in the classroom, not anywhere, at any time. Period.

But from a historical perspective, the presence of large numbers of women in the workplace is a relatively new phenomenon,
and it's come at a time of rapidly shifting attitudes toward courtship
and male-female relations in general. Given the different sexual
mind-sets of most men and most women, a certain level of sexual
confusion, friction and crossed erotic wires seems inevitable. What
some men think of as harmless sexual banter or mild sexual flirtation, with no offense or follow-up intended, may seem offensive and
tendentious to some women. Some women enjoy male badinage
when it is truly harmless. Or at least they did, until they were told
they were being harassed. As with rape, in our earnest, long-overdue
attempt to right a wrong, we may sometimes be committing new
wrongs; we may be overreacting, distorting definitions and, yet
again, turning modest pleasures into venal sins.

Did Bob Packwood, the former Oregon senator, "sexually ha-
rass" the nineteen women whose charges against him were supported by "substantial credible evidence" in the words of a biparti-
san Senate Select Committee on Ethics? Some of Packwood's
defenders, including Ruth Shalit, an associate editor at the *New
Republic,* have argued that it's "unfair to persecute the charmless
Packwood for his kissings and fondlings while tolerating the over-
tures of his more glamorous colleagues." Few men, Shalit argues,
"know whether their advances will be reciprocated until they try." I
vigorously disagree. As I said earlier, I think that most women know
when a man is coming on to them and most men—if they want to—
can read the signals of possible receptivity or rejection well before
things reach the kissing and fondling stage. More important, any
boss—any man in a position of authority and power, as Packwood
certainly was—may seem threatening to his employees, no matter
that he may be as benign as he is boorish. So, yes, I think that what
Packwood was accused of doing amounted to a clear case of sexual
harassment. If he hadn't resigned (under pressure), I think the Senate
should have expelled him. Other civil and criminal penalties should
also apply if the Senate committee is correct that he "intentionally

altered" his diaries when he "knew or should have known that the committee had sought or would likely seek [them] as part of its preliminary inquiry."

I felt the same way about Clarence Thomas's treatment of Anita Hill—for the same reason—although I reject her as some kind of feminist heroine. What Thomas did was despicable. I believe her account completely. But her behavior wasn't exactly admirable either. She'd hitched her wagon to Thomas's rising star, and she wasn't about to unhitch it over a few pubic hairs on a Coke can. When she decided to remain cordial to Thomas, to stay on the job, to move with him to another job, she put her career above both her personal dignity and her feminist principles. Men have made similar decisions for centuries, but that doesn't make it right—and it doesn't make them heroes any more than it makes her a hero.

Thomas survived Anita Hill's charges and wound up on the Supreme Court, where his narrow-minded, vindictive approach to the law will no doubt torment us for another two or three decades. Clearly, he has neither the character nor the temperament nor the intellect to be sitting as a justice of the United States Supreme Court. But denigrating him doesn't require glorifying her.

I also think that John Fitch, a sixty-two-year-old superior-court judge in the central California town of Fresno, was guilty of sexual harassment when he made offensive remarks to female court reporters and clerks about their breasts, buttocks and legs. When a judge pats a female court reporter on the ass and says, "Your butt looks good in that dress," he's way out of line, and he should be censured—as Fitch was, by the California Supreme Court, in 1995.

I don't mean to suggest that only the most egregious forms of sexual harassment should be punished. I realize that the worst, most degrading forms of this behavior can sometimes be subtle—and all the more insidious because of that subtlety. They, too, are inappropriate—detestable and contemptible.

But is it sexual harassment when someone puts a photograph of his cousin on his desk at work—just because the cousin happens to be a very pretty cheerleader for the Dallas Cowboys? Is it sexual harassment when a fireman, between calls, reads a copy of *Playboy* magazine in the fire station? Is it sexual harassment when a cus-

tomer in a restaurant quietly reads *Playboy* at his table? Is it sexual
harassment if a female employee just happens to overhear one male
employee tease another male employee about being "pussy-
whipped"? In each of these cases, women have argued that they
were indeed sexually harassed. To me, those charges are absurd on
their face. I find the Dallas Cowboy cheerleaders a group of plastic
automatons—about as sexy as the Cowboys owner—but I suppose
it could constitute sexual harassment if women employees had to
look at a giant, prominently displayed blowup of a particularly sexy,
scantily clad Dallas Cowboy cheerleader. And I suppose the same
would be true of a giant, prominently displayed blowup of a nude
Playboy playmate. But a desktop photo? A single magazine? Come
on. Fortunately, the American Civil Liberties Union rode to the rescue of the fireman.

"If he sits there by himself and just reads the magazine, that's
protected [by the First Amendment]," said Ramona Ripston, executive director of the ACLU in Southern California, where the *Playboy*-loving fireman lives.

I have long regarded Ripton as a true heroine for her many
courageous battles on behalf of free speech, and I certainly supported her on this matter. But I was a bit unsettled when even she
suggested that if the fireman "takes the centerfold and opens it up
for all to see and says, 'Hmmm!' or 'Hey, look at this!,' that's offensive."

"Hmmm!" is offensive? My God, what are we coming to?
Can't a fella express his pleasure in the female form without risking
his job? Obviously, if he makes a habit of it, does it loudly or provocatively, runs around waving the magazine and urging the women
firefighters to "check out these hooters," he's out of line and he
should be disciplined. But "Hmmm!"? Couldn't the female firefighters just ignore him? Or ask him to keep his appreciation to himself?
Or just tie a knot in his hose?

As for the *Boston Globe* reporter who teased his colleague
about being "pussy-whipped," that was clearly bad—bad taste, bad
judgment, bad timing and, worst of all, bad, sexist thinking. But
"sexual harassment"? If he'd made his comment *to* a woman—or if
he'd made it intending for the alleged "pussy whipper" herself to

hear the comment—one could make that argument. But it seems downright balmy for a woman to charge sexual harassment just because she happens to overhear a comment, however inappropriate, that wasn't directed to her or intended for her consumption in the first place.

Richard Bernstein, in *Dictatorship of Virtue,* tells an even more harrowing tale, from academe. An English professor at the University of New Hampshire told his class, "Focus is like sex. You zero in on your subject. You seek a target. You move from side to side. You close in on the subject. You bracket the subject and center on it. Focus connects experience and language. You and the subject become one."

This is not scholarship or rhetoric worthy of Aristotle. It's sexist, stupid, repetitive and in execrable taste. It wasn't directed at any specific student, though. It didn't involve any attempted flirtation, seduction or intimidation. The professor didn't touch or proposition anyone. But when outraged female students began grumbling, other accusations were made against the same professor—including the charge that he made an allegedly offensive remark to one female student who said she never heard any such remark. Result: The professor was found guilty of sexual harassment; he was fined $2,000 and ordered to submit a written apology to the offended students and to undergo a year of weekly counseling with "a professional psychotherapist approved by the university." The professor appealed and won, then lost the next round and was suspended for a year without pay and still had to undergo counseling with a university-approved psychotherapist.

As I said, there was nothing admirable in what this professor said. But throughout academe these days, the once-robust intellectual marketplace of ideas is being turned into a cheap bazaar of political correctness. The joy of untrammeled intellectual discourse and debate is being undermined by excessive sensitivity on matters of gender, race, religion and sexual orientation. I think we should be—must be—sensitive to the rights and the feelings of others; thoughtless (and calculated) words can lead to improper, discriminatory, sometimes violent action. But most words just lead to more words, and words—thoughts, discussion, disputation—are at the heart of intellectual pursuit, especially on a university campus. Stifling open debate in the name of sensitivity, because someone, somewhere, might be offended, is *over*sensitivity; it's destructive to the pleasure of dialogue and to the knowledge and the progress that such exchanges often and ultimately produce.

I think women have the inalienable right to spend their days (and nights) free of unwanted sexual attentions, physical *or* verbal, and free of embarrassment, humiliation, intimidation and a hostile or abusive environment, whether in the home, the workplace, the classroom or anywhere else. But I worry that between sexual harassment suits and sexual conduct codes and the characterization of virtually all sexual byplay as oppressive, we are losing a lot of what makes life enjoyable—intellectually, psychologically, emotionally and aesthetically.

I am a voyeur. I freely admit to that. I enjoy looking at a beautiful woman, just as I enjoy looking at a beautiful waterfall or sunset or Gothic cathedral. (No, more!) I don't think I'm alone in my appreciation. In recent years, several researchers have suggested that the greatest single predictor of success in life is not brains, money, race or family connections, but physical appearance. This is true for men and women alike. Studies conducted for the National Bureau of Economic Research by Daniel Hamermesh of the University of Texas and Jeff Biddle of Michigan State University have shown, for example, that men and women who were rated below average in physical attractiveness by job interviewers earn 12 percent to 15 percent less than those rated above average. Psychologist Jean Ritter of California State University in Fresno found the same appeal applies even between mother and child. Ritter's study of 144 infants and their mothers showed that moms whose children were attractive were routinely more affectionate with their children than were moms who had homelier babies. Ritter and her colleague, Judith Langloisk, also found that parents with less attractive children were more likely to perceive their children as a hindrance in their lives than were parents of more attractive children.

I'm certainly not suggesting that this is good—for anyone. Clearly, it is not. But it is reality. Yes, beauty *is* only skin-deep. And it's wrong to treat people—children, dates, job applicants, anyone—

differently just because they are not attractive. I wish I could say I
had never done so. But I know that while I would defend to the
death a homely woman's right to equal opportunity and equal treatment—and have tried to behave accordingly on all substantive matters—I know, too, that I have occasionally been guilty of smiling
more readily at or chatting more animatedly with a pretty waitress
or salesclerk than a dumpy one.

As someone who genuinely likes to pay compliments—"Super
dinner, sweetheart," "Nice tie, Larry," "Great story, Ruth"—I used
to enjoy telling women I knew when I thought they looked particularly good. I took pleasure in paying the compliments, and I had the
distinct impression that they took pleasure in receiving them. I still
compliment my wife and women I know really well on their physical
appearance. But I think twice—three times, four times—before I tell
a female colleague or a relatively new acquaintance (or, Dworkin
forbid, a stranger) that I think she or her dress or her hair looks
especially pretty, even if I've also (perhaps often) praised her professional, intellectual or aesthetic performance. And I sure as hell don't
tell any risqué jokes or offer any specific anatomical praise or observation, not even the most innocent, benign, humorous or well intended.

Recently, I was discussing restaurants with a female colleague
who is, I would guess, in her mid to late forties and whom I've
known for many years although never well. We pass in the hallway.
We say hello. We occasionally ask after the health of our respective
spouses and children. Because she knows of my passion for eating
well, she also asks me for restaurant recommendations from time to
time. But that's it. On this particular occasion, she was saying she
would love to go to a particular restaurant, but, in a very self-depre-
cating manner that was painful to see, she said she wouldn't allow
herself to do so until "I finish Weight Watchers and lose about
twenty pounds." This woman is not fat. She's not thin either. She's
what the Yiddish would call *zaftig*—well rounded, plump, but very
pleasant, attractive, somewhat sexy. She has a pretty face, a warm
smile and a nice manner and she is always nicely dressed and well
groomed; it's clear that her physical appearance is important to her.
I wanted to say something—not flirtatious, not tendentious, not of-

fensive—but something that would make clear that I thought she was attractive and should feel good about herself. But in today's climate, I was afraid to say anything more specific than a lame "You don't look like you need Weight Watchers to me,"—and as I said even that, I worried that it might be misinterpreted.

It wasn't. But I think it's most unfortunate that we were both deprived of the genuine pleasure of the physical compliment, paid and received.

I realize that some men are offensive in their behavior toward and around women. But I also realize that some women like the way they look in clinging and/or revealing clothes. That is their inalienable right, and I revel in their exercise of it. They cannot, however, dress provocatively, in a way that deliberately draws attention to a specific part of their anatomy—wearing, for example, a dress with a neckline that scoops closer to the navel than the neck or a skirt so short that it looks like little more than a wide belt—and then claim to be "offended" if someone takes notice of the anatomical assets so highlighted. Under such circumstances, a smile—indeed, on occasion, a leer—does not seem inappropriate. You don't want leers? Don't flash your assets in the sartorial equivalent of neon.

I remember watching Lainie Kazan sing in nightclubs fifteen or twenty years ago, before she went from voluptuous to fat. She used a lot of double entendres in her between-songs patter, threw her ample breasts around with a knowing abandon and sang in a husky voice that was as full of seductive promise as it should have been, given where it had just been. Kazan also wore dresses so tight and so low-cut that I was sure it had taken the best work of two Nobel Prize–winning physicists and a whole school of structural engineers just to keep her breasts from falling out every time she smiled— which she did, often and lasciviously. One night, Kazan came to the ringside table where my wife and I and another couple were sitting and, in the course of a particularly throaty torch song, she leaned over and playfully nestled my head between her breasts. When the song was over, in the course of chatting up the audience—with my head still firmly in her bosom—she mentioned that one part of her was Russian and one part was Jewish. My mouth was as close to her breasts as to her microphone—her choice, not mine (although I wasn't complaining)—and I couldn't help myself. "How can you tell which one of these is which?" I asked in what I thought was a whisper. But my words were picked up by her microphone and boomed throughout the room, to gales of laughter from the audience. Kazan jerked her microphone (and her mammaries) away from me and stormed back to the stage, muttering aloud about my "boorish" behavior. I don't know if she was really offended by my reference to her breasts or if she was just using that to cover the real source of her annoyance—that my wisecrack got a bigger laugh than anything she'd said all night.

I don't, of course, think that a woman in an office—or in a bar or on a street or almost anywhere else—should have to put up with the same kind of wisecrack as an entertainer who deliberately makes erotic interaction with her audience an integral part of her shtick. Men do not have the right to make vulgar comments or unwanted sexual advances, no matter how a woman is dressed. Women should discourage such behavior, and if the louts persist, the louts should be disciplined, fired if necessary. But the misbehavior of some shouldn't turn an office into a sterile environment for everyone. Racial sensitivities, political correctness and fears of sexual harassment charges are turning many workplaces into humorless, impersonal laboratories. Like so much else in the most extreme feminist positions, the legitimate battle against sexual harassment is also undermining genuine romance. Many people meet and fall in love at work. But an increasing number of employers have become so concerned about the possibility of lawsuits for sexual harassment that they now forbid dating among employees. As the *Wall Street Journal* reported in 1995, "Today's fling may turn into tomorrow's filing."

The irony in all this is that women are once again being treated as frail flowers, too fragile to listen to words that have sexual connotations. I thought we were trying to end the double standard, not return to our Victorian roots. I thought a major objective—and a major victory—in the struggle for sexual equality was to liberate women, to allow them to have the same sexual freedoms as men, the same opportunities to act (or not act) on their sexual impulses.

As Nadine Strossen argues in *Defending Pornography: Free Speech, Sex and the Fight for Women's Rights,* "The growing presumption that a woman is demeaned or harassed by any sexual reference to her, or in her presence, hardly advances women's rights. When women cry 'sexual harassment' at any passing reference to sex, they trivialize the issue, make it a laughingstock and deflect attention and resources from the serious ongoing problems of gender discrimination in employment and education."

Strossen quite rightly notes that "the accelerating presumption that the mere presence of sexual words or pictures in the workplace or on campus is somehow inherently incompatible with women's full and equal participation in those arenas resurrects the very traditional, and very disempowering, notion that sex is intrinsically demeaning to women." Rather than advancing women's equality, Strossen argues, "this growing tendency to equate any sexual expression with gender discrimination undermines women's equality. Women are, in effect, told that we have to choose between sexuality and equality, between sexual liberation and other aspects of 'women's liberation,' between sexual freedom and economic, social and political freedom."

BLUENOSES
AND
BLUE PENCILS

*T*hirty years ago, my sister bought me a subscription to *Playboy* as a birthday present. I had seen the magazine sporadically before then without its making much of an impression, but by the time my one-year gift subscription had expired, I was hooked. I liked the pictures. I liked the monthly interview. I liked the pictures. I even found some of the articles interesting. I liked the pictures. But what really intrigued me was the sense that *Playboy* was both chronicling and symbolizing a transition in America's attitudes toward sex. I wanted a record of that passage. Although I'd never been much of a collector—no stamps or coins, baseball cards only briefly—I decided I had to have every copy of *Playboy*.

I haunted secondhand magazine stores for several months until I had the full set, dating back to December 1953. Later, I also bought a hardcover index to the entire *ouvre*. Many friends teased me about my collection, especially as the women's movement increasingly (and quite rightly) criticized *Playboy* for its sexist objectification and denigration of women. But over the years, its sexist philosophy notwithstanding, *Playboy* managed to publish some very good journalism, and I was always amused when the reporter friends who most frequently teased me (and most often criticized the magazine) would ask to look at my *Playboy* index and then borrow one old issue or another to use as reference material for a story they were working on.

By the 1980s *Playboy* seemed increasingly anachronistic, though—more representative of an outdated culture than of an evolving one. I was tempted to let my subscription lapse, but I figured my collection was probably worth some money, so I kept renewing, to keep the collection complete, even though I seldom looked at the magazine anymore, except for a quick glance at the pictures. Finally, three years ago, I realized that my *Playboy*s had to go. Forty years' worth of magazines, all in leather binders, were taking up valuable bookshelf space that I needed for the various books, magazines, newsletters, auction catalogs and related publications of a much newer hobby—wine. Besides, with a young son, I had less time for magazine reading, and I was pruning my massive subscription list. When my then-current subscription to *Playboy* expired, I didn't renew. I advertised my collection in a couple of publications that cater to antique collectors (how appropriate) and sold it relatively quickly. And just in time. Catharine MacKinnon and a few of her more radical feminist colleagues declared war on pornography about that time; I might have wound up in jail if I'd hung on to my *Playboy*s much longer.

MacKinnon argues that sexually explicit material is not only offensive but is tantamount to—no, the equivalent of—rape. Making leaps that might earn her 10s in the Winter Olympics but Fs in a freshman logic class, she has said:

"Pornography is masturbation material. It is used as sex. It therefore is sex."

This is MacKinnon's basic approach to so-called obscene or pornographic materials. MacKinnon, who compares pornography to the lynching of blacks and to Nazi atrocities against the Jews, not only argues that pornography makes men commit sexually violent acts against women—a theory oft advanced but never proved—she goes one step further: to her, pornography is itself a sexually violent act. Pornography is not words and pictures. Pornography is not entitled to First Amendment protection. Pornography *is* the systematic rape, humiliation and degradation of women—the actual acts, not merely a depiction of those acts. The words and pictures *are* the acts.

MacKinnon defines pornography as "graphic, sexually explicit materials that subordinate women." But she's not talking only about the truly ugly porn—rape and bondage materials, snuff films and depictions of violent rape fantasies that no reasonable person could stomach. She says her definition is "coterminous" with such magazines as *Playboy,* because in those magazines, "women are objectified and presented dehumanized as sexual subjects or things for use" by men. That's true. Is it also true of Manet's classic painting *Déjeuner sur l'Herbe,* in which fully clothed men are picnicking and frolicking with nude women? It's certainly true of much advertising in the Western world today. The same March 13, 1994, issue of the *New York Times Magazine* that contained a lengthy interview with MacKinnon on her views about pornography had an inside front cover photo, in full color, of a barefoot young woman, stripped to the waist, the curve of her breast barely visible as she lay languorously on a rocky precipice overlooking the sea. Express Jeans were all she wore, and "Express Jeans" were the only words in the advertisement. The next two pages contained the same words—once with a woman wearing only shorts, rolled up high on her buttocks, the other with a woman naked except for a shirt open almost to the navel, barely covering her nipples. The look of abandonment and rapture on the woman's face bears no resemblance to the stern, focused visage of Ms. MacKinnon peering out from the magazine forty pages later, but each provided pleasure for *Times* readers that morning. What sets the two apart is that (1) the money from the ads in which the model appeared helped make it possible for MacKinnon to present her views to more than 2 million readers, and yet (2) if MacKinnon had her way, such ads would probably not be published since they certainly present women as sex objects.

Because MacKinnon is so corruscatingly intelligent in so many ways, it is difficult to understand how she and other radical feminist censors can be either blissfully ignorant of or willfully indifferent to a simple set of facts: The societies that suppress pornography the most vigorously (the Islamic nations, for example) also suppress women the most vigorously. Some of the societies that permit the most salacious forms of pornography (the Scandinavian countries among them) take a far more respectful and egalitarian approach to women. Japan, with rape and bondage material far more widely available—and far more vivid, far more violent—than in the United States, nevertheless has a far lower incidence of rape and other violent crimes than does the United States.

I'm not suggesting there is a cause-and-effect relationship between graphic pornography and low crime rates. But some experts do theorize that pornography may help *prevent* rape, that men who use it to masturbate do so instead of looking elsewhere for sexual satisfaction. A study in Denmark several years ago concluded that there was a correlation between the increased availability of pornography there and a decline in sex offenses.

My father had a pornography collection. It consisted of hundreds of small, grainy, black-and-white photos of naked women, a few of them engaged in sex acts with men. Some of the pictures were amusing—a woman nude except for a funny hat, a man with eyeglasses perched on his erect penis. None were what we would today call hard-core. No penises in vaginas (or any other bodily orifices). Certainly no scenes of rape or bondage or any group sex that I can recall. It was all pretty tame by today's standards.

My father kept his collection in two large brown envelopes, locked in his old U.S. Army footlocker. Looking at them gave him great pleasure. I never saw him, whang in hand, crouched over his footlocker, but given what he had told me (and what I had sensed) about my mother's attitude toward sex, I suspect that they were his primary, if not his only, sexual outlet during a significant portion of their twenty-six-year marriage. But Catharine MacKinnon and her colleagues insist that such material should be declared illegal, and they would characterize my father's use of it, all by himself, as "rape."

Suppose the experts are wrong about pornography as a deterrent to rape? That still doesn't mean pornography *causes* rape. Pornography is usually sexist and often odious, but the true value of the First Amendment clearly lies in the protection it provides for unpopular, even potentially dangerous speech. George Will—no libertine he—has written that the First Amendment "is a nullity if it protects only expression that is without consequences, or that has consequences universally considered benign."

If someone derives pleasure from looking at *Playboy,* who is Catharine MacKinnon to tell him he can't do so? What kind of society are we creating when we see rape, harassment and debasement in every word and deed? I read about a college professor who argued that a magazine article on the sinking of the *Titanic* amounted to "one of the worst sexist violations in print" because it said "an iceberg slashed a 300-foot gash in her starboard side." Using the female gender to describe a ship in that context, said P. J. Corso of Hunter College in New York, "recreated an act of violence against a female, not a luxury liner."

Right. The iceman—pant, pant—cometh.

Nadine Strossen argues that women's rights are "far more endangered by censoring sexual images than they are by the sexual images themselves." Freedom of sexually oriented expression is "integrally connected with women's freedom," Strossen says, "since women traditionally have been straitjacketed precisely in the sexual domain. . . . During the first wave of feminism in this century, Margaret Sanger, Mary Ware Dennett and other pioneering birth control advocates were prosecuted (and, in some cases, convicted, fined and imprisoned) for disseminating birth control information. Significantly, this information was held to violate *anti-obscenity* statutes. Such laws were used not to promote women's equality but rather to erode it."

Wendy McElroy uses similar language in her provocative 1995 book *XXX: A Woman's Right to Pornography.* "Sexual freedom—especially pornography, which is sexual free speech—is an integral part of the battle for women's freedom," she says. "The censoring of sexual words and images does not simply lead to the suppression of women's sexual rights. It is an attempt to control women themselves. For women's rights have traditionally been phrased in terms of their sexuality: marriage, abortion, birth control."

Historically, as historian Judith Walkowitz wrote in *Prostitution and Victorian Society: Women, Class and the State,* "protection" of young women by the state "inevitably led to coercive and repressive measures against those same women." Thus, more contemporaneously—in 1984—when the city of Indianapolis enacted an antipornography ordinance based on a draft by MacKinnon and Andrea Dworkin, the American Civil Liberties Union argued that it was both unconstitutional and discriminatory. The law, the ACLU said, "presumes a natural and inevitable vulnerability of (weaker) women to the unbridled and voracious sexual appetites of (stronger) men and accordingly promises to 'protect' all women." Such protection, the ACLU said, perpetuates gender-based stereotypes and inhibits "the evolution of genuine equality between the sexes."

Fortunately, a federal appeals court ruled the Indianapolis ordinance unconstitutional. Another Dworkin-MacKinnon inspired ordinance, in Minneapolis, was vetoed by the mayor. But the two women helped radical feminists in Canada shape arguments that persuaded the Canadian Supreme Court to rule in 1992 that sexual material deemed "degrading" to women could be banned as obscene. As a result of that decision and subsequent legislation, authorities have seized a wide range of sexual material, including two of Dworkin's own books. Much of the material seized has involved gay and lesbian sexual activity, and several lesbian leaders have expressed sadness and outrage that an effort purportedly intended to protect women has wound up interfering with the rights of some women. After police arrested the owner and cashier at a gay bookstore in Toronto, the manager of the store complained that authorities shouldn't be focusing on a "little gay and lesbian bookstore that is there to help educate the community."

To their credit, many feminists in Canada have taken a lead role in both Censorstop and Feminists for Free Expression, organizations dedicated to fighting censorship efforts that they regard as "invasive and paternalistic." In the United States, almost two hundred progressive feminists—Betty Friedan, Adrienne Rich, Judy Blume, Nora Ephron and Anne Bernays among them—have banded together in a similar campaign as the Ad Hoc Committee of Feminists for Free Expression.

Ironically, as Wendy McElroy, former president of Feminists for Free Expression/Canada, points out in XXX, feminism and pornography were longtime "fellow travelers on the rocky road of unorthodoxy." Both feminism and pornography "flout the conventional notion that sex is necessarily connected to marriage or procreation," McElroy writes. "Both view women as sexual beings who should pursue their sexuality for pleasure and self-fulfillment."

McElroy rejects radical feminist arguments that pornography is degrading and exploitive and leads to violence. She says pornography actually "benefits women, both personally and politically," by, among other things, "serving as sexual therapy"; allowing women to "safely experience sexual alternatives"; providing "a different form of information than can be found in textbooks or discussions"; stripping away the "emotional confusion that so often surrounds real-world sex," and breaking "cultural and political stereotypes so that each woman can interpret sex for herself."

But McElroy says that "liberal feminists" who oppose the censorship of pornography "meet with abuse and dismissal" from their radical sisters; feminists who "actively enjoy pornography or who speak out for the rights of pornographers are treated with special contempt," she says.

To be fair, it must be noted that radical feminists are not exactly pioneers in the campaign for censorship of sexually based materials. What makes their stance unusual is that until some feminists decided that Hugh Hefner was the twentieth-century equivalent of Genghis Khan, most censors of sexually based material came from the Right side of the political spectrum, not the Left.

Censorship of such material dates from at least the early seventeenth century, if not earlier, and its casualties through the years have included such literary luminaries as Chaucer, Shakespeare, Baudelaire, Walt Whitman, Oscar Wilde, James Joyce, Henry Miller, Vladimir Nabokov and J. D. Salinger, to name but a few. Film, music, drama, periodicals, live performers of various kinds—over the centuries, all have felt the painful sting of the censor's blind blade. In the United States in particular, as Robert Hughes observed in *Time* magazine in 1995, "the arts have always had to prove how moral they are." Almost fifty years before Tipper Gore began worrying that rock lyrics would corrupt today's innocent young children, NBC ordered 147 pop tunes banned from its radio network because of the implicit sexual content of their lyrics. The 1940 blacklist also included a number of instrumental tunes, prohibited because their very titles were thought to be inappropriately suggestive ("Lavender Cowboy"? "Dirty Lady"? "But in the Morning, No"?). Some songs could be played but only if certain lyrics were excised, as in the case of "Thank You Father" and its verboten lines, "Though your father's name was Stanley, / Thank God that he was manly."

Today's rap lyrics are infinitely more specific than this. They are ugly, vicious exhortations to violence and to the degradation, subjugation and brutalization of women; the record companies that release these records should be ashamed of themselves—about as ashamed as Robert Dole, the Senate Hypocrisy Leader, should be of himself. Dole, you may recall, excoriated Hollywood moviemakers and rap music companies last year for promoting "nightmares of depravity" and a pervasive culture of violence, while he simultaneously advocated a repeal of the federal ban on assault weapons.

Record company executives who take self-righteous refuge behind the First Amendment and the "demands of the marketplace" are being equally hypocritical. But if I were going to advocate censorship—which I'm not—I would censor violence, not sex. Although I do think child pornography should be banned—whether on film, in print or on the Internet—I tend to be a First Amendment absolutist where adults are concerned. Even with children, I worry far less about the (allegedly) harmful effects of their seeing an adult couple making love on-screen than I do about the (demonstrably) harmful effects of the 100,000 acts of violence—including 8,000 murders—that the average American child sees in the media by the time he leaves grade school. I know from personal experience that even cartoon and comic book violence can have an effect on young children. We banned the television program *Mighty Morphin Power Rangers* from our house when we noticed that Lucas, then four, was demonstrably more aggressive—more likely to hit and kick—after watching it.

I can think of no greater waste of time than surfing the Internet in search of filthy words and pictures, but I thought Congress was dead wrong when it passed legislation that would impose fines of up to $250,000 and prison sentences of up to five years on anyone who made "indecent" material available over computer networks that are accessible to minors. The courts have previously held that efforts to protect children from the (allegedly) harmful effects of lewd material "may not reduce the adult population . . . to reading only what is fit for children," as Justice Felix Frankfurter ruled in a 1957 U.S. Supreme Court decision that struck down an antiobscenity statute in Michigan. Besides, hard-core sexual images on the Internet are neither as pervasive nor as accessible as critics contend. Congressmen supporting restrictive legislation on cybersmut cited a study that said "83.5 percent of all images posted on the Usenet are pornographic." *Time* magazine published a cover story based largely on the same study, referring to it as the work of "a research team at Carnegie-Mellon University." But the "research team" turned out to be primarily one undergraduate student with a degree in electrical engineering and no relevant academic credentials, and his study was not subjected to routine peer review. The study was widely discredited.

Usenet is a worldwide computer network made up of about fifteen thousand discussion groups, and as *Time* later conceded, the student "grossly exaggerated the extent of pornography on the entire Internet by conflating findings" from public networks like Usenet and Internet with those from private bulletin board systems that require credit cards and proof of age; the private systems are off limits to minors and cannot be reached through commercial on-line services. In effect, the student looked primarily at the user groups, both private and public, that specifically bill themselves as being erotic or sexual in nature, and he then said that 83.5 percent of their images were erotic or sexual in nature. That's like spending an evening at Yankee Stadium and then making the startling announcement that 83.5 percent of the people there were baseball fans. Pornographic images are actually present in only about 3 percent of all messages on the Usenet, and researchers—real researchers—at Vanderbilt University said that fewer than .5 percent of all messages posted on the Internet are pornographic.

The sexual information and imagery that are available on public computer networks are not the sort of material that an innocent young child is likely to stumble upon accidentally. One must know how to navigate the often arcane paths of the electronic highway system to find them. I'm sure that many computer-literate whiz kids can learn to do so. But I don't think we need sweeping new legislation to limit the access of the very young to the most depraved examples of on-line smut. There are a growing number of software programs, passwords and other screening and filtering devices that can block access to certain kinds of material, and I think technology will make even more—and more effective—monitoring and V-chip-type screening devices available very soon, especially if the alternative is even more government-imposed censorship. But parents have responsibility, too. I know that mom and dad can't sit home all day, peering over their children's shoulders to make sure they're not tainted by images of intercourse on the Internet. But parents *can* use the filtering and screening devices already available and they *can* teach their children some standards and insist on adherence to those standards. This may seem naive, but on this issue, as on so many others, I favor parental judgment, standards, discipline and example to federal legislation. As for adults who object to being exposed to obscenity and pornography themselves—whether on the Internet or at the corner liquor store, in the movie theater or on a rap CD—I have a few simple words of advice: Don't look at it. Don't listen to it. Don't buy it. And if you think it's harmful to society, try persuasion, peaceful protest, public denunciation and economic boycott, not government censorship.

For the most part, those who advocate censorship and who seek to stifle and stigmatize the literary, artistic or commercial representation of sex tend to be the same as those who seek to stifle and stigmatize the pleasure of sex itself. That is the one bond that some radical feminists on the Left share with many bluenoses on the Right. I've sometimes wondered if the very intensity of the pleasure associated with sex is so great that it can only be stifled by the combined efforts of the Left and the Right. Does that, perhaps, explain why some feminists have joined the traditional fearmongers and Fundamentalists among us in the battle against pornography, thus providing the final proof that sex makes even stranger bedfellows than politics?

Not surprisingly—until recently at least—extreme religionists have taken the lead in censorship as aggressively as they have taken it trying to stifle other manifestations of human sexuality. As far back as 1559, the Catholic Church maintained an Index of Forbidden Books *(Index Librorum Prohibitorum)*, a list of literary works thought harmful to the Catholic faith. Through the centuries, the index included many of the great thinkers and writers in Western history—Locke, Hobbes, John Stuart Mill, Rousseau, Voltaire, Kant, Descartes, Milton, Victor Hugo, Flaubert, Dumas, Balzac. This list, finally abolished in 1965, also included many religious works—among them, eight different versions of the New Testament in various languages. The index was designed to proscribe allegedly heretical religious thought, not sexual representation. But the Catholic Church took aim at the latter as well, through its Legion of Decency, which from 1934 until well into the 1960s told Catholics which movies were forbidden, largely because of their sexual content. (The Office for Film and Broadcasting of the United States Catholic Conference still gives a "C" [for "Condemned"] rating to certain movies, but these ratings don't seem to influence moviegoers *or* moviemakers the way those issued by the Legion of Decency once did.) Many other religious orders have also sought to keep their faithful from being exposed to sexual representation in art and literature. The movie industry has even imposed a de facto censorship on its own product, dating back to the enactment of the first Motion Picture Producers and Distributors of America Code (known as the Hays Code) in 1930. Although this code, like the strictures of the Catholic Church, lacked the force of law, it, too, was enormously persuasive. Theoretically, the Legion of Decency sought only to discourage Catholics from seeing certain movies, but since Catholics are the largest single denomination in the United States, this prohibition served at times as a powerful disincentive to Hollywood. The Hays Code and its various successor rating systems have operated in much the same way—in the beginning by specifically forbidding sexual themes that would "stimulate the lower and baser element" and, more recently, by imposing restrictive ratings (first X and now NC-17) that would eliminate the lucrative teenage market. (Movie codes have also imposed restrictive ratings on movies for violence or obscene language, but Hollywood—like the rest of American society—

has always been much more censorious of making love than of making war.)

One could argue that religious and political censorship are more pernicious than sexual censorship. But the censorship of sexual material strikes most directly at pleasure *qua* pleasure. Moreover, virtually all forms of censorship—political, religious *and* sexual—ultimately impinge in one way or another on our right to read, and reading is not only one of the great pleasures in life but, in my view, the single most valuable intellectual tool we can give our children. Reading, I am convinced, is the one skill that would do more than any other to solve, on an individual basis, the problems of poverty, juvenile delinquency and unemployment in our society. Teach people to read and you enable them to participate in life, not sit on the sidelines, where they may be tempted by less exalted pursuits.

I certainly don't mean to suggest that prohibiting someone from looking at *Hustler* magazine will turn him into a drug-dealing gangbanger. But censorship has always been a slippery slope. You start with *Hustler*—or worse—and before you know it, you're censoring *Catcher in the Rye, Lady Chatterley's Lover, Ulysses, The Sun Also Rises, The Grapes of Wrath, As I Lay Dying* and countless other literary works that have been banned, despite the valuable insights they offer into the human condition. Look what America Online did last fall. As part of the effort to remove all "obscene or vulgar" language from the Internet, America Online purged its entire system of the word "breast." That meant that in addition to removing all sexual references to breasts, the company removed—and prohibited—all references to breast cancer, thus depriving many of its female users and subscribers of valuable information they had been sharing with one another through America Online bulletin boards and interest groups. Fortunately—in this case—howls of outrage from justifiably enraged women quickly persuaded the company to modify its purge. But I suspect that we will see many more such foolish, potentially harmful—and more long-lasting—acts of censorship as the new puritans continue their drive for control of our minds and bodies.

Censorship strikes at the creator as well as the consumer, of course. Language is both powerful and rich in nuance, and for a writer, few pleasures compare with the unfettered use of the full range of the language. Censorship undermines that pleasure.

Censorship causes harm even beyond its interference with pleasure and enlightenment; it seeks to make all art conform to "acceptable" standards—an effort that undermines the very idea of art . . . and of the intellectual marketplace for which writers write, an arena where conflicting ideas and varying standards collide for the ultimate benefit of us all. But we now hear that the children's classic *Peter Pan* is offensive to American Indians, that *The Adventures of Huckleberry Finn* is offensive to blacks, that *A Chorus Line* is offensive to gays. In California, the State Department of Education banned *Am I Blue?* by Alice Walker, the Pulitzer Prize–winning author of *The Color Purple,* because it was thought to be "anti-meat-eating."

Religious and political censorship undermine man's most basic freedoms: his relationship with God (who governs his spiritual life) and his relationship with government (which governs his temporal life). But one's relationship with one's own body and one's own mind—and one's mate—should also be cherished and inviolate. Moreover, just as those societies that suppress pornography the most aggressively tend to suppress women the most aggressively, so—all through history—those societies that censor sexual material tend to censor religious and political material as well. Repressive regimes are intolerant of any activity they cannot monitor and control, any activity that gives its citizens the slightest semblance of freedom or pleasure. Repressive regimes suppress anything that does not serve their immediate, self-perpetuating purpose. In the past sixty years alone, we have only to look at Nazi Germany, at the former Soviet Union and its Iron Curtain empire, at China and Iraq and Iran and various other dictatorships around the globe.

Most tyrannies have a "puritanical nature," says Pete Hamill, the New York journalist and author, who cites in particular the "iron-fisted puritanism" of such dictators as Stalin, Hitler and Mao. "They wanted to smother the personal chaos that can accompany

sexual freedom and subordinate it to the granite face of the state,"
he says. "Every tyrant knows that if he can control human sexuality,
he can control life."

Democracies are not immune to such instincts either. Over the
past four decades, the list of popular artists and performers whose
invocations of sex have been decried by bluenoses in the United
States is as long as it is shameful. Allen Ginsberg. Elvis Presley. Jerry
Lee Lewis. Lenny Bruce. George Carlin. Richard Pryor. Howard
Stern. 2 Live Crew. Madonna. Robert Mapplethorpe. These are just
the first ten names that pop into my head as I sit here today; I would
not argue that any of them—or all of them collectively—are the
bedrock of Western civilization. Scores more names—some more
illustrious and perhaps more deserving of our sympathy and defense—could easily be listed. In the last few years alone, censors
have pilloried more than a dozen performance artists, photogra-
phers and filmmakers whose names would probably not be recognized by the general public (Ron Athey? Karen Finley? John Fleck?
Merry Alpern?). In 1995 the Republican-led Congress slashed funding for the National Endowment for the Arts; many conservatives
would like to eliminate it altogether, largely because they view it as
"state-subsidized porn."

Does one have to like (or even approve of) a given artist or
work of art to recognize the value of federal subsidies for the arts—
and the dangers of state-sponsored censorship?

No.

Art—culture—is one of the true measures of a civilized society,
and it is worthy of the collective support of that society. But art
survived—at times thrived—before the national endowments were
created in 1965, and they will do so again, no matter how vigorously Congress tries to Newt-er them. It's the impulse behind the
congressional action—the desire for censorship itself—that worries
me the most.

Personally, I was a big Elvis Presley fan—and I thought Lenny
Bruce a gifted comic who brilliantly laid bare the foibles and hypoc-
risies of a society just beginning to deal with sexuality outside the
confines of the marital bedroom. (Bruce was, after all, the man who
said, "I was arrested for using a ten-letter word that began with 'C,'

but I would marry no woman who was not one.") One need not admire the work of these artists to be offended by efforts to censor them, though. I find Stern puerile and disgusting, for example—about as talented as a thirteen-year-old boy who scribbles "fuck" on the blackboard when his teacher's back is turned. I'm not much more impressed with Mapplethorpe; photographs of a whip or an arm inserted into an anus or of a finger inserted into a penis or of one man urinating into the mouth of another is not my idea of art. I find these pictures repulsive. As for 2 Live Crew, well, songs that celebrate a man forcing anal sex on a woman and later making her lick his feces are so loathsome, so repellent, so contrary to what any decent human being should want to do *or* listen to, that I can't imagine anyone getting pleasure from it. So I don't buy it or listen to it. But if some sicko out there wants to do either, that's his own (lamentable, depraved) business. The government has no business telling people what they can or can't listen to, look at or read in the privacy of their own homes.

Interestingly, the news media—those bastions of First Amendment freedom—are among the most successful (and most hypocritical) of our contemporary censors. In 1993 two obscenity cases involving 2 Live Crew made headlines across the country. So did the trial (and acquittal) of a Cincinnati museum director charged with obscenity for exhibiting a number of Mapplethorpe's photographs. But no major daily paper printed any of the allegedly obscene 2 Live Crew lyrics and very few described the lyrics in anything but the most general terms. Nor did any major daily newspaper publish any of the most controversial Mapplethorpe photographs in full; many refused even to describe the photos in more than general terms, even though newspaper editors generally insist that their reporters be specific and detailed in their stories, especially on controversial issues.

Newspapers and magazines—the *New York Times Magazine* in particular—routinely publish photographs that depict scantily clad women, women whose heaving bosoms are fairly bursting out of their bras, women who sometimes appear sexually aroused. But those photos appear only in advertisements. Never mind Mapplethorpe; neither the *New York Times* nor any other mainstream newspaper would consider publishing these lingerie photographs in their news columns, not even to illustrate a story in which the woman's attire is absolutely critical to the story. The (immoral) moral: using sex to make money is okay; using sex to tell a story is not. There is a centuries-old tradition of using sex to make money; it's called prostitution. But the men who wield the blue pencils at the nation's newspapers and magazines would self-righteously reject any such interpretation of their actions.

Journalists tend to be liberal on most matters, especially on those matters involving freedom of speech and artistic expression. They routinely wave the First Amendment flag to defend not only their own actions but the actions of artists and political dissidents everywhere. Traditionally—stereotypically—most journalists have also been hard-boiled cynics, given to graveyard humor about the most brutal murders, earthquakes, hurricanes and explosions. But with rare exception, the editors I've known are all more comfortable with dead bodies than with naked bodies. As Bill Kovach—former Washington bureau chief for the *New York Times,* former editor of the *Atlanta Journal and Constitution,* now curator of the Nieman fellowship program at Harvard—acknowledged to me a few years ago, "We can talk about death, murder, war, cancer and suicide, but . . . we certainly are constipated as journalists when it comes to dealing with sex . . . especially as editors."

Too often, this constipation leads to censorship—not censorship as grave or as damaging to the body politic as that which has historically been imposed in the cultural and political arenas, to be sure, but a peculiarly invidious sort of censorship nonetheless. Because I'm a journalist, because I write about the media, because editors' actions on many stories involving sex seem so hypocritical, I've always found it a subject worth exploring.

Why are editors so discomfited by matters sexual? An editor at my newspaper offered an intriguing theory a few years ago when I was researching a story on this very question. Specifically, I was writing about why it is that every time the media cover a story involving sex—be it about AIDS, child molestation, the William Kennedy Smith rape trial or the sex lives of Bill Clinton and Gary Hart—they fuck it up. When this editor heard what I was working on, he sent me a message by intraoffice computer.

"Most newspapers are run by middle-aged white guys," he said. "They have boring sex lives. So when they're confronted with a story about sex, they get uncomfortable or upset or even envious and they fumble the ball."

That seemed a pretty provocative remark, but since the editor had not made it in the course of a formal interview, I felt obligated to ask his permission to use it—and his name—in my story.

"Sure," he said. "Go ahead. Use it."

But the next morning—belatedly realizing, I guess, that *he* is a middle-aged white guy—he tried frantically to reach me, begging me not to use his name with his quote.

"I have a great sex life," he said. "I wouldn't want anyone to think I was talking about myself—or my wife."

At least twice in ensuing weeks, this editor—whom I did not know well at all—volunteered to me, over the office's computerized message system, that he had enjoyed spectacularly good sex with his wife the previous night. Once, when he suggested we have lunch, he asked that I choose a place "close by, since I'm not sure how well my legs work today, after what we did last night."

Like most editors, this fellow has never struck me as the sort who has much fun in life. Like most editors, he seemed both suspicious and envious of those who eagerly indulge in any pleasures of a sensual nature. I think that's a leitmotiv—and not so *leit* at that—running through the attitudes of most of the busybodies who are so determined to restrict people's sexual activities and many other enjoyable activities as well. Yes, I know all about—and have already mentioned—our Puritan roots and Victorian heritage, and yes, I know that many Americans have genuine, deeply rooted religious beliefs that honor scriptural strictures against adultery, fornication and various forms of lewd behavior. I realize that these beliefs influence how they feel about many sexual issues. But I remain unalterably convinced that, beyond Oliver Cromwell and Jerry Falwell, beyond piety and sincerity, there are strong streaks of nose-to-the-grindstone earnestness and an "I'm not having any fun, so you shouldn't either" attitude in the average American that are inevitably at odds with pleasure in any form. Many Americans seem to think that any activity that provides pleasure must be wrong—indeed sinful—and newspaper editors are by no means immune to this anhedonic virus. In fact, in some ways, they may be its most virulent carriers. Certainly, I've always sensed a certain unease among many editors over my outspoken enthusiasm for the sensual pleasures provided by fine food, wine, cigars—and sex.

Ironically, from the 1960s onward, conservative critics blamed the news media for the sexual revolution that was taking place in the United States. Simply by reporting what was happening in society, the media came to be seen as legitimizing nudity and "perversity"— teenage sex, extramarital sex, pornographic sex, gay sex, group sex. But the truth, as anyone who has worked in the news media knows, is quite different. Most high-ranking news executives are cautious and conservative by nature. As in any bureaucracy, they didn't rise to the top by taking bold stands and challenging the status quo. On sex in particular, they were—and increasingly are, in the cautious nineties—squeamish and confused.

I first became aware of this phenomenon in the mid-1960s and, more acutely, in the early 1970s, when I became the *Los Angeles Times*'s unofficial staff sex pervert.

It all began with Carol Doda, the topless dancer I mentioned in my introduction.

I first encountered Ms. Doda in the fall of 1964, when I took a young woman to San Francisco for a weekend to see a college football game and have dinner with friends. After dinner, one of our friends suggested a stroll along North Beach, where—he assured us, with a knowing leer—we could get a great espresso, "among other things."

The next thing I knew, we were being hounded by barkers outside one topless joint after another, each promising thrills beyond the imagination of a very literal-minded twenty-one-year-old. At our friend's urging, we decided to favor the Condor Club with our custom, and there we discovered the newly celebrated Ms. Doda.

Both the voyeur and the reporter in me were fascinated by the experience, and when we returned to Los Angeles, I tried to interest my editors in a story on the topless phenomenon.

Not a chance.

I was working on a small daily newspaper (26,000 circulation then, now defunct) in suburban Los Angeles. It was my first full-time newspaper job—I was also a full-time college student—and my editors weren't about to shake up their readers, most of them elderly transplants from the conservative Midwest, with a rookie reporter's wide-eyed tales of unsheathed bosoms. I tried again two years later, when I'd graduated from college and had moved up to a medium-sized daily newspaper (circulation about 150,000) in a larger Los Angeles suburb. Not a chance there either. Most of our readers were from Iowa, my editor told me—as if Iowans don't have or enjoy sex.

"What are you, Shaw, a pervert?" the editor asked.

Then he asked another question:

"Are there any good topless places around here where we could go for lunch?"

I didn't think it was the mere mention of bare breasts in print that worried my editors; I think they were alarmed by my suggestion that my story not be merely a titillating account of bobbing breasts and panting patrons.

"It won't stop here," I said. "We should tell our readers what's going to happen next."

"What's that?" they all asked nervously.

"Bottomless," I said.

"Bottomless?" one editor asked, stunned. "You mean you think they're going to dance with their, their—their . . . *thing* showing?

"What are you, Shaw, a pervert?" this editor asked, in what was beginning to become a familiar newsroom refrain. "They'll never do it and the cops would never allow it."

By the time I joined the *Los Angeles Times,* in late 1968, Carol Doda had been dancing topless for more than four years. She still kept her *thing* covered—although barely. Thousands of other dancers were far less modest. They had traded in their G-strings for G-notes. Bottomless dancing was the order of the very lucrative day.

I spoke to my editor about doing a story on it. After all, I was then working for the Orange County edition of the *Times,* and Orange County—hotbed of Goldwater Republicanism, with more churches than you could shake a collection plate at—was one of the incongruous centers of the bottomless movement. My preliminary research—a dirty job but someone had to do it—had disclosed that bottomless bars in the county routinely made a 50 percent profit and were driving many traditional bars into bankruptcy. Clearly, the not-so-good burghers of Orange County preferred tits and ass to Scotch and soda.

Before embarking on more detailed research, I repeated to my editor at the *Times* an updated version of what I had said to my previous editors: "I don't think we should just write about naked women dancing. I want to talk about the unusual legal tactic the district attorney is using to fight these bars, and I want to get into the economics of the business—and I want to tell the reader what's going to happen next."

My editor thought the legal and financial angles were indeed worth examining. He wasn't so sure about my skills at sexual prognostication.

"Just what do you think will happen next?" he asked, terrified that I'd really tell him.

"I don't know. I'll tell you when I'm done with my reporting."

A few weeks later, I was done. But I didn't know how to tell my editor what I'd found. Ted was very smart and he was very good to me, but he was a remarkably straitlaced fellow, so uptight that when he first interviewed me for my job, I thought immediately of a colleague's description of his father-in-law: "He wouldn't say 'shit' if he had a mouthful."

Editors argue that they have a "special responsibility" to their readers and their readers' children; they are, in effect, the juvenile vice squad of the pleasure police. At all costs, they say, they must safeguard the sensibilities of the children in their communities, as if (1) any young children read newspapers these days, (2) those old enough and interested enough to do so wouldn't already know anything about sex that they'd be likely to find in even the most licentious daily newspaper and (3) the mere mention of a woman's bare breasts—or, horrors, visible pubic hair—would stunt their growth and permanently retard their intellectual development.

A few years later, I learned firsthand of the folly inherent in this presumption of journalistic *in loco parentis*. The *Los Angeles*

Times published a story on Frasier, a physically debilitated lion at the local wild animal park. Despite being seventy-five years old in human terms, Frasier had cut an enviable swath through the female population of Lion Country Safari, siring more than thirty cubs with six different mates in eighteen months. The *Times* published a photograph of Frasier, along with a modest account of his exploits. The photo was no Mapplethorpe; it simply showed Frasier lying on his back, napping under the "watchful eye of one of his wives," in the words of a caption writer who obviously specialized in reading the minds of lady lions.

But between editions, the watchful eye of another *Times* editor noticed that Frasier's genitals were clearly visible in the photo. He ordered them "airbrushed"—eliminated—for the next edition, seemingly on the theory that the mere sight of Frasier's cub-making equipment might have caused lasting psychological damage to any child who happened to see the picture.

That evening, I showed the Frasier story to Leonard, the ten-year-old boy who then lived next door and who had seen Frasier on a recent family outing to Lion Country Safari. He read it with great amusement. It was a nicely written story, done by a colleague with a deft touch. But when Leonard looked at the photo, an expression of unmistakable confusion and concern appeared on his face.

"But, Mr. Shaw," he asked, "what happened to his balls?"

As gatekeepers—and guarantors of their publishers' investment—editors actually worry that children might not know about such matters; editors insist that it is their sworn duty to shelter children from that knowledge, so when I walked into Ted's office to report on the results of my journalistic inquiries amid the Orange County dens of iniquity, I knew that I would not find it easy to persuade him to publish my findings.

"I've got the answer to that question you asked me about what's going to happen next with the bottomless dancers," I said.

He looked up, his brow furrowed, his face flushed and his eyes narrowing.

"Yes?"

He managed to make the one syllable sound like a question, a warning and an expression of extreme anxiety, all at the same time.

You would have thought I was his teenage son about to report that I'd smashed up the family car and run over two toddlers in the process.

"Well, Ted, I don't think you're going to like this, but my sources tell me the novelty of bottomless dancing is already beginning to wear off. The bar owners think they have to juice up their shows to keep the customers coming in."

"Yes."

This time it wasn't a question. It was a threat: "Don't you dare."

"Well," I said, plunging blindly ahead, "they think they're going to start having live sex shows. Onstage."

His face was now beet-red. So was his entire bald head. I could swear I saw smoke coming out his ears. He glared at me, obviously struggling for control.

He tried to speak twice, cleared his throat both times, thought better of it, then tried again. What came out was a squeak.

"And you intend to write about this in the pages of the *Los Angeles Times*."

Again, it was not a question.

"Sure. Why not? It's news, isn't it?"

He looked at me as if I'd just dropped in through the skylight, with horns, a tail and a giant, gift-wrapped turd.

"No."

"But—"

"No."

"Ted—"

"Shaw, I could swear you said you spoke English when I hired you. Clearly, you overstated your language skills. Which part of my answer didn't you understand—the *N* or the *O*?"

Further attempts at discussion over the next week or two proved fruitless. I wrote my story, carefully eschewing any mention of the public fornication about to be visited on our unsuspecting county.

"Topless and bottomless bars are big business in Orange County," the story began, and it went on to detail the growth, early profitability and current slump at the clubs. The story also explained how District Attorney Cecil Hicks—frustrated by First Amendment lawyers in his attempts to shut the bars down by arresting bottomless dancers for "indecent exposure" and "lewd and dissolute conduct"—was invoking the Red Light Abatement Act, the civil statute used to close down bordellos in Northern California almost sixty years earlier. That law empowered authorities to seek court action against any business establishment in which "lewdness, assignation or prostitution" took place. Such action, the law said, was considered "a public nuisance." My story quoted lawyers and bar owners and dancers and city officials. But it didn't say a word about live sex acts. It was—and remains—the only story I've ever written in which my editor ordered me to omit the single most interesting, relevant, provocative piece of information I had.

But time—and *Times* editors—change. Sort of. A year later, I had been promoted to the main office of the *Times,* in downtown Los Angeles, and Ted had been passed over for promotion—not, I am sure, because he had forced me to leave our readers woefully ignorant about what would happen next in the Orange County barroom division of the sexual liberation movement. I was chatting one morning with Bill Thomas, then the metropolitan editor, and he said, "David, I heard the craziest thing the other day. There's a bar next to one of the places in Hollywood where carrier boys pick up our papers, and the guy who runs the office tells me that couples actually—"

He broke off, uncertain just how to phrase what he was about to say. Bill is the son of a small-town, midwestern banker, a real straight arrow. He's not uptight like Ted—far from it—but neither is he the sort of fellow with whom you'd sit around swapping dirty jokes.

He raised an eyebrow, lowered his voice and rushed through what he had to say, as if by saying it quickly, he wasn't really saying the embarrassing words at all: "Theyhavesexonstage."

I laughed.

"That's the story I tried to do for Ted in Orange County last year."

"Well, do it for me now."

"I'd rather not."

Bill seemed surprised. I'd only been working for him for a few months, but we'd already established a good relationship. I thought he was the best editor I'd ever worked for—in eighteen months he'd be named editor of the entire paper—and he seemed to like my stories. He knew of my personal and journalistic interest in the then-nascent sexual revolution, and he couldn't figure out why I didn't want to do this story.

"I don't want the same hassles I've had before on this," I told him. "I know all this public sex stuff has to stop someplace and maybe this is where it stops—with live sex shows. But if it isn't, if there's a next stage, I want to say so and I don't want to be told again that we can't tell our readers what we know."

Bill seemed taken aback.

"Why? What do you think will happen next? What could possibly happen next? What's left after . . . this?"

"I haven't a clue."

"Then don't worry about it. Do your reporting. Write your story as you see it. If there's a problem, we'll deal with it then."

I respected Bill enormously. He was a superb journalist and a man of his word. I knew, however, that the *Los Angeles Times,* like most big-city newspapers, took what it saw as its civic responsibility Very Seriously. I also knew that Los Angeles, for all its wide-open ways in the 1960s and 1970s, had a history that could weigh heavily on the editors. This was, after all, a city that once had strict regulations on dancing in public, that had rigidly enforced laws prohibiting fornication and that had been "overrun with military moralists," in the words of one writer. Would a newspaper in a city that once had formal regulations saying that ballroom dancers' cheeks could not touch be willing to publish a story that described nude couples screwing in public?

I went to work on the story, starting with the beer bar on Melrose Avenue, near Western Avenue, next door to the *Times* Hollywood delivery station. There I met a young woman I came to call Sue. She was twenty-one, "an exquisitely proportioned blonde with sparkling blue eyes and the fresh-scrubbed beauty of a high school homecoming queen," as I described her in the first paragraph of my subsequent story. Sue and her boyfriend "Joe" were professional dancers who had put together a forty-minute act, complete with music, costume and choreography. About midway through the act, as I wrote, "Joe and Sue remove their costumes—and when the act ends, they are lying down, nude, unmistakably engaged in sexual intercourse."

I found a number of similar men and women, all engaged in similar activities, right out in public, including a twenty-nine-year-old professional actor who had spent five months screwing onstage in San Francisco . . . with one week out to play Richard III in a Shakespeare festival in Colorado. Journalistically and sociologically, I found all this fascinating. But I was somewhat less enchanted personally than my colleagues seemed to assume. Much as I like to look at a beautiful woman—especially a beautiful naked woman—I don't particularly want to watch strangers making love. In my view, sex is for participants, not spectators. A surprising number of friends, associates and news sources volunteered to help me with my research on this story, though—Mr. District Attorney, Cecil Hicks, among them.

"I should see just what these people are doing," he said earnestly, when I called to ask if he thought authorities would use the Red Light Abatement Act against the live sex shows. "I can't go to one of those shows in Orange County. Someone might see me. Can I go with you in L.A.?"

I was tempted to suggest that since his interest was clearly as personal as it was professional, he might consider abandoning his role as local chief of the pleasure police. But hectoring friends is a good way to lose friends. Besides, I like Cecil and thought it would be fun to spend an evening cruising sex shows with him. So I just laughed and said, "Sure. When do you want to go?"

Late one night the next week, we went to a bar in the suburban San Fernando Valley that I'd visited the previous afternoon to interview the owner and the "dancers." (That's how they styled themselves—not "actors," not "strippers," not "lovers"—"dancers.") When we walked in, the owner was standing behind the bar. I told him that my friend—name and occupation unspoken—wanted to see the show. He picked up the phone that connected him to the dancers' dressing rooms.

"Hey, Jake," he said, "that reporter from the *L.A. Times* is back. Think you can get it up for one more show?"

A few minutes later, Jake and a statuesque brunette walked out, stepped onstage and began dancing. Normal dancing to loud rock music. They danced for much longer than they had the previous afternoon. My friend began drumming his fingers impatiently. He hadn't come all the way to the deepest, darkest San Fernando Valley to watch a waltz. I craned my neck, trying to spot the owner. He came over and shrugged. "Hey, look, they just did it twenty minutes ago. Jake probably needs a few more minutes to be, you know, ready."

Finally, Jake nodded. He was ready. They began to disrobe. They got down on the floor. They started to make love. But it was two o'clock in the morning by then, and in California, Alcoholic Beverage Control laws specify that any establishment that serves liquor must stop serving—and stop all entertainment—at two o'clock. All of a sudden, the owner stepped onstage, grabbed Jake by the bare collarbone, yanked him into an upright position and said, "Okay, Jake, two o'clock. Finish it in the dressing room if you want."

Jake and his partner jumped offstage—while Cecil howled in dismay and disappointment.

I didn't write about that particular night in my story. But I did write about Jake and several other "dancers." And about what the law was trying to do to curb them, starting with the Red Light Abatement Act. I also pointed out that shrewd entrepreneurs had discovered that if they put their sex shows on in a theater, instead of a bar, there wasn't much the authorities could do to stop them. In a theater, they had First Amendment protection; the spirit of Thomas Jefferson made screwing onstage a constitutionally inviolate expression of free speech.

And what was next?

In San Francisco, I saw a movie in which a woman had sex with a dog, a pig and a horse—not, Jefferson be praised, simultaneously. In the Hollywood beer bar where my research began, I saw a man, a woman and a dog take turns having sex with each other—and then invite people in the audience to come onstage and choose whichever of the three they wanted as a partner. Soon, sexual activities of this kind might be taking place throughout California, my sources told me.

Personally disgusted but pleased that I finally had an answer to my question, I wrote that into my story with a trepidation that was subsequently fully justified.

"Animals?!?!" Bill yelped when he got to that part of the story. True to his word, he didn't take it out, though.

His boss did.

"Nick [the soon-to-retire editor of the paper] says he's not having our readers read any story in his newspaper about people having sex with farm animals, not while they drink their morning coffee," he told me when he emerged from Nick's office.

"Dogs aren't farm animals," I responded feebly.

He shook his head.

Nick Williams, I knew, was reputed to have one of the finest collections of erotic art in the state. I reminded Bill of this. I grumbled about the hypocrisy—and the arrogance, the elitism—so obviously embodied in Nick's judgment that it was perfectly fine for him to ogle sexually explicit material but that he had every right to play sex cop for his presumably fragile and benighted readers.

Bill just shrugged. I reminded him that the story was his idea. I reminded him that I hadn't wanted to do the story—and why. I reminded him of his promise.

"I'll talk to Nick again," he said.

"I'll talk to Nick myself," I said.

"No you won't."

He came back thirty minutes later and spoke to another high-ranking editor. A series of negotiations ensued. By day's end, Bill had hammered out a compromise agreement with his two superiors.

"You can say what's coming next," he told me, "but you can't say exactly what kind of animals are involved and you can't say specifically what the people did with the animals."

"I can't use the words 'dog' or 'pig' or—"

"Right."

"What can I say?"

"One word," he said. " 'Bestiality.' "

"Bestiality?"

"Yes. Nick is convinced that no one will know what it means, so no one will be offended."

"Great. We're in the communications business, and the editor of the paper wants me to use a word only because he knows it won't communicate."

But I had read a great deal about the checkered history of the *Los Angeles Times,* and I remembered another occasion, almost a century earlier, when the paper had used "bestiality" in another controversial story. In 1886 the *Times* had prominently displayed a story about a political opponent of the publisher allegedly cavorting with three male companions and "four common prostitutes [in a scene of] . . . almost sickening bestiality."

"The four drunken male brutes and three of the four drunken female brutes were sprawled, almost nude, all in the most atrocious attitudes, about the front room," the story said. "The man who now asks your suffrage as Secretary of State, almost stark nude, was endeavoring to arouse the waiter to go and get a photographer for obscene purpose."

But that was a different *Times,* a *Times* routinely used to further its publisher's political and social agenda—and to punish his enemies—the dictates of good taste, good judgment and good journalism notwithstanding. The "new" *Los Angeles Times* was a model of journalistic rectitude. *My* "bestiality" would appear as an effort to avoid giving offense, not as an effort to humiliate a political rival. We had gone from being political arbiters to being moral arbiters, from being kingmakers (and breakers)—unprincipled custodians of our readers' votes—to being "principled" custodians of our readers' sensibilities.

That didn't make me feel any better about the mandated linguistic obfuscation, but in truth I wasn't displeased by the ultimate outcome. I hated to lose the juicy details—I fought futilely for them for another twenty minutes after Bill told me what he and Nick had worked out—but I'd really never expected the paper to publish my story in any form, given my past experiences. I realized that this wasn't exactly the Pentagon Papers, but just getting the story into the paper, with or without animals, would be a small moral victory.

"Nick said we can run the story, right?" I asked.

"He's not nuts about it. He hates it, in fact. And he thinks the readers will be outraged. But, yes, we can run it."

Bill looked a bit sheepish.

"But?" I asked.

"Well, he said we can't start it on page one."

"Okay."

"Or on the front page of any other section."

"Okay."

"Or at the top of any page anywhere."

"Is that all?"

"No. He also said that no headline on the story, not the main head or any of the jump heads [the headlines on those portions of the story that would be continued to subsequent pages] could be more than two columns [wide]."

Bill seemed more troubled than I was by these bizarre and, so far as I could tell, unprecedented restraints on his authority.

Nick's attitude reminded me of what I'd heard about a similar situation at the *New York Times* several years earlier. John Corry had written a lengthy account of *Human Sexual Response,* the book based on the massive sex research done by Dr. William Masters and Virginia Johnson. As Corry later described the ensuing struggle in his memoir *My Times,* he submitted a four-thousand-word story, as assigned, only to have a top editor order it cut to eight hundred words and insist that "under no circumstances would it run on page one." Corry's immediate supervisor had argued with the higher-ranking editor, much as Bill argued with Nick, and after many re-writes and much haggling, Corry finally produced a story deemed fit to print in the great, gray lady—"except for one word," Corry wrote. "That was 'penis.' 'Vagina' was acceptable, but 'penis' had to be replaced by 'male sex organ.' "

Clearly, the men who ran Corry's *Times* were more uncomfortable with specific references to their own genitals than to a woman's genitals. Big surprise. On the other hand, my editors didn't want any mention of penises *or* vaginas. Of course, Corry's story had been based on serious scientific research; mine was based on watching couples fuck on barroom stages.

I asked Bill if Nick had asked for any cuts in the story other than the animal material and the specific references to genitals.

"No."

"Did he say we couldn't use the word 'sex' in any of the heads?"

"No."

"Then I'm not terribly worried. It's a long story. It'll jump two or three times. We'll have 'sex' in every head; people will find the story—and they'll read it."

Sure enough, the main head on the story said:

Explicit Sex on the Stage:
Pay Attracts Performers

The jump heads—more like labels really, in keeping with the paper's style at the time—said "Sex Performers" and "Sex on Stage" and, for the final portion of the story, just "Sex."

But Nick was right about readers' reaction. I received more angry letters on that story than on any other story I'd written in the first decade of my journalistic career.

It is precisely this sort of reader response—or the fearful anticipation thereof—that makes most editors squeamish about stories involving sex in general and obscenity in particular.

•   •

Having long since graduated from the sex beat, my job at the *Los Angeles Times* for the past twenty years has been to examine the performance of the media, my own newspaper most specifically included. About three years ago, I went to Shelby Coffey, who had succeeded Bill Thomas as the editor of the *Times,* with my aforementioned idea to do a story on how the news media invariably screw up any story involving sex. Shelby quickly agreed that it would make an interesting and provocative story. "And be sure," he said, "that you also write about sex-based language."

I asked if he meant "obscenity."

He said he did.

"I think I'll pass," I said. "I'm not going to write a story about how newspapers are afraid to use obscene words, even when they're crucial to a very important story, and then not be able to use those words in my own story." Shelby assured me that I could use those words.

Hah!

Three months later, I turned in my story—a three-part series: Part one examined the media's mishandling of sex stories in general. Part two explained how and why female editors are generally much more sensible and much less timid than male editors in dealing with such stories. Part three dealt with obscenity. Shelby said he liked all three stories and he commended me, in particular, for my "restraint" and my "reasonable" handling of the part on obscenity—despite its containing, among many other Anglo-Saxon expressions, all of the seven dirty words that comedian George Carlin once said you can't say on television. That conversation with Shelby took place, as I recall, on a Friday. That afternoon, George Cotliar, the managing editor—the number two editor at the paper—took my series home so he could read it over the weekend. After the paramedics managed to get George's heartbeat back below 300 and his cardiologist took him off the defibrillator, George told both Shelby and me that under no circumstances should the obscenity story—or the entire series for that matter—appear in the newspaper.

This was not the first time that George and I had clashed over obscenity—or over other stories I had written on the media. But I had always liked him and respected him, all the more so for telling me to my face when he didn't like what I had written. Fortunately, Shelby, like Bill Thomas before him, has always been very supportive of my work, even when he disagreed with my conclusions (and even when my stories brought him considerable in-house criticism). Like Bill, he has always dealt fairly and honestly with me—and he has given me great freedom to do my work as I see fit. But over the course of the week following George's comments on my obscenity story, Shelby asked me each day to shorten the obscenity piece a little bit more—although he assured me each time that his purpose was not to remove the allegedly "obscene" words themselves. By week's end, however, Shelby told me that all the dirty words would have to come out. "I thought I was ready to use them, but I guess I'm not," he said. "I would only authorize using them if they were essential to the nature of a particular story."

He then told me—with a straight face—that he did not think obscene language was essential to a story on obscene language. So all the words came out. The last one to go was "cunt." I think that is one of the few genuinely obscene words in the English language. But I wanted to include it because it had figured prominently in an incident that could have served as a paradigm for my entire story.

A year earlier, another reporter at the *Los Angeles Times* had been examining transcripts of radio transmissions between police cars; she'd found that in addition to their many racist remarks, the cops had referred to a woman as a "cunt." The reporter wrote a story about this as part of the paper's continuing critique of police department practices, an inquiry engendered by the cops' beating of Rodney King and the subsequent riots in the city. Shelby had ordered the word "cunt" excised from the story. He said it was "sexist and derogatory . . . too offensive to women." A delegation of women had then visited him and insisted that the word should be published precisely because it was so offensive; it would demonstrate just how the cops thought about women. Shelby refused. I wrote about that incident in my obscenity story. Shelby said I could use the incident but not the word "cunt." I had to substitute "a four-letter vulgarism for vagina."

In the final version of my story, I inserted seven paragraphs explaining how my story had come about and how it had been censored. I wrote that Shelby had suggested a story on obscenity, had liked the resultant story and had then changed his mind and censored the story. To Shelby's great credit, that insert ran in my story—uncensored (although Shelby did reject my suggestion for a headline on the story; I told him that I thought the headline should say, "Chickenshit Times Editor Says 'No Shit in My Newspaper' ").

I do not mean to single Shelby out here. As much as I objected to his hyperkinetic blue pencil, I understood why he acted as he did, and I appreciated the latitude he gave me to express my extreme displeasure over his decision, both in print and to his face. Shelby is, alas, but one of many in a long line of newspaper editors made uneasy by obscene language.

In the summer of 1995 the most volatile development in the O. J. Simpson double-murder trial involved the racist, sexist comments made on audiotapes by Mark Fuhrman, the former Los Angeles police detective whose ugly utterances virtually hijacked the trial for several weeks. In addition to his vile disparagement of African Americans, Mexicans, women and virtually everyone else who wasn't a brutal, corrupt, white, Anglo-Saxon cop, Fuhrman said that Margaret York, the highest-ranking woman in the LAPD (and Judge Lance Ito's wife), had "screwed her way to the top." For at least a day, it looked as if Fuhrman's comments about York might force Ito to recuse himself from the rest of the trial, which legal analysts said would almost certainly lead to a mistrial. Newspapers across America made this front-page news. But not one major paper published Fuhrman's obscene comment about York. Most paraphrased it or used euphemisms—or, in the case of the *Atlanta Journal and Constitution,* flatly misstated it as "talked her way to the top."

Five months later, newspapers across the country headlined stories about three National Football League players using "obscene" words on television in postgame interviews. Some viewers and conservative social critics said the players, their teams, the TV stations and/or the entire National Football League should be penalized for such gross transgressions. It was a big story amid the annual hype leading up to the Super Bowl. But not one newspaper that I searched in the computerized databases told its readers just what it was that the football players had said to warrant all this attention. (I believe that one player said his coach had prepared him to "kick some ass"; another said his coach had taken a lot of "shit" from critics, and a third—using what the *Chicago Sun-Times* described only as "the mother of all swear words"—spoke of winning "the fucking Super Bowl." Although no newspapers reported these words, some did quote William Bennett, our old friend from the drug wars (and from the Department of Education), as calling the use of such language "one more notch, one more guardrail knocked down," one more step toward the destruction of civilization.

Journalistic bowdlerizations were especially common in the 1960s and 1970s, turbulent times when the country's Puritan heritage collided with the sexual revolution. Hester Prynne meets Abbie Hoffman. Editors, like other Americans, often felt uncomfortable with (and uncertain how to respond to) the rapidly changing sexual mores of the time. So they rewrote—or repressed—history, omitting obscene words even when they were crucial to some of the most important and/or most provocative stories of the day:

- In 1963 a Dallas police officer called Jack Ruby a "son of a bitch" just as Ruby shot Lee Harvey Oswald, two days after Oswald had assassinated President John F. Kennedy. There was much speculation at the time—and ever since—about Ruby's relationship with Oswald and with the police; the officer's exact language might have given a clue, however vague, to that relationship. But most newspapers either omitted that phrase from their stories or changed it to "s.o.b."
- In 1968 Mayor Richard Daley of Chicago became so angry over Senator Abraham Ribicoff's criticism of Chicago police tactics during the Democratic National Convention that he leaped to his feet and shouted at Ribicoff, "Fuck you, you Jew son of a bitch, you lousy motherfucker, go home." The outburst was certainly relevant—essential—to the proceedings and their impact on the Democratic Party and American society, both then and for a generation to come. But no daily newspaper in the country quoted what Daley actually said.
- In 1970, when eight radicals were being tried on conspiracy charges arising out of the Chicago demonstrations, one defendant, David Dellinger, snapped "Oh bullshit" in open court after testimony that he objected to. The judge admonished Dellinger and revoked his bail for the rest of the trial. The outburst was clearly "central to the day's events," in the words of J. Anthony Lukas, who was covering the trial for the *New*

York Times. But neither the *New York Times* nor any other major daily newspaper quoted Dellinger. Instead, the *Times* said Dellinger had uttered "a barnyard epithet."

- In 1976 Secretary of Agriculture Earl Butz was quoted in *Rolling Stone* as having made an obscene, racist remark—specifically, that Republicans could not attract more black votes because, he said, blacks only want "three things . . . a tight pussy . . . loose shoes and . . . a warm place to shit." Butz was forced to resign because of those disgusting remarks. Newspapers throughout the country put the story on their front pages. But only the *Toledo (Ohio) Blade* and *Madison (Wis.) Capital Times* told their readers just what Butz had said that prompted his resignation. Every other paper resorted to euphemisms and obfuscation.

- In 1978 the United States Supreme Court upheld the right of the Federal Communications Commission to ban from the radio the obscene language contained in the George Carlin monologue satirizing "the seven dirty words you can't say on television." But no metropolitan daily newspaper in the country except the *San Francisco Chronicle* told its readers just what those words were. (They were "fuck," "shit," "piss," "cunt," "tit," "motherfucker" and "cocksucker.")

Almost a decade later, the United States Supreme Court upheld the right of a high school in the state of Washington to suspend a student for comments he made during a speech. But few newspapers told their readers what the student said. They reported only that he made "sexual references" (the *Boston Globe*) or "sexually suggestive" remarks (the *Chicago Tribune*). A few newspapers provided more detail, but it was the *New York Times* that provided the most precise account of the student's speech. The *Times* said he had described a friend who was running for student office as being "firm in his pants . . . a man who takes his point and pounds it in . . . a man who will go to the very end—even to the climax—for each and every one of you."

Many journalists were surprised to see the *New York Times*

take the lead in specificity on this story. The *Times* has long been the most rigid of any major newspaper in the country in its refusal to publish vulgarity, obscenity or profanity. Such language, *Times* editors have repeatedly said, is inappropriate—not in keeping with the paper's slogan, published on the front page every day: "All the News That's Fit to Print."

This policy is so deeply ingrained that the paper made news when it abandoned it for one day in 1974, during the Watergate scandal; on that day, taped transcripts were released of President Richard Nixon's conversations with top aides about the Watergate cover-up. Nixon's exact words, quoted in the *Times* and elsewhere, were: "I don't give a shit what happens."

The *Times* published that quote verbatim. When reporters from other news organizations asked A. M. Rosenthal, then the executive editor of the paper, why he had departed from the *Times*'s historic prudishness to do so, Rosenthal said:

"The *New York Times* will take 'shit' from the president of the United States but from nobody else."

And shit is about all the *New York Times* will take, even from the president of the United States.

In 1976, when President Jimmy Carter was quoted in *Playboy* as saying, "Christ says, don't consider yourself better than someone else because one guy screws a whole bunch of women while the other guy is loyal to his wife," most major papers quoted him verbatim; the *New York Times* dropped the word "screws" and substituted "a vulgarism for sexual relations." (When it became clear that some readers mistook that to mean "fuck," the *Times* published a notice explaining that it had meant a "five-letter vulgarism for sexual relations," thus taking eleven words over two days to dance awkwardly around what could have been stated plainly the first day with one word.)

The *New York Times* has been equally obfuscatory when far milder vulgarisms have crept into the daily news flow.

- In 1979, when Billy Carter, the late brother of President Jimmy Carter, said that American Jews who criticized him for hosting a Libyan goodwill mission could "kiss my ass," many major newspapers printed his exact quote; the *New York Times* used a dash instead of the word "ass."

- In 1980, when President Carter said that if Senator Edward M. Kennedy entered the presidential race, "I'll whip his ass," most major newspapers used the quote. Not the *New York Times*.

- In 1984, when then-Senator Barry Goldwater sent an angry letter to William J. Casey, then director of the Central Intelligence Agency, complaining that Casey had not told him about an important White House policy decision affecting a major congressional debate, Goldwater wrote, "I am pissed off." The *Washington Post, Los Angeles Times* and *Wall Street Journal,* among others, quoted Goldwater verbatim. The *New York Times* said he wrote, "I am [expletive deleted]."

- In 1995, in a lengthy article explaining why New York City was probably the "most foul-mouthed city in the nation," the *Times* quoted or cited everyone from Spike Lee and a variety of credentialed academics to a "cherubic toddler" named Nellie on the subject of the pervasive use of profanity in the city. But nowhere in the article did the *Times* manage to give a single specific example of just what it is that people say when they swear in New York. (Do those prolific cursers in the Big Apple, for example, favor any oaths unknown to less sophisticated swearers elsewhere?)

It's not just allegedly obscene words that the *New York Times* deems unfit to print. The paper often avoids even the most clinical references to sex. In 1995, almost thirty years after *Times* editors refused to publish the word "penis" in John Corry's account of the Masters and Johnson research, it took almost a month for a new generation of *Times* editors to decide it was okay to tell its readers just what it was that British actor Hugh Grant had done to get himself arrested with a prostitute. I didn't expect the *Times* to run a headline saying "Brit Gets Blow Job," but it might have been informative to use the phrase "oral sex" instead of the vague "lewd act" that the *Times* prissily insisted on until Frank Rich finally slipped "oral sex" into his op-ed column twenty-nine days after Grant's arrest.

Over the years, a few "lesser" newspapers have tried to be as specific as possible on sex-based language—obscene or not—regardless of whether those specifics might have offended readers.

In 1975 a Treasury agent in Dayton, Ohio, angrily accused another Treasury agent of "fucking with my family . . . fucking with my future," whereupon he shot the other agent dead. The *Dayton Journal Herald* printed the agent's words verbatim.

"We reported the story of a savage argument in which the obscene word was directly crucial to the outcome, a fatal fight. . . . They were the last words of a man drawing his gun to kill a fellow agent and friend," said Charles Alexander, editor of the Dayton paper.

The owners of the paper didn't share Alexander's views. They said they'd lost confidence in his judgment. He'd offended his—their—readers. He "resigned."

What is offensive or obscene is often in the eye of the beholder, though. When a Florida state senator used the words "fuck" and "nigger" in 1984, *Washington Journalism Review* substituted "f——" for "fuck" but published "nigger."

By what standard is "nigger" *less* obscene than "fuck"? To me, "nigger" is the most obscene word in the English language.

But newspapers throughout America made a similar choice last year when they published some of Mark Fuhrman's comments about African Americans; they used the word "nigger" repeatedly but omitted or used dashes or asterisks for his more obscene adjectival modifiers—hence "——— niggers." In this case, however, it could at least be argued that the racist words were essential to the story; they were what the story—the entire issue—was about. It was Fuhrman's racism, not his foul mouth—his use of "niggers," not of "fucking"—that was crucial to the defense case.

Sometimes, editors don't limit themselves to excising obscene words; they change "obscene" *numbers,* too. I can still remember the foggy morning, perhaps twenty-five years ago, when there was a 69-car pileup on a Los Angeles area freeway. The story was the main banner headline on the front page of that day's "late final" (i.e., street sales) edition of the *Los Angeles Times* and it remained on the front page, albeit with a smaller headline, in the next day's home edition. But in both editions, in headlines and stories alike, the *Times* called the accident a "70-car" pileup.

When I asked the editor who arbitrarily changed 69 to 70 why he had done so, he told me he had wanted to avoid "titillating or offending readers" by reminding them of the sex act of the same name—er, number.

Obscene words have long been taboo in polite society, whether in the morning newspaper, over the evening meal or anywhere or anytime in between. Traditionally, swearing in particular has been a definite no-no, especially with women and/or children present; many a young child has had his mouth washed out with soap for daring to utter one of the dread four-letter words himself, whether he knew what it meant or not. Many conservatives saw the partial (but by no means complete) breakdown of this taboo in the 1960s as symbolic of a general breakdown in standards and values. John C. Burnham, in his book *Bad Habits,* argues that proponents of an entire constellation of what he calls "minor vices"—drinking, smoking, gambling, recreational drug use—regarded "bringing offensive language into common use in the United States as a symbolic victory, a signal that standards of all propriety had indeed been turned upside down."

Burnham links the use of swearing to the "lower orders and the underworld," an argument similar to the one advanced by my sainted high school journalism teacher, Mrs. Viola Bagwell, a devout Southern Baptist who—when she wasn't teaching me the fundamentals of newspapering—alternated between trying to persuade me to abandon profanity and to believe in Christ. ("You can still be Jewish," she said repeatedly during the latter campaign. "Just accept Jesus, too.") The profane, the obscene and the scatological have always come easily—and frequently—to me, and I can still hear Mrs. Bagwell saying, "Now, David, you know that the only people who talk like that are loose girls, bad boys and students with weak vocabularies." But I didn't fit any of those categories. I was clearly not a girl—loose or otherwise—and my obvious respect and affection for Mrs. Bagwell herself, combined with my almost-straight-A record and my position as editor in chief of her beloved campus newspaper, the *Chimes,* clearly marked me as a "good boy." Most frustrating of all to her, I am sure, my cocky, adolescent emulation of my father's sesquipedalian habits often sent her scurrying to the dictionary, so she couldn't very well accuse me of swearing to cover up a feeble vocabulary.

I have always found swearing to be one of life's more enjoyable (if decidedly minor) pleasures, both a colorful, evocative way of speaking and a harmless way to release anger or tension. In the latter instance, it is surely a more socially acceptable form of behavior than throwing something, hitting someone, breaking something or ramming your car into the goddamncocksuckingmotherfuckingasshole who just cut you off on the freeway. Robert Graves once wrote that swearing has "a definite physiological function"; it serves as a realistic and honorable adult alternative to the tears and tantrums of a child and the silence of a stoic or a coward. Others have likened obscene oaths to pimples—better that they come out, to cleanse the system, than that they stay inside and "angry up the blood" (as Satchel Paige, the great baseball pitcher, once said of fried foods).

In the aforementioned *New York Times* story on New York as "the most foul-mouthed city in the nation," experts suggested that so many people swear so often in New York because life there is "so much trouble that we need some expletive to fill the need," in the words of Leonard R. N. Ashley, an English professor at Brooklyn College and a student of language usage among the city's underclass.

Just as the stress of life in New York has made profanity prevalent, so the anonymity of life in New York has increased most people's tolerance of profanity, the *Times* said. In New York, profanity seems both less personal and more routine. Shakespeare would no doubt approve. (Quoth the Bard: "When a gentleman is disposed to swear, it's not for any standers-by to curtail his oath.") In fact, I've never understood why so many people get so upset by "obscene" language. Why should anybody care if someone says "Shit" instead of "Shoot," or "I hate this fucking job" instead of "I hate this boring job"—or "I hate this zbqvmlgt job"? I puzzled anew over this absurd waste of outrage recently when Lucas and I were taking a bubble bath together and he asked me what a "fart" was. I explained it and then told him that it was "not a nice word" and that he shouldn't use it because it bothered some people.

"Why, Daddy?" he asked.

Good question.

Unlike various racial, religious, ethnic and gender slurs, which are ugly and obscene because they embody—and convey—contempt and even hatred for other human beings, the so-called obscene words used for sexual activity and bodily functions are merely arbitrary configurations of letters that some people have imbued with the freight of the forbidden. Most of the power of these words comes from their taboo. If people who find them so offensive would just ignore them, they'd soon lose their taboo quality and they'd probably disappear, no longer able to shock or offend. But the language police and other self-appointed arbiters of morality in our society can't wait that long. In their tyranny of virtue, patience is one virtue they lack. They want to stamp out overnight every instance of pleasure, freedom and self-expression, no matter how small or symbolic; they're determined to tell us all just how to lead our lives.

I realize that many religious people object to profanity because they see it as "taking the Lord's name in vain." But I would think that such an invocation-cum-confirmation of the Almighty's power would actually please His followers. "God damn it!" does, after all, implicitly acknowledge God's power to condemn whatever "it" is. As for remonstrations against sexual and scatological obscenity of a nonprofane nature, the most benign interpretation I can come up with is that these four-, six-, eight- and ten-letter words give a public name to what their critics think should be private (copulation, defecation and the body parts involved therein). I agree that these matters should be private. But the folks who most vigorously argue this position often mean something else indeed. It is not mere coincidence that the folks who object most strenuously to obscenity in conversation are the same folks who object most strenuously to obscenity in art and literature—who are the same folks who object most strenuously to sex itself, even in the privacy of one's own bedroom. They don't want people doing it, writing about it, painting it, photographing it, singing about it or talking about it. They don't want sex in bed, onstage, in a museum, on a record, in a joke or in an oath.

May God have (some) mercy on their miserable fucking souls.

A SELECTED BIBLIOGRAPHY

ASBURY, HERBERT. *The Great Illusion: An Informal History of Prohibition.* Garden City, N.Y. Doubleday & Co., 1950.

BEAUVOIR, SIMONE DE. *The Second Sex.* Paris: Librairie Gallimard, 1949.

BENNETT, LINDA AND AMES, GENEVIEVE. *The American Experience with Alcohol: Contrasting Cultural Perspectives.* New York: Plenum Press, 1985.

BERNSTEIN, RICHARD. *Dictatorship of Virtue: Multiculturalism and the Battle for America's Future.* New York: Alfred A. Knopf, 1994.

BREYER, STEPHEN. *Breaking the Vicious Circle: Toward Effective Risk Regulation.* Cambridge, Mass.: Harvard University Press, 1993.

BROWNMILLER, SUSAN. *Against Our Will: Men, Women and Rape.* New York: Simon & Schuster, 1975.

BRUMBERG, JOAN JACOBS. *Fasting Girls: The Emergence of Anorexia Nervosa as a Modern Disease.* Cambridge, Mass.: Plume, 1989.

BURNHAM, JOHN. *Bad Habits: Drinking, Smoking, Taking Drugs, Gambling, Sexual Misbehavior, and Swearing in American History.* New York: New York University Press, 1993.

CARSON, RACHEL. *Silent Spring.* Boston: Houghton Mifflin Co., 1962.

CLARK, ROBERT. *James Beard: A Biography.* New York: HarperCollins, 1993.

CLINE, SALLY. *Women, Passion and Celibacy.* New York: Carol Southern Books, 1995.

CORRY, JOHN. *My Times: Adventures in the News Trade.* New York: G. P. Putnam's Sons, 1993.

CROSSEN, CYNTHIA. *Tainted Truth: The Manipulation of Fact in America.* New York: Simon & Schuster, 1994.

DENFELD, RENE. *The New Victorians: A Young Woman's Challenge to the Old Feminist Order.* New York: Warner Books, 1995.

DIAMOND, JARED. *The Third Chimpanzee: The Evolution and Future of the Human Animal.* New York: HarperCollins, 1992.

DOUGLAS, MARY, AND WILDAVSKY, AARON. *Risk and Culture: An Essay on the Selection of Technical and Environmental Dangers.* Berkeley, Calif.: University of California Press, 1979.

DWORKIN, ANDREA. *Pornography: Men Possessing Women.* New York: G. P. Putnam's Sons, 1979.

———. *Intercourse.* New York: Free Press, 1987.

DWORKIN, ANDREA, AND MACKINNON, CATHARINE. *Pornography and Civil Rights: A New Day for Women's Equality.* Minneapolis: Organizing Against Pornography, 1987.

EASTERBROOK, GREGG. *A Moment on the Earth: The Coming of Age of Environmental Optimism.* New York: Viking, 1995.

EDWARDS, ALLEN. *Erotica Judaica: A Sexual History of the Jews.* New York: Julian Press, 1967.

Encyclopedia Judaica. Jerusalem: Ketter Publishing House, 1972.

EPSTEIN, DIANE, AND THOMPSON, KATHLEEN. *Feeding on Dreams: Why America's Diet Industry Doesn't Work and What Will Work for You.* New York: Maxwell Macmillan International, 1994.

EPSTEIN. L. M. *Sex Laws and Custom in Judaism.* New York: Ktav Publishing House, 1968.

ESTRICH, SUSAN. *Real Rape.* Cambridge, Mass.: Harvard University Press, 1987.

FARB, PETER, AND ARMELAGOS, GEORGE. *Consuming Passions: The Anthropology of Eating.* Boston: Houghton Mifflin Co., 1980.

FAUSTO-STERLING, ANNE. *Myths of Gender: Biological Theories About Men and Women.* New York: Basic Books, 1985.

FILSTED, W. J., ROSSI, J. J., AND KELLER, MARK, eds. *Alcohol and Alcohol Problems: New Thinking and New Directions.* Cambridge, Mass.: Ballinger Publishing, 1976.

FISHER, M. F. K. *The Art of Eating.* New York: Vintage Books, 1976.

FRENCH, MARILYN. *The Women's Room.* New York: Summit Books, 1977.

FRIEDAN, BETTY. *The Feminine Mystique.* New York: W. W. Norton & Co., 1963.

FUMENTO, MICHAEL. *The Myth of Heterosexual AIDS.* New York: Basic Books, 1990.

————. *Science Under Siege: Balancing Technology and the Environment.* New York: William Morrow & Co., 1993.

GLASSNER, BARRY. *Bodies: Overcoming the Tyranny of Perfection.* Los Angeles: Lowell House Books, 1992.

GOLDMAN, ALBERT. *Elvis.* New York: McGraw-Hill Book Co., 1981.

GRAHAM, SYLVESTER. *A Lecture to a Young Man, on Chastity.* Boston: C. H. Pierce, 1834.

GREELEY, ANDREW. *Sex: The Catholic Experience.* Chicago: Tabor Publishing/Thomas More, 1994.

GREENWALT, KENT. *Fighting Words: Individuals, Communities, and Liberties of Speech.* Princeton, N.J.: Princeton University Press, 1995.

GREER, GERMAINE. *The Female Eunuch.* London: MacGibbon & Kee Ltd., 1970.

GURALNICK, PETER. *Last Train to Memphis: The Rise of Elvis Presley.* Boston: Little, Brown & Co., 1994.

GUSFIELD, J. R. *Symbolic Crusade: Status Politics and the American Temperance Movement.* Champaign, Ill.: University of Illinois Press, 1963.

HALBERSTAM, DAVID. *The Fifties.* New York: Villard Books, 1993.

HARDIN, GARRETT. *Filters Against Folly: How to Survive Despite Economists, Ecologists, and the Merely Eloquent.* New York: Viking Penguin, 1985.

————. *Living Within Limits: Ecology, Economics, and Population Taboos.* Oxford: Oxford University Press, 1993.

HENRY, WILLIAM A. III. *In Defense of Elitism.* New York: Doubleday, 1994.

HENTOFF, NAT. *Free Speech for Me—but Not for Thee: How the American Left and Right Relentlessly Censor Each Other.* New York: HarperCollins, 1992.

HOLLAND, BARBARA. *Endangered Pleasures: In Defense of Naps, Bacon, Martinis, Profanity, and Other Indulgences.* New York: Little, Brown & Co., 1995.

Holy Bible. American Standard Revised Edition. New York: Thomas Nelson & Sons, 1901.

HUGHES, ROBERT. *The Culture of Complaint.* New York: Oxford University Press, 1993.

KASS, LEON R. *The Hungry Soul: Eating and the Perfecting of Our Nature.* New York: Free Press, 1994.

KEARNEY, PATRICK J. *A History of Erotic Literature.* Hong Kong: Paragon Book Service, 1982.

KELLOGG, JOHN HARVEY. *Rules for "Right Living."* Battle Creek, Mich.: Health Extension Department, Battle Creek Sanitarium, 1935.

KINSEY, ALFRED, POMEROY, WARDELL, AND MARTIN, CLYDE. *Sexual Behavior in the Human Male.* Philadelphia: W. B. Saunders Co., 1948.

———. *Sexual Behavior in the Human Female.* Philadelphia: W. B. Saunders Co., 1953.

KLEIN, RICHARD. *Cigarettes Are Sublime.* Durham, N.C.: Duke University Press, 1993.

LAWRENCE, D. H. *Pornography and Obscenity.* New York: Alfred A Knopf, 1930.

LEWIS, H. W. *Technological Risk.* New York: W. W. Norton & Co., 1990.

LIPP, MARTIN, AND WHITTEN, DAVID. *To Your Health: Two Physicians Explore the Health Benefits of Wine.* San Francisco: HarperCollins West, 1994.

LONG, H. W. *Sane Sex Life & Sane Sex Living.* New York: Eugenics Publishing Co., 1919.

LOTH, DAVID. *The Erotic in Literature.* New York: Julian Messner, 1961.

MACKINNON, CATHARINE A. *Sexual Harassment of Working Women: A Case of Sex Discrimination.* Cambridge, Mass.: Harvard University Press, 1979.

———. *Feminism Unmodified: Discourses on Life and Law.* Cambridge, Mass.: Harvard University Press, 1989.

———. *Toward a Feminist Theory of the State.* Cambridge, Mass.: Harvard University Press, 1989.

————. *Only Words.* Cambridge, Mass.: Harvard University Press, 1993.

MASTERS, WILLIAM, AND JOHNSON, VIRGINIA. *Human Sexual Response.* Boston: Little, Brown & Co., 1966.

MCELROY, WENDY. *XXX: A Woman's Right to Pornography.* New York: St. Martin's Press, 1995.

MCWILLIAMS, PETER. *Ain't Nobody's Business If You Do: The Absurdity of Consensual Crime in a Free Society.* Los Angeles: Prelude Press, 1993.

MICHAEL, ROBERT T., GAGNON, JOHN H., LAUMANN, EDWARD O., AND KOLATA, GINA. *Sex in America: A Definitive Survey.* Boston: Little, Brown & Co., 1994.

MILLETT, KATE. *Sexual Politics.* New York: Doubleday, 1970.

MORISON, SAMUEL ELIOT. *The Puritan Pronaos: Studios in the Intellectual Life of New England in the Seventeenth Century.* New York: New York University Press, 1936.

NADER, RALPH. *Unsafe at Any Speed: The Designed-in Danger of the American Automobile.* New York: Grossman, 1965.

PAGLIA, CAMILLE. *Sexual Personae: Art and Decadence from Nefertiti to Emily Dickinson.* New Haven: Yale University Press, 1990.

————. *Sex, Art, and American Culture.* New York: Vintage Books, 1992.

————. *Vamps & Tramps, New Essays.* New York: Vintage Books, 1994.

PFEIFFER, JOHN. *The Emergence of Society.* New York: McGraw-Hill Book Co., 1977.

POST, ROBERT. *Constitutional Domains: Democracy, Community, Management.* Cambridge, Mass.: Harvard University Press, 1995.

RIDLEY, MATT. *The Red Queen: Sex and the Evolution of Human Nature.* New York: Macmillan Publishing Co., 1993.

ROIPHE, KATE. *The Morning After: Sex, Fear and Feminism on Campus.* Boston: Little, Brown & Co., 1993.

Rossi, Alice S., ed. *The Feminist Papers: From Adams to de Beauvoir.* New York: Columbia University Press, 1973.

Rosten, Leo. *The Joys of Yiddish.* New York: McGraw-Hill Book Co., 1968.

Rugoff, Milton. *America's Gilded Age: Intimate Portraits from an Era of Extravagance and Change.* New York: Holt, 1989.

Sabato, Larry. *Feeding Frenzy: How Attack Journalism Has Transformed American Politics.* New York: Maxwell Macmillan International, 1991.

Sandberg, Ryne, with Rozner, Barry R. *Second to Home: Ryne Sandberg Opens Up.* Chicago: Bonus Books, 1995.

Schwartz, Hillel. *Never Satisfied: A Cultural History of Diets, Fantasies, and Fat.* New York: Anchor/Doubleday, 1986.

Shilts, Randy. *And the Band Played On: People, Politics and the AIDS Epidemic.* New York: St. Martin's Press, 1987.

Sommers, Christina Hoff. *Who Stole Feminism: How Women Have Betrayed Women.* New York: Simon & Schuster, 1994.

Stacey, Michelle. *Consumed: Why Americans Love, Hate and Fear Food.* New York: Simon & Schuster, 1994.

Stephens, Mitchell. *A History of News: From the Drum to the Satellite.* New York: Viking, 1988.

Stoltenberg, John. *The End of Manhood: A Book for Men of Conscience.* New York: Dutton, 1993.

Strossen, Nadine. *Defending Pornography: Free Speech, Sex and the Fight for Women's Rights.* New York: Scribner, 1995.

Suchocki, Marjorie. *The Fall to Violence: Original Sin in Relational Theology.* New York: Continuum, 1994.

Sullivan, Andrew. *Virtually Normal: An Argument About Homosexuality.* New York: Alfred A. Knopf, 1995.

TAVRIS, CAROL. *The Mismeasure of Woman: Why Women Are Not the Better Sex, the Inferior Sex, or the Opposite Sex.* New York: Simon & Schuster, 1992.

TELUSHKIN, JOSEPH. *Jewish Wisdom: The Essential Teachings and How They Have Shaped the Jewish Religion, Its People, Culture and History.* New York: William Morrow & Co., 1994.

TIGER, LIONEL. *The Pursuit of Pleasure.* Boston: Little, Brown & Co., 1992.

TISDALE, SALLIE. *Talk Dirty to Me.* New York: Doubleday, 1994.

VISCUSI, W. KIP. *Smoking: Making the Risky Decision.* New York: Oxford University Press, 1992.

WALKOWITZ, JUDITH. *Prostitution and Victorian Society: Women, Class and the State.* Cambridge, Mass.: Cambridge Univeristy Press, 1980.

WATTENBERG, BEN J. *The Good News Is the Bad News Is Wrong.* New York: Simon & Schuster, 1984.

WHORTON, JAMES C. *Crusaders for Fitness: The History of American Health Reformers.* Princeton, N.J.: Princeton University Press, 1984.

WOJTYLA, KAROL. *Love and Responsibility.* London: William Collins and Sons Co. Ltd. and Farrar, Straus & Giroux, 1981. (Revised English-language edition; originally published in Polish, 1969.)

INDEX